Confederate Guerrilla
Sue Mundy

Confederate Guerrilla Sue Mundy

A Biography of Kentucky Soldier Jerome Clarke

THOMAS SHELBY WATSON
with PERRY A. BRANTLEY

Foreword by James M. Prichard

McFarland & Company, Inc., Publishers
Jefferson, North Carolina, and London

FRONTISPIECE: Born in southwestern Kentucky's Simpson County, Jerome Clarke was orphaned at age eleven and reared by family members. On his 17th birthday in 1861, he enrolled in the Confederate Army and was an infantryman, but later became a cavalryman under Colonel Adam Rankin Johnson, then Brigadier General John Hunt Morgan. After fleeing Cynthiana, Ky., the result of a Union victory over Morgan's forces, Jerome was separated from regular Confederate forces and was pursued by federal forces as a "guerrilla." Newspaper editor George Prentice attached the fictitious name "Sue Mundy" to Clarke. (Information from the Filson Historical Society, Louisville, Ky.)

LIBRARY OF CONGRESS CATALOGUING-IN-PUBLICATION DATA

Watson, Thomas Shelby.
    Confederate guerrilla Sue Mundy : a biography of Kentucky soldier Jerome Clarke / Thomas Shelby Watson with Perry A. Brantley : foreword by James M. Prichard.
        p.   cm.
    Includes bibliographical references and index.

    ISBN 978-0-7864-3280-6
    softcover : 50# alkaline paper ∞

    1. Clarke, Marcellus Jerome, 1844–1865.   2. Guerrillas — Confederate States of America — Biography.   3. Guerrillas — Kentucky — Biography.   4. Soldiers — Confederate States of America — Biography.   5. Kentucky — History — Civil War, 1861–1865 — Underground movements.   6. United States — History — Civil War, 1861–1865 — Underground movements.   I. Brantley, Perry A., 1949– II. Title.
    E470.5.W38   2008
    973.7'13092 — dc22
    [B]   2007047036

British Library cataloguing data are available

On the cover: Marcellus Jerome Clarke (Filson Historical Society, Louisville, KY); Tintype frame and background ©2007 Shutterstock

Manufactured in the United States of America

McFarland & Company, Inc., Publishers
  Box 611, Jefferson, North Carolina 28640
  www.mcfarlandpub.com

This book is dedicated to all those who made it possible; from the descendants of people whose names appear within these pages, to others who offered specific information and to the brillant Kentucky historians who gave of their time and knowledge.

Acknowledgments

In recognition of Dr. Lowell H. Harrison, Owsley Brown Frazier, Jerry and Linda Bruckheimer, the late Dr. Thomas D. Clark, J. Winston Coleman, Frank G. Rankin and Marcellus Jerome Clarke of Anchorage, Ky., great-nephew of our subject, for their encouragement and trust in this project.

And in remembrance of and gratitude to L.L. Valentine, Robert E. McDowell, Phil Hunter, Elmer Stevens, Orville Watson, Ottis Goodwin, Emma Wilson Brown, Emily Dawson, Lowell Ashe, Ilda Ashe, Fred Miles, Pauline Peck, Edgar Jacobs, Fred Ford, B. James George, Sr., Nathalie Gardner, Kathryn Cox Johnson, Jack Muir, Howard Gray, Frank Rankin, Joe Creason, Joe Wakefield, Mark Wakefield, Joe Morry Wakefield, Mary Wakefield Eggen, Edgar Sullivan, Pete Downs, Walter Magruder, Mrs. Lee Hamilton and the John Langford family.

These acknowledgments must also include: Susan Watson, Bill Samuels, John Peck, Gwendolyn Burks, Ollie Talbott, Sue Sutherland, Nancy Inman, the Robert Harper family, the F.B. Mitchell family, A.J. Alexander, Mildred Holmes, Kenny Popp, Al Miller, Roy Herndon, Curtis Ochs, J. Robert Crume, H.S. Green, Dr. Robert Hendren, Judge Tom Dawson, Dr. Robert P. Moore, Frank Walker, Warren Larue, Byron Crawford, Grace Snider, Bob Fay, Davis Lee and Bonnie Downs, Cathy Barton and Dave Para, Shirley Roberts, Leroy King, Tim Ballard, Dixie Hibbs, David Hall, Mary Francis Brown, Berttye Brown and Sarah B. Smith.

Also: Carl Breihan, Rick Mach, Carl Flowers, Charlie Long, Richard S. Brownlee, Donald R. Hale, William A. Settle, Jr., Jane Cecil, Helen McKinley, Harry D. Tinsley, Don Wilkinson and the *Ohio County News*,

Acknowledgments

of Hartford, Ky., Marty Rice, Larry Raymond, Nettie Oliver, the Filson Historical Society, the Kentucky Historical Society, Jim Prichard, Kentucky Department of Libraries and Archives, Kenneth Spencer Research Library, Max Allen, Rex Allen, Roxanne Pleva, Ron D. Bryant, Catherine Brantley, Allan Leach, Eula Ray Kirkland, the Kentucky, Kansas and Missouri Historical Societies, National Archives Old Military Records; Spencer, Nelson, Shelby, Anderson, Washington, Larue and other county historical and genealogical groups, to mention a few people and organizations whose cooperation and assistance in making this book a reality was exceptional.

Table of Contents

Table of Contents

Foreword by
James M. Prichard

His daring course as a rebel guerrilla was colorful but brief. His death on the gallows was swift and sudden. Yet, when he mounted the scaffold on March 15, 1865, 20-year-old Marcellus Jerome Clarke was well on his way to becoming an enduring legend.

Known to history as "Sue Mundy," the Simpson County, Kentucky, native rivals Confederate General John Hunt Morgan as one of the state's most memorable Civil War figures. His youth, daring and tragic death led that postwar champion of the Lost Cause, John Newman Edwards, to accord Clarke a place of honor in *Noted Guerrillas*, his glorified history of William C. Quantrill, the James Brothers, the Youngers and other noted Missouri veterans of border warfare. Indeed, Clarke is virtually the only Kentucky guerrilla chieftain to be mentioned in most modern historical studies of the Civil War in the Bluegrass State. As Kentucky entered a new century, the bold rider was further immortalized in print by Kentucky poet and novelist Richard Taylor.

Ironically, the nickname "Sue Mundy," which brought Clarke far greater notoriety than any other guerrilla who operated in Kentucky, also distorted the historical picture. "Sue" was in reality the creation of George D. Prentice, the veteran editor of the pro–Union *Louisville Daily Journal*. The former disciple of Henry Clay was a bitter critic of the Lincoln administration throughout the conflict.

As late as the dawn of the 20th century, one could still find lurid accounts of "Kentucky's Female Guerrilla," typified by a 1902 *Washington*

1

Post article that described "Sue Munday's" legendary "acts of cruelty" and deadly skill with a pistol. Recent historical works have exposed Prentice's myth-making, but the ruthless nature of the guerrilla warfare that ravaged the heart of Kentucky during the war was a grim reality for both civilians and fighting men alike.

This work strips the war of glory and romance to reveal a nightmare struggle in which Clarke, "One-Arm" Berry, Henry Magruder and other Confederate irregulars, including the notorious Quantrill himself, spread terror throughout the heart of Kentucky. The equally ruthless anti-guerrilla measures and prisoner execution of U.S. Brigadier General Steffen Burbridge, as well as the brutal search and destroy missions of Union partisans such as Captain Ed Terrell and Major Jim Bridgewater, further underscore the bleak nature of a struggle marked by both reckless bravery and unspeakable brutality on both sides. In many ways, these desperate fighters helped sow the seeds of violence that plagued Kentucky long after the struggle ended.

This work is the first to offer an in-depth, historical account of Clarke's actual exploits and Quantrill's final operations in Kentucky. Journalist and historian Thomas Shelby Watson has long been recognized as an authority on "Sue Mundy" and guerrilla warfare in central Kentucky. As Research Room supervisor at the Kentucky Department of Libraries and Archives in Frankfort, I came to know his associate, Perry A. Brantley, as a masterful, tireless researcher with an encyclopedic knowledge of partisan warfare. Together they uncovered a wealth of previously unpublished primary source material and photographs that create a stark, vivid portrait of the youthful guerrilla chief.

Determined to cut through the myths surrounding Clarke, Quantrill and other daring, ruthless partisans, the two have produced a valuable work that sheds new light on the war within the war in Kentucky. This is work that proves that historical fact can be as dramatic and compelling as the legends of Kentucky's past.

A free-lance historian in Louisville, James M. Prichard has served as research room supervisor at the Kentucky Department for Libraries and Archives since 1985. He is the author of numerous articles on Civil War guerrillas.

Preface

This unique Civil War book is a non-fiction work that is a study of Confederate guerrillas and those who pursued them. It serves as an adjunct to research of the war because of the precise nature of the information offered. It paints a clear picture of the ruthlessness of detached soldiers who spilled blood on the porches and in the homes of their enemies, rather than on the battlefields.

The book centers on Kentucky native Marcellus Jerome Clarke, a member of the Confederate Army, who by someone else's doing, became more notable than thousands of other soldiers during America's Civil War.

He was given the name "Sue Mundy" by Louisville Journal newspaper editor George Prentice and portrayed near the close of the conflict as a young woman guerrilla who became a thorn in the side of the Union Army.

The fictitious name, "Sue Mundy," could have been applied to any of several long-haired young Rebels who had become detached from their units and were roaming the countryside. The reason for the female name being created by Prentice and why it was attached to Jerome Clarke will be explored in this study of the "other war," or "guerrilla war."

Jerome Clarke had distinguished himself in battle and was serving under Gen. John Hunt Morgan at the time he was forced to flee Morgan's command at Cynthiana, Ky. Clarke remained in north-central Kentucky, much of the time, just a few miles south of Louisville where a large force of Union troops was quartered.

The name "Sue Mundy" should not be construed in any manner to refer to an actual woman, to a man who dressed as a woman or to a man with the physical body of a woman. Jerome had what some called feminine facial features and long hair. "Sue Mundy" was, and will be for all time, a fictitious name. Its origin is explained within these pages, and while it is known who coined the name, the precise objective for it is difficult to fathom.

Perry A. Brantley and I have joined forces to compose a work that offers new findings from a portion of American history that heretofore has not received the attention we believe it deserved. We discovered common interests through phone conversations and emails, then researched together in Kentucky libraries, courthouses and the National Archives. Trips were made to several states to gather information.

I have extensive research on guerrilla leader William Quantrill and other irregulars, and previously unreported information from descendants of people with whom they interacted, while Perry's work produced information, both from military records and geneological digging. His attention to Morgan and his men over the years aided the project, while we had explored Jerome Clarke's career and the Sue Mundy story at length. Perry's research and my years of collecting interviews and photographs combined to produce a wealth of information that begged to be published. With a combined four decades in the broadcast industry and as an Associated Press writer, I tackled the job of turning it all into this book.

I interviewed members of families with particular information, such as the late Marcellus Jerome Clarke of Anchorage, Ky., whose namesake and kinsman was called "Sue Mundy." I also talked with relatives of many other Rebel irregulars and victims of guerrilla outrages. The interviewees included the son of one of the men who was with Quantrill at the farm where the guerrilla chief was mortally wounded and the nephew of one of Quantrill's attackers.

We did more than simply quote from existing books in composing this new work of Civil War history. Assistance and advice came from historians like Dr. Lowell Harrison, the late Dr. William Settle and the late Dr. Thomas D. Clark.

Existing books on Quantrill do not correctly cover the Quantrill–Jerome Clarke connection, nor do they explain the confusion created when Quantrill used the alias "Captain Clark," as he rode with Jerome Clarke. This book, the culmination of many years of trying to unravel the facts about Clarke and Quantrill, explains it. Research is the key to finding the truth, and whether the subject is the American Civil War or anything else of historical importance, we must never stop looking.

When we begin to feel satisfied that our efforts have produced enough information to adequately tell a story — that is the time we must redouble our efforts and keep working: The goal of a historian is to uncover every detail possible. While this book is not perfect, it represents a genuine effort to seek the truth about the past.

Introduction

It is not possible to analyze the American Civil War in a few paragraphs, but a brief examination of the events that formulated Kentucky's position in the conflict is necessary to set the scene for the story that follows.

A war was fought decades earlier in the name of freedom from tyranny and oppression. Many sided with the British as loyalists during the American Revolution, seeking to take no active part in the conflict, while those who opposed British rule called themselves "patriots." It was the descendants of loyalists, patriots, German mercenaries and others, who fought each other in the War Between the States.

From 1861 to 1865, the North and South fought over differences concerning a race of people being held in bondage that numbered some 4,000,000 in 1861. The war was also a result of the eroding rights of the individual states.

The War Between the States, also called the War of the Rebellion, or in the opinions of some zealots, War for Southern Independence or War of Northern Aggression, took an immense toll in human life and personal property. Kentucky was a Union state during the American Civil War, although its General Assembly had twice voted in favor of neutrality.[1] A clear majority of Kentuckians were Unionists, but many of them opposed Lincoln. Even in 1864, Kentucky voted strongly anti–Lincoln.

The Bluegrass State did not take sides until armies from both the North and South crossed her borders. It was September 3, 1861, when Confederate troops under Major General Leonidas Polk occupied Hickman and Columbus in western Kentucky.

Then, two days later, by order of Brigadier General Ulysses Simpson Grant, Union forces claimed the western Kentucky city of Paducah. The General Assembly voted September 11, 1861, to demand that Governor Beriah Magoffin order both Union and Confederate troops to be withdrawn from the state immediately. In a separate vote, it was demanded by the legislature that Confederate or "Tennessee troops" be withdrawn from Kentucky unconditionally.[2] Magoffin vetoed the action but a strong Union majority in the legislature overrode the veto.

An effort was made to form a Confederate government in Kentucky and delegates from across the state, mostly self-appointed, met in the western Kentucky city of Russellville. The pro-secessionists elected George Washington Johnson of Scott County, in the bluegrass section of the state, as their provisional governor.[3] The Kentucky Rebels selected Bowling Green as their provisional state capital. Kentucky was admitted as a member state of the Confederacy December 10, 1861. When the Confederate army withdrew from the state in February, 1862, Kentucky's Confederate government went into exile and Johnson then left Kentucky to fight in the war.

Governor Johnson was sworn into the ranks as a private in Company E of the Fourth Kentucky Confederate Infantry Regiment on the eve of the Battle of Shiloh, Tennessee. He saw action in the battle, was wounded April 7, 1862, and died a day later. Major Richard Hawes, Jr., 65, of Bourbon County, Ky., a member of Brigadier Humphrey Marshall's staff, was elected by Kentucky's Provisional Confederate Council as the new Rebel governor and began serving in that capacity in the summer of 1862. General Braxton Bragg installed Hawes, who didn't have much time to get organized, because Bragg pulled his forces from the state in October, 1862. Nevertheless, when Bragg and General Kirby Smith had their armies in Kentucky, they did something that would not be replicated in any other state during the war by occupying the state's capital, in this case Frankfort.[4]

The Confederates had hoped to put a conscription law into effect, but they didn't hold Frankfort long enough to complete the task. The number of volunteers the Rebels succeeded in adding to the ranks during the summer was considerably fewer than the number of casualties they suffered during the campaign.[5]

The Unionists solidified control of the General Assembly and Magoffin became weary of having his vetoes overridden. He chose to resign after some political maneuvering that ensured his successor. The lieutenant governor had died and the president of the Senate was next in line. Magoffin would not accept John Fisk, the Senate speaker, as his successor, but would accept Senator James Fisher Robinson. Fisk resigned as speaker, but remained in the Senate and when Robinson was elected speaker August 18, 1861, Magoffin resigned. Robinson was sworn in as governor and Fisk was re-elected speaker.[6]

The terror of the war to civilians was made especially horrific by the actions of guerrillas and others with no respect for human rights or human life. It is hoped that a closer look at these soldiers of fortune, and the people with whom they interacted, will add to the knowledge of the American Civil War. The story of "Sue Mundy" is one of the most unusual and captivating of the war.

It involves an otherwise highly respected newspaperman's obvious disregard for journalistic ethics, as we know them today, by reporting something he knew was untrue. As he persisted with the falsehood, his motive became as mysterious as the character he created.

It was a fabrication that transformed unknown Confederate cavalryman Marcellus Jerome Clarke of southwestern Kentucky into the infamous guerrilla "Sue Mundy."

Jerome's family tree included many achievers and some black sheep. Marcellus Jerome Clarke was born August 25, 1844, in Simpson County, Ky., the seventh and last child of Hector Marcellus Clarke (born June 30, 1795, Chesterfield County, Va.; died September 26, 1855, Simpson County, Ky.) and Mary Hail (born 1798, Halifax County, N.C.; died February 28, 1847, Simpson County, Ky.). Hector Clarke remarried October 18, 1848, to Elizabeth Caroline Robey, born in North Carolina, but a resident of Simpson County when she took the vows. Jerome's siblings were Eliza Jane (born February 15, 1829; died September 16, 1843), Julia Ann (born October 11, 1831; died January 28, 1864); John Thomas (born January 28, 1833; died February 20, 1926), Emily Catherine (born October 5, 1835; died December 19, 1915), Mary Susan Elizabeth (born March 30, 1838; died July 10, 1914) and William Beverly (born May 15, 1840; died January 10, 1863). Jerome's paternal grandparents were Charles Clarke Jr. (born September 1751 in Powhatan County, Va.; died 1828, in Simpson County, Ky.) and Nancy Martin (born December 14, 1760, in Virginia; died December 23, 1843, Simpson County, Ky.).

Jerome's first cousin, Beverly Leonidas Clarke, served in the Kentucky General Assembly during 1841–42, was a U.S. Representative 1847–49 and in 1855 was the Democrats' nominee for governor. He was defeated by Charles S. Morehead of the "Know Nothing" or "American" party.[8] Beverly Clarke was assigned to the post of Minister to Guatamala in 1858 and died there March 17, 1860. Confederate Colonel John Singleton Mosby, known as "The Gray Ghost," married Mariah Louisa Pauline Clarke, a daughter of Jerome's cousin, Beverly Clarke. Another first cousin of Jerome, William Branch Clarke, was indicted for an 1858 murder in Madisonville, Ky., but "Branch" Clarke's case was moved to McLean County and he failed to appear every time it was called. The case was removed from the dockett in September, 1860, and Branch Clarke was never tried, according to the Kentucky Department of Libraries and Archives. Branch Clarke's son, Tandy, was convicted of robbing the mails and was sentenced to the penitentiary just before the Civil War began.[9] Just eleven when his widowed father died, Jerome Clarke was taken to McLean County, where his two older brothers had married great nieces of Mary Tibbs. After a short stay with brother John Thomas Clarke, Jerome became a resident in the home of Mary Tibbs at Crow's Pond, Ky.

John Thomas Clarke married Elizabeth Lashbrook and William Beverly Clarke married her sister, Surilla Lashbrook. Mary Tibbs, in her mid–70's, had no problem taking in the orphaned Jerome. She was already rearing her great-nephew, John L. Patterson of Sebree in McLean County, Ky., who was nine years older than Jerome and came to be considered as an older brother.[10] An assistant engineer on the steamer *Peytona* when the war broke out, Patterson enlisted in the Confederate service in 1861 at the age of 26 in Company B, 4th Kentucky Infantry Regiment under Captain Frank Scott and went with Scott to Camp Burnett, in Montgomery County, Tennessee.

Jerome Clarke was enrolled at Camp Burnett on his 17th birthday, August 25, 1861, in Confederate Captain James Ingram's Company B, 4th Kentucky Infantry Regiment. Jerome and John Patterson found themselves in the same infantry company and later both rode with Colonel Adam Rankin Johnson's cavalry. At one point, they were so close to Crow's Pond in McLean County the two went home to visit, taking some fellow soldiers with them.

The morning following the visit, on the ride toward camp at Slaughtersville, Patterson was cut off by a squad of federals. A Yankee on foot grabbed the reins of Patterson's horse and forced the Rebel to surrender. A federal guide rode up and fired into Patterson's head, and although the wound was not fatal, Patterson was left blind.

Patterson recovered and dealt with the blindness, but Jerome, it was said, swore to never take another prisoner alive.[11] Many of the guerrillas who operated in Kentucky and other states near the close of the war were former Confederate soldiers who had become battle weary and chose to fight "on their own hook," in the phraseology of the time.

Some of the guerrillas who roamed about during the latter stages of the war were local toughs who sought to take advantage of the civil disorder for personal gain. Most of those covered in this book were soldiers, cut off from their ranks, reeling from a bitter defeat and not eager to again hear the roar of cannons or face charging Union cavalry. Some were following orders to remain in certain areas of Kentucky to recruit for the Confederacy while discouraging Negro enlistment in the federal army.

The guerrillas were provided a new spark for violence when the Union army began executing Confederate prisoners in retaliation for the murders of northern sympathizers and innocent civilians. The Union executions produced an even more dangerous period of bloody disorder while polarizing the attitudes of some Kentuckians in favor of the Rebel cause.

The guerrillas sought out and killed individual Union soldiers who had been discharged or given temporary leave and it didn't matter if they were walking home on crutches. They hunted down federal troops who were en route to new assignments or who were on leave to attend family emergencies. They battled patrols that hunted them and sometimes attacked Union forces of similar strength.

Some guerrillas were tried for murders, rapes, robberies and other crimes. Some were hanged for their unlawful acts and others served prison terms. Basil Wilson Duke, in his book *A History of Morgan's Cavalry*, had a somewhat peculiar, romanticized definition of a guerrilla: "A guerrilla was, properly speaking, a man who had belonged to some army, and had deserted and gone to making war on his private account. He was necessarily a marauder, sometimes spared his former friend, and was much admired by weak young women who were afflicted with a tendency toward shoddy romance."

By Union definition, one of the more notorious guerrillas of the Civil War was Kentuckian Henry Clay Magruder.

The alleged confession of Magruder, dictated after the guerrilla's capture in 1865 to the Rev. Jeremiah Jedediah Talbott of St. John's Episcopal Church in Louisville, and published by his federal captor, Major Cyrus James Wilson, gives clues to the movements of the guerrillas in central Kentucky.[12]

Three Years in the Saddle is disjointed to some extent, but Magruder's recollections of events is extraordinary, since he was relying on memory alone. With the many skirmishes fought by Magruder, Jerome Clarke and other guerrillas, it is inevitable that the Bullitt Countian would fail to recall every detail. If Magruder had been considered a Partisan Ranger, there would be disagreement over whether he committed crimes or acts of war. Partisan Rangers were Confederate soldiers who operated in a detached manner from regular forces.

The book is very valuable as a research tool and contains enough information to serve as a partial guide through the career of Magruder and those men with whom he rode, including Jerome Clarke.

Wilson's insertion of the subtitle "The Original Sue Munday" under Magruder's name and the labeling of Magruder as "alias Sue Monday" in the introduction could be construed as an attempt to sell books. Outrageous acts during the closing months of the war weren't committed exclusively by Confederate guerrillas. The federal command in Louisville had difficulty keeping thieves and rowdies among Union troops under control.

There were scoundrels among the thousands of Union troops stationed in the city, as evidenced by the many published reports of theft and violence during their stay.[13] Federal soldiers were blamed for what the *Louisville Daily Journal* called, in its January 25, 1865, edition, "The most extensive riot we were ever called upon to chronicle..." when chaos reigned over the entire three-mile length of the Portland community in northwest Louisville along the Ohio River.[14]

"The proprietors and owners of stores and saloons closed their doors, but they were broken open and robbed of their most valuable contents," Prentice noted in his coverage of the riot.

Ed Burke, identified by Prentice as "a keeper of a little groggery," was fatally shot and an Italian confection store owner wounded, but the name and condition of the confectioner were not reported.

"The greatest excitement continued all day," Prentice reported. "We understand that citizens were knocked down in the streets and robbed, baker wagons were rifled, and depredations committed too numerous to detail. These soldiers have been robbing for several days past, but on a smaller scale," he wrote. The military brass instructed guards to shoot down any soldier caught in the act of even a misdemeanor. Loafers, not among the soldier presence, were ordered to get out of town.[15]

When on patrol away from the city, the worst of the lot were on their worst behavior. Union troops were not always kind to residents, although Kentucky had remained loyal. Citizens were chastised, insulted and robbed by regular federal soldiers and citizens hired by the government to hunt down Rebel irregulars.[16] Confederate sympathizers received the brunt of the ill treatment by the Union troops, as would be expected.

The Confederate guerrillas were excellent riders and generally accomplished marksmen and fighters despite the opinions of some authors to the contrary. So effective were the Rebel guerrillas as cavalrymen and marksmen and so many were their supporters and hiding places, the government was forced to hire decoy guerrillas of similar skills to hunt them down.

These local mercenaries, such as Edwin Terrell of Shelby County, Ky., killed and pillaged to the extent that citizens feared Terrell and his men as much, if not more, than the Rebel guerrillas. The Union command's use of such men was a way of fighting fire with fire. Many Kentuckians viewed creation of the decoy guerrillas a Union mistake, but another decision by federal authorities near the close of the war made it pale by comparison. Citizens could scarcely believe the Union's campaign of retaliation executions. They were horrifying and an embarrassment to most Kentuckians.[17]

The personalities of the Southern soldiers of fortune varied from the ruthless to some who had no heart for guerrilla violence and seemed trapped in it by virtue of the circumstances. If they surrendered and sought paroles, they could be hanged or shot by a firing squad. If they started home, they faced a gauntlet of Union patrols.

"Sue Mundy" was the product of the fertile imagination of George Dennison Prentice, editor of the *Louisville Daily Journal,* who coined the name October 11, 1864, in his newspaper. Prentice applied the name to Jerome Clarke after the long-haired Rebel took part in the robbery of a stagecoach near Harrodsburg, Ky., and was mistaken for a woman by the driver, Billy Wilkinson.[18]

Another story said Clarke became known as Sue Mundy after putting on a dress and riding sidesaddle through the streets of Bloomfield, Ky., to the delight of his comrades. It was also proposed that Clarke made such a ride through Bloomfield in women's clothing on May Day, but he was not there in May of 1864 because he was serving as a regular Confederate cavalryman, and he was not there in any subsequent May. Still another version in court-martial testimony said a girl by the name of Sue Mundy stole a horse and started a report that it was Jerome Clarke who did it.

The name "Sue Mundy" in relation to Clarke came many weeks after Prentice coined the fictitious name, leaving his readers to believe "Sue" was a wild-riding, gun-slinging female of unknown identity.

In the court-martial proceedings of numerous guerrillas, there is no mention of Clarke's ever having been seen dressed as a woman.[19] Author and former *Louisville Courier-Journal* City Editor Young E. Allison wrote in 1935 that the question of the actual sex of Sue Mundy took three years to answer.[20] That was not possible, because Clarke only lived six months after the name "Sue Mundy" was attached to him.

So, where did Prentice come up with the name Sue Mundy? A published report, often repeated, said Prentice based the name Sue Mundy on Susannah Mundy, a black woman who had been in trouble with the authorities on numerous occasions.[21] In 1887, Allison wrote: "The real woman who bore the name of Sue Mundy seems to have been a notorious courtesan, living in the vicinity of Bloomfield, in Nelson County, Ky. She was a large woman, with the face and figure of an Amazon, piercing black eyes, and a profusion of black hair. She suddenly disappeared from her haunt, and it was understood had gone to join [Confederate Brigadier General] John Morgan and offered her services in the capacity of a spy, work that had been made popular by the reports of Belle Boyd's success."[22]

The name "Susan Mundy" appears in a list of relatives of some of the followers of Confederate guerrilla leader Captain William Clarke Quantrill, when a three-story brick building being used as a women's prison collapsed August 14, 1863, in Kansas City, Mo. Since the Kansas City incident appeared in print, it's possible, but not likely, that Prentice chose the name "Sue Monday" from that.[23] Jerome himself said that a girl by the name of Sue Mundy stole a horse and started a report that he did it, but it was Prentice who made the name "Sue Mundy" the stuff of infamy.[24]

Prentice, although once a friend and supporter of President Abraham

Lincoln, had become weary of the Union occupation of Louisville and state-wide federal military rule. That perhaps led to a reasonable, logical and likely explanation for the creation of the Sue Mundy character. It concerns Union Colonel Marcellus "Marc" Mundy and reports that women, in disguise as men, joined the federal army across the Ohio River from Cincinnati, Ohio, while Mundy was in charge of a northern Kentucky garrison.[25]

Mundy later served as Kentucky Provost Marshal in Louisville, where he was consistently critical of Prentice and sought to have the editor censured. Prentice could have been retaliating by naming his character after the Union officer who wasn't able to tell female recruits from males. At first, Prentice spelled his character "Monday," but said later he had learned the correct spelling was "Mundy," which just happened to be the way Marc Mundy spelled his surname. None of the theories of where Prentice came up with the name "Sue Mundy" appeared to be feasible for various reasons except for the Marc Mundy scenario. Allison's account of the origin of the name, written years after Clarke's guerrilla career, was like so many others that lacked corroboration.

It is possible Prentice had never thought of creating such a character until the report of Jerome Clarke at the stage robbery near Harrodsburg. Prentice's son, William Courtland Prentice, was killed while fighting under Morgan.[26] It may have been the newspaper editor was endeavoring to make the federal forces look foolish and to extract a degree of revenge for his son's death as Yankees tried and failed to capture a guerrilla that Prentice attempted to persuade his readers was female.

The biggest debate among Civil War historians concerning the Sue Mundy legend is whether Jerome Clarke was or was not a guerrilla. Clarke's service record proves that he was a legitimate Confederate soldier, but courts-martial proceedings indicate he rode with Confederate guerrillas and acted in that capacity. If he was acting as a Partisan Ranger, Clarke's status in the closing months of the war could be debated.

A great-grandnephew of Clarke, the late Marcellus Jerome Clarke of Anchorage, Ky., said he did not believe his kinsman was a marauding guerrilla. Jerry Clarke said his namesake was a scapegoat of the Union army, which had been embarrassed by the exploits of others.

He did not believe that the young Confederate soldier was the person Prentice was talking about when he invented the Sue Mundy character, nor did he believe his kinsman was tried, and was of the opinion that a document purporting to be a U.S. court-martial transcript was fake.[27]

The modern-day Marcellus Jerome Clarke made some interesting points. Occasionally, Prentice didn't recognize Jerome Clarke as Sue Mundy because in his stories he sometimes placed Clarke at one place and Sue Mundy in another at virtually the same time. Some of the confusion was caused by the alias used by Quantrill after he entered Kentucky January 1, 1865. He called himself "Captain James Clarke of the 4th Missouri Cavalry." Quantrill, 27, had killed a Colorado Union soldier by the same surname and had taken his identity papers. Quantrill and his men usually wore Union uniforms to conceal their identities. Quantrill was actually a Confederate cavalry captain, also referred to as a "captain of scouts or guerrilla," enrolling in the Rebel army January 29, 1862.[28]

There was also some confusion over a soldier named "Flowers," and some believed Jerome Clarke was using that name as an alias, but there was a Thomas Flowers among the guerrillas with whom Jerome and others associated.[29] When the name "Sue Mundy" appeared in print, Prentice did not immediately link the name to Jerome Clarke, but in the same story in which the character was created, he identified "Sue" as having previously been with Captain Gabriel Slaughter Alexander.[30] Jerome Clarke had been with Alexander, but Sue Mundy, not created then, had not. Prentice guessed Jerome's age at 22, although his correct age was 20. The fun Prentice was obviously having with his "Sue Mundy" character was tempered by the report that the editor's son, Major Clarence Joseph Prentice, had been lodged in a Confederate stockade after killing a fellow soldier. It was an incident that prompted Prentice to get special permission, possibly from President Lincoln, to travel through Union patrols into Rebel territory and visit his son. Clarence Prentice was soon freed, most likely through the influence of the powerful newspaper editor.

The question of why George Prentice violated the ethics of journalism to create the character Sue Mundy has never been answered to the satisfaction of Civil War historians. There was no woman guerrilla named Sue Mundy. It seems likely that after the stage robbery near Shaker Village, Jerome Clarke was the person Prentice was thinking of when he invented the character and Clarke's chances of surviving the war ended the day Sue Mundy took to the saddle.

To the people of the era, Sue Mundy was a mysterious and romantic character. In his post–Civil War book, *Noted Guerrillas, or the Warfare of the Border*, John Newman Edwards painted a portrait of the legend, referring to Sue Mundy as:

> A quiet, gentle, soft-spoken dandy, with his hair in love-knots six inches long, a hand like a school-girl, and a waist like a woman. Sometimes he

Left: This photograph of Marcellus Jerome Clarke was donated to the Filson Historical Society in Louisville in 1932 by Prince Wells of Bloomfield. Wells said in a statement attached to the back of the image that Clarke gave the photo to his father, Jessie S. Wells, who ran a general store in Bloomfield. Prince Wells claimed Clarke, as Sue Munday [*sic*], entered his father's store dressed as a woman just before the Battle of Perryville and was seeking a Union uniform, which he did not get there, but obtained later by "flirting with a soldier" and "leaving the soldier wearing just what he came into the world in." The Battle of Perryville was fought in early October 1862. Jerome Clarke was serving in other theaters of the war prior to and during the Perryville battle. The fictitious character "Sue Mundy" was not created until 1864. *Right:* The powerful editor of *The Louisville Daily Journal*, George Dennison Prentice, was known for his stinging editorials and eloquent poetry, but did something curious during the Civil War. The Connecticut-born Prentice created a character he called "Sue Monday" [*sic*], but later changed the surname spelling to "Mundy" and appeared to be trying to make Union officer Marc Mundy appear foolish for allowing women to sneak into the army. Prentice eventually attached the "Sue Mundy" name to Jerome Clarke. The late Kentucky Historian Laureate Dr. Thomas D. Clark, said Prentice could be "the Devil incarnate" or "like a little cherub" (both photographs from the Filson Historical Society, Louisville).

dressed also as a woman, hence the sobriquet of Sue. As a spy he came and went as a wind that blew. So many were his shapes and disguises, so perfectly under control were his speech and bearing, that in some quarters his identity was denied, in others his sex was a matter of doubt, in all, those who did not fear him had an improbable idea both of the man's prowess and personal appearance.

Mundy was a cool, brave, taciturn, experienced soldier, well acquainted with the country where he operated and utterly fearless. In addition, he was also a thorough fatalist. His smooth, open, rosy-cheeked face made almost any disguise easy of encompassment. His iron nerve carried him easily through many self-imposed difficulties that without it extrication could not have come through a regiment of cavalry. When he fought he fought savagely.

Beneath an exterior as effeminate as a woman of fashion he carried the muscles of an athlete and the energy of a racer. His long hair in battle blew about as the mane of a horse. The dandy in a melee became a Cossack; in desperate emergencies a giant.

There is Sue Mundy, the legend, but this is Sue Mundy, the true story ... based on fact. There were irregular Southern soldiers who became infamous to the federal authorities and citizens of Union persuasion, but they were adored by many Kentuckians and residents of other states as well. In recent years, a Quantrill Society was formed in Missouri that holds meetings and takes field trips to the sites where their hero spilled Yankee blood or wrote love poems to country girls.

Quantrill and others mentioned herein are subjects of great interest to Civil War students, historians and enthusiasts, but Jerome Clarke is the main character of this narrative. The question to be answered is whether Jerome Clarke should have been recognized as a Southern soldier, separated unwillingly from his ranks, or as the infamous Rebel guerrilla Sue Mundy, the scourge of Kentucky.

CHAPTER 1

Riding with the Thunderbolt

As thousands of Kentuckians left their homes and families to become part of the Civil War, a majority chose to fight as loyalists. Some 90,000 natives of the Bluegrass State joined the Union army or were drafted. The estimated 25,000 who became Confederate soldiers chose the South for a variety of reasons.[1]

Many followed their family's convictions or their own feelings about the issues involved. Younger men, of those not conscripted, were often influenced by forces that entered the state.

Brigadier General John Hunt Morgan had a significant number of Kentuckians in his command, adding more every time he returned to his native soil. The dashing Rebel, with his plumed hat and bravado personality, easily gained new followers.[2] Morgan's rapid movement of troops led to the sobriquet the "Thunderbolt of the Confederacy."[3]

When astride "Black Bess," the thoroughbred horse given him by Woodford County horseman Major Warren Viley, he presented a striking military figure.[4]

Jerome was put into the Fourth Kentucky Infantry, then detailed by Brigadier General Simon Bolivar Buckner to report with a detachment being sent to Bowling Green. He was a member of what would eventually become Kentucky's "Orphan Brigade."[5] The detachment remained in Bowling Green some two months, then a portion of it was converted into an artillery company under the command of Captain Rice Evans Graves.[6] Jerome was drilled two more months as an artilleryman before moving out to Fort Donelson, Tennessee, on the Cumberland River. There, in the winter of 1862, he fought in the four-day battle that was won by the Union on February 15. The loss was a hard one for Rebel forces, who had been whipped ten days earlier at Fort Henry, also on the Tennessee River.

The Union victories were the result of the undermanned condition of the Confederate forces and the Union gunboats that hammered the Rebel gun emplacements. The federal troops in those fights also had a tenacious leader in Brig. Gen. Grant.

Brigadier General Gideon Johnson Pillow, in a report to Captain Clarence Derrick, assistant Confederate adjutant general, wrote of the carnage witnessed by those who fought at Fort Donelson.[7]

> Such was the condition of the two armies at night-fall after nine hours of conflict, on the 15th instant [February, 1862], in which our loss was severe, and leaving not less then 1,000 of the enemy dead upon the field. We left upon the field, nearly all of his wounded, because we could not remove them. We left his dead unburied, because we could not bury them. Such carnage and conflict has perhaps never before occurred on this continent....

The Confederate force was estimated at 13,000, while with reinforcements the Union had as many as 40,000 soldiers for its use at Fort Donelson. Jerome joined Rebel combatants who found it necessary to surrender. They included his boyhood friend John Patterson and Brig. Gen. Buckner. They were taken to Camp Morton, Indiana, but escaped by overpowering guards after being taken to the White River to bathe. From there, Jerome and John returned to Kentucky.[8]

Jerome soon after made his way to Tennessee, where he was assigned the role of an infantryman in the Rebel army and ordered to report to Vicksburg, Mississippi. Later, Jerome was able to swap places with another soldier and join the Second Kentucky Battalion under the command of Captain John Dillard Kirkpatrick. He thus became one of Morgan's men.

Morgan had been appointed commander of the southwestern part of Virginia and a section of east Tennessee.[9] As a cavalryman in Morgan's command, Jerome saw action at Chattanooga and Ringold in Tennessee, then went to Decatur, Georgia, a small village outside Atlanta, where he recruited briefly for the Rebel army.

Jerome was a member of General Hylan Benton Lyon's command by April and on a march through Georgia, South Carolina and North Carolina. On that trek, Jerome and his compatriots fought no battles and the men caught up on their enjoyment of Southern hospitality. In early May, federal forces moved toward the Confederate capital of Richmond, Virginia, by way of a road to Dublin Depot over the New River bridge. Other Yankees moved in the direction of Saltville, Virginia. Generals William Woods Averell and George Crook commanded the federals, who appeared intent upon capturing both the saltworks and the lead mines near Wytheville, Virginia, while cutting off the Rebel forces from communication with Richmond.[10]

Jerome was with the "Morgan Brigade," then composed of 600 Rebels and commanded by Kirkpatrick and Major Jacob T. Cassell. Lieutenant Colonel Robert Augustus Alston brought the brigade up to reconnoiter with another under the command of Colonel Henry Liter Giltner.[11] The intention was to stop Averell, 32, a former drug clerk from Cameron, N.Y., and 1855 graduate of the U.S. Military Academy at West Point. Morgan's old division, some 400 dismounted cavalry, had made Dublin Depot, Virginia, and awaited Crook's arrival.

It was May 9, 1864, when scouts reported to Morgan that Averell appeared to be moving on Wytheville rather than Saltville. The next day, Morgan began tracking Averell and developing a plan in which a small force would be left behind to pin him down in the mountains.

Morgan took a shortcut, reaching Wytheville first.[12] He found a detachment of Rebel Brigadier General William E. "Grumble" Jones' brigade of cavalry in the town and placed them under the command of Colonel George Crittenden.

Morgan then ordered the small force to occupy a pass the federals would have to use to reach Wytheville and to stop them from advancing. Averell would have to take a wide detour if the plan worked. The entire command of Morgan moved into Wytheville the afternoon of May 11, 1864. The town had been captured previously by the Union army and part of it was burned.

Morgan found an item that had not been destroyed during the earlier raid and he believed it could prove very useful to the Southern cause. Basil Duke described his general's ingenuity upon discovering an old "six pounder" cannon that belonged to the town. The Rebels had brought no cannons with them because of the anticipated difficulty of getting them across the mountains. "General Morgan, having no artillery, at once took

21

charge of it and called for volunteers to man it," Duke wrote after the war. "Edgar Davis and Jerome Clarke of Captain (James E.) Cantrill's company and practical (*sic*) artillerists come forward and were placed in command of the piece."[13] At 3:30 that afternoon, gunfire erupted at the gap where Crittenden's men were stationed, marking the arrival of the federals.

The rest of the force double-timed to the gap, skirted through the woods and threatened the federals' rear. A fire fight raged for some time with Union sharpshooters on high ground making it hot for the Rebs. The federal troops fell back some 500 yards and fired from behind a house and other structures on a farm. Clarke and Davis were busy firing the commandeered piece of artillery, when Morgan himself pitched in to help.[14]

Once victory was assured, Morgan put his force on a march that soon took them back into Kentucky. The so-called June Raid was intended to regain prestige lost on the previous major raid, which reached into Ohio. Morgan also needed more men and wanted to recruit as many Kentuckians as he could while procuring horses for all who had none.[15]

Morgan reported to Richmond that he wanted to initiate a movement within the lines of U.S. Brigadier General Edward Henry Hobson, who left Mount Sterling on May 23, 1864, and was moving toward Louisa, 73 miles distant, with some 3,000 men. Another 2,500 federals were reported in Louisa, awaiting the arrival of Hobson. A uniting of federal forces at Louisa, plus support from Averell and Crook, would give the Yankees a decided edge in any future attempts to capture the saltworks and lead mines of southwestern Virginia.[16]

Morgan wrote to the Confederate adjutant general:

> This information has determined me to move at once into Kentucky, and thus distract the plans of the enemy by initiating a movement within his lines. His army, then numbering 2,200 men, would endeavor to avoid the force out of Louisa and expected only a "few scattered provost guards" to retard his progress. By the time he left in late May, his army may have numbered as many as 2,500 men. The Rebel division moved out in three brigades with Giltner at the head of about 1,100.

Lieutenant Colonel James William Bowles joined Majors Cassell and Kirkpatrick in leading their 600 men in three small battalions of the "old Morgan division." Alston also commanded part of the force that included two battalions of some 800 dismounted men from the other commands, mainly the second brigade. The two battalions of the third brigade were led by Lieutenant Colonel Robert M. Martin and Major George R. Diamond. The third brigade was commanded by Colonel Dabney Howard Smith.[17]

Jerome Clarke saw duty as a cavalryman in the Old Morgan Division as Morgan sought to reach Mount Sterling ahead of Burbridge, who lumbered from the extreme eastern part of Kentucky with artillery pieces. The Southerners marched through rugged mountain terrain, averaging as many as 27 miles a day.

Giltner reported losing some 200 horses in his brigade alone as the animals broke down because of the steep, rocky mountainsides. The strength of the horses was also depleted due to a lack of forage.[18]

The Rebels entered Kentucky and passed through the mountain town of Whitesburg. As the force moved toward central Kentucky, Morgan sent out 50 men to destroy the bridges on the Frankfort and Louisville Railroad and Captain Peter M. Everett was dispatched with 100 men to capture Maysville to the north. Morgan sought to magnify his strength and in doing so, bewilder Union officers.[19] There was time in Winchester for the Rebels to rob the Simpson and Winn Bank, where the loot wasn't all cash, but also included Charlotte F. Buckner's $2,500 in bonds.[20]

On June 8, 1864, telegraph lines were cut and the Rebels allowed no one to enter or leave Mount Sterling. A charge that morning drove federal Captain Edward C. Barlow of the 40th Kentucky Infantry and his troops from their defensive positions in the town. Jerome was among the Rebels rounding up prisoners, capturing several horses and destroying stores of supplies. Citizens were robbed and so was the Farmers' Branch Bank, which gave up an estimated $80,000.[21]

Everett's men tried to rob the Maysville branch of the Northern Bank of Kentucky while detached from the main force, but found the cash and securities had been moved.

They burned the Maysville fairground building and also raided Flemingsburg while Morgan took the second brigade and headed for Lexington, leaving the remainder of the force at Mount Sterling. The unmounted cavalrymen were in deplorable condition with only faith in their leader and the Southern cause to keep them going. They had marched 230 miles in ten days from Huyter's Gap, Virginia to Mount Sterling. Their shoes were worn to pieces and their feet were raw and bleeding.[22] Union Brigadier General Stephen Gano Burbridge had moved to central Kentucky much faster than Morgan had anticipated, reaching the edge of Mount Sterling before dawn June 9, 1864.

"I pursued, and, by marching ninety miles in twenty-four hours, came upon him at Mount Sterling yesterday morning, and defeated him," Burbridge wrote in a June 10, 1864, report to Major General Henry Halleck in Washington. "By stealing fresh horses he (Morgan) reached Lexington at 2 o'clock this A.M. Our forces held the fort, and Rebels did but little damage. He left here at 7 A.M. for Versailles. I start in pursuit with a fresh force this evening, and hope to capture his command,"[23] Burbridge said in his report.

Duke said after the war that Morgan arrived in Lexington the next morning and rousted defenders under the command of Colonel Wickliffe Cooper, then burned the government depot and stables. He said Morgan captured enough horses to mount all of his dismounted men in the first and second brigades. Jerome Clarke was with Morgan in Lexington and took part in the skirmish that forced the 4th Kentucky Union Cavalry to retreat to Fort Clay in the suburbs.[24]

The Branch Bank of Kentucky was forced to hand over $10,000 to the Rebel cause. Stores and citizens were relieved of goods, valuables and money. From Lexington, Morgan sent a company to Frankfort to "demonstrate," then directed his troops toward Georgetown.[25] Union Colonel George W. Monroe and 250 regular Union troops defended the capital along with militia, one unit of which included Governor Thomas Bramlette. The Rebels passed through Georgetown and about daylight on the morning of June 11, 1864, Morgan's troops arrived at Cynthiana and attacked from three directions.

A force of 300 men was on hand at the Harrison County seat of government to guard it from invading Rebels. They were home guardsmen and men of the 168th Regiment Ohio Volunteer Infantry.

The defenders occupied at least 25 houses that were quickly set afire by the invading Confederates. A covered bridge leading into town was well defended until a force of Morgan's men crossed the Licking River and began driving the federals back into town along the railroad.

North of town, at the burned Keller's railroad bridge, Giltner was made aware of a train headed for Cynthiana that was hauling as many as

1,500 federals under the command of Brigadier General Edward Henry Hobson. A second train was following with horses and supplies. Giltner's men fired on the first-arriving train as Morgan began circling the enemy by crossing the river.

Morgan took Cassell's battalion, got behind Hobson, and forced him to surrender. Federal casualties numbered as many as 80, with 500 prisoners rounded up by Morgan's forces. Some of Hobson's men successfully retreated, while others fled into the countryside. Hobson was taken to Cincinnati to be exchanged for Confederate officers but the plan didn't work. Hobson was freed and the Rebels who had escorted him were held captive for several weeks. After stores of supplies were captured and burned at Cynthiana, the bone-weary Morgan troopers sought rest.

Several had been sent as prisoner escorts and guards, others were still busy destroying track and bridges of the Kentucky Central Railroad as Morgan's force shrunk to 1,200 men. Basing his decision on two- and three-day-old reports by scouts of the location of Burbridge, and thinking there was no need for immediate concern, a Rebel lieutenant colonel made a tactical error. Robert M. Martin had ordered that 50 men establish a rear guard about a mile from camp with pickets to patrol the road. They were to protect the dismounted men from surprise attack, but the rear guard was placed not more than 200 yards from the vulnerable camp.[26]

It was three o'clock in the morning on a warm and mostly clear 10th of June, 1864.[27] The exhausted foot soldiers lay by their campfires. Suddenly, without warning from the pickets, Burbridge's advance stormed the camp. Some of the groggy Rebels were shot where they slept as Union cavalrymen rode over them. The dazed struggled to find their weapons, only to be trampled.

After an hour of fighting, the surviving Rebels made their way out of Mount Sterling, leaving 14 commissioned officers and 40 privates dead or wounded. Many were too badly wounded to be moved, a hundred others were taken prisoner and more than a hundred dispersed.[28] Giltner's command on the Paris road had tried to fight the 5,200-man Union force, but the Rebels were running out of ammunition. The cartridges captured the day before did not fit their guns. Morgan had instructed Giltner to take the seized guns as well as the ammunition. Giltner decided instead to hold onto the "better rifles" his troops already had. Morgan ordered a retreat on the Augusta Road, but the mounted reserve, trying to cover the retreat, came under heavy fire. The Rebels fought back, taking cover behind a stone fence on Ruddle's Mill Road and inflicting casualties on the Yankee force. The men in gray were also stained with crimson, including Jerome Clarke, who was wounded in the hand.[29] Bowles was overrun and Smith retreated through Cynthiana only to find himself surrounded on three sides. The only escape was the Licking River.

Basil Duke wrote: "Seeing the condition of affairs, the men became unmanageable and dashed across the river. Having been re-formed on the other side, they charged a body of cavalry which then confronted them and made good their retreat, although scattered and in confusion."

A report by Burbridge on the flight of Morgan's men also said many drowned trying to cross the river. Morgan paroled his prisoners on the Augusta Road and, gathering as many of his remaining force as possible, ordered a retreat.

Morgan moved out toward Claysville with Colonel Israel Garrard and his First Brigade in pursuit until he reached the mountains and made his escape. Jerome fled toward the west, unattached and soon to be called a "guerrilla."

CHAPTER 2

Lighting the Fire of Reprisal

Without direction or command, the unattached Morgan cavalrymen nonetheless remained loyal to the Southern cause and with or without their general, the Rebels strove for victory.

Both sides had "pressed" horses since the beginning of hostilities in 1861, but an incident five days after the Cynthiana fight helped fuel the fire of billowing guerrilla terrorism.

Jerome Clarke was not identified as being among those involved in the incident, but he would feel the reverberations caused by it, as would all Confederates separated from their units.

Virginian John R. Jones, 79, and his second wife, Anna (Grant), 42, had been married 40 days. Jones' young wife must have made him feel younger, listing his age as 68 on his marriage license. He was a Union man and with Confederate troops occasioning the neighborhood in northeast Nelson County, he feared for the safety of his wife and 18-year-old grand-daughter, Elizabeth.[1]

The family occupied a beautiful two-story, 15-room brick house that Jones built on the Bloomfield-Springfield Turnpike in 1857. It sat upon a large tract of prime agricultural land.[2] It was Friday, June 17, 1864, and Confederate Lieutenant Colonel George McCracken Jessee, a regimental commander under Morgan, was leading a group of the Morgan cavalry who survived the Cynthiana fight. Jessee began adding area farm boys to his ranks and discouraging blacks from joining the federal army. High-ranking Union authorities immediately labeled Jessee and his followers "guerrillas."

A Union report from Illinois and Indiana units serving in Kentucky called Jessee and his Rebels "...a fierce-looking lot of bearded mountain men, escaped prisoners, Copperheads with prices on their heads, farmers who had seen their homes go up in smoke, deserters and former cavalry troopers."[3]

They were compared by the Union to William Quantrill and his followers in Missouri, but Jessee and his force had militarily moved into a detached structure in Kentucky, similar to that of Confederate Colonel John S. Mosby in Virginia. They headquartered in Owen County, not far from Jessee's home place in adjacent Henry County, but their recruiting base knew no bounds. Jessee had served in the Kentucky General Assembly from 1857 to 1859 and was a respected farmer in the north-central counties, giving him legitimacy for recruiting purposes.

Jessee and a large contingent of cavalry had camped about three miles south of Bloomfield. Jerome Clarke's whereabouts at the time was uncertain, but events were unfolding that would eventually take on life or death consequences for the young Kentuckian. The force was estimated at 150 that stopped at or near Camp Charity, where Morgan's Rifles had been organized at the beginning of the war. The camp was along a meandering stream off a road between Bloomfield and Bardstown.

Jessee was sending out patrols to find fresh horses and one of them was told to inquire at Confederate sympathizer Green Duncan's mansion a short distance from camp. The patrol, instead, arrived at the Jones place, less than a mile from Duncan's, at 10 P.M. Finding only a mule, they awakened the slaves, asking what saddles and bridles there were. The slaves told the Rebs that only their master would be able to answer their questions.[4] Then, a young Negro boy, unaware that he was igniting a fuse that would lead to deadly results, innocently spoke of Jones' fancy saddle that he kept in the house.

The Confederates dismounted, walked onto a rear porch, knocked on the door and hallooed, but there was no answer. Private Thomas McIntire and his companions threatened to break down the door with an ax if Jones did not "deliver up" all his saddles and bridles. When Jones continued to remain silent, they threatened to burn his house. Jones would not comply, and instead loaded his gun.

Suddenly, two shots were fired from inside the house, the bullets crashing through the flags beside the door, striking McIntire and taking him down.[5] The bone above the elbow in McIntire's left arm was shattered, causing extensive bleeding and trauma. McIntire was taken to the nearby town of Chaplin, where a doctor found it necessary to amputate the mangled arm.[6] The wounded soldier was then transported to the Chaplin home of Confederate sympathizer Elias Hobbs some five miles east of Bloomfield, where he soon died from loss of blood.

When Jessee received word of the young cavalryman's death he was incensed and ordered that Jones be shot and his house burned. Three soldiers returned to the scene of the McIntire shooting and set fire to the light, wooden framework of the house. Apparently becoming fearful that his wife and granddaughter would die in the fire, Jones volunteered to surrender. Jones opened the door and stepped onto the porch, where the three Rebels opened fire, their bullets striking Jones in the heart and the abdomen. Jones fell dead without a groan.[7] After the Confederates left, neighbors came and helped the family put out the fire.

In a letter written June 21, 1864, to her grandmother and sisters, Nelson Countian Josephine "Josie" Thomas described the chaos. "The Negro (*sic*) men all run off and Mrs. Jones screamed and hollowed till they heard them at Pences.... She had sent two of the Negro women after Pence and he and his wife ran there. Mrs. Pence, barefooted, knocked her toe out of joint."

Josie also wrote that the Jones shooting indirectly resulted in the death of an acquaintance who went to tell a neighbor about the excitement. "They said she talked very calmly about the affair, but they had talked about it about 15 minutes when she made some little complaint and they went to her and she did not breathe but once or twice and was dead. She was affected with heart disease and I suppose becoming excited hastened her off."[8]

Burbridge became commander of the Union Military District of Kentucky and, in that position, kept hearing public outcries for action against citizen killings, but the course he chose proved to be a most unpopular one. On July 16, 1864, Burbridge issued General Order 59, which was a factor in fueling Kentucky's guerrilla war.

It said: "When an unarmed Union citizen is murdered, four guerrillas will be selected from the prisoners in the hands of the military authorities and publicly shot to death in the most convenient place near the scene of the outrage."

Burbridge wasted no time in seeing that the order was carried out. On July 19, 1864, Pierman Powell and Charles W. Thompson were taken from the Military Prison at Louisville and executed by firing squad. They were shot at Henderson for the killing of a "Union man" they had never met. Word of the executions spread throughout the region and a report that the Union would retaliate in Bloomfield put fear in the hearts of many of the community's most enthusiastic Rebel sympathizers who thought they might be shot. But it was two Confederate soldiers who were selected from a Union prison in Lexington to be executed in retaliation for Jones' death.

One version of how the selection was made said there were two red beans and many white beans in a hat that was passed around to all the prisoners.[9] All selected white beans except the two who would die and they did not know at the time for what they had been chosen. Another version of the selection process said they were required to draw straws.[10] Still another said names were drawn from a hat. Before getting around to Bloomfield, Burbridge ordered two soldiers executed in Scott County, July 27, 1864; two at Russellville July 29, 1864 and four at Eminence August 12, 1864.

John May Hamilton, a 37-year-old veteran Confederate soldier who had a wife and children back home on the farm in Johnson County, was unlucky at the draw for the Jones retaliation. So was 20-year-old Richmond Berry of Livingston County. Hamilton was captured March 6, 1864, near his mountain home. He had been discharged after a year's enlistment and was serving as a partisan ranger. Hamilton was attached to Company G, 7th Battalion, Confederate Cavalry under Captain Sidney Cook of Carter County. Hamilton's association with "Sid" Cook, labeled by some as a guerrilla with operations mainly in Elliott and Morgan Counties, didn't help his chances of staying alive. Cook, during the summer of 1863, rode with the 7th Confederate Cavalry Battalion, commanded by Lieutenant Colonel Clarence Prentice, son of the *Louisville Daily Journal* Editor George Prentice.[11] It was ironic that Cook served under the son of the anti–Confederate and bitterly anti-guerrilla editor.

Major Francis Henry Bristow of the Eighth Kentucky Cavalry was sent to Bloomfield to carry out the executions. He and his men arrived Aug. 13, 1864, and camped on Sallie Stone's farm.[12] Hamilton and Berry were sent from Lexington to Lebanon and placed in the care of Hobson.[13]

As soon as the prisoners arrived and the detail that brought them to Bloomfield made contact with Bristow, they lined up for a march and it didn't take long for the group to reach a spot on Bunker Hill on the south side of town.[14] Berry began to weep and was chastised by Hamilton.

"Don't cry," Hamilton said. "Die like the brave Southern soldier you are."[15] Berry asked permission to dictate a final note to his father and Bristow agreed. It said:

Dear Pa:

I am to be executed in a few moments. I do not want you, ma and the children to grieve after me; bear it with as much fortitude as possible. I think I am prepared to die. I have been living as a Christian ever since I have been in prison, reading my testament and praying. So don't grieve for any sake. Assure yourself that I am prepared and not scared.

Your son,
R. Berry.[16]

Berry had a knife in his pocket that had gone undetected.

He told one of the guards escorting him, "Take this, it is all I have to give you."[17] Berry and Hamilton stood facing a firing squad whose weapons had been loaded in advance. Some had real loads, others didn't. Those firing would not know who had the live loads that would inflict the mortal wounds. Berry is reported to have asked Bristow not to shoot him in the face because it would make it so hard on his mother.

The same report said Bristow agreed.

"Ready! Aim! Fire!" was quickly ordered by Bristow and the two prisoners fell to the ground. Hamilton was shot in the head and chest and exhibited no signs of life, but Berry moaned in pain from a mortal chest wound and it appeared his soul would not take flight immediately. Bristow quickly walked forward, took aim with his revolver and fired five shots into Berry's face.[18] The description of the execution spread far and wide, generating volatile anti–Union sentiment. The federal troops left town immediately and the people of Bloomfield retrieved the bodies.

They took them to Colonel Isaac Stone's residence in town where drops of blood spilled on the floor and according to local legend, would not fade away.[19] Stone bought two coffins and after appropriate preparations, the bodies were made available for public viewing at the Masonic Lodge. The whole town wept for the young men.[20]

The two were given Christian burials in Bloomfield's Maple Grove Cemetery; however, the family came a short time later and took Berry's body back home. Hamilton was allowed to rest in peace at Bloomfield.

The retaliation executions became commonplace and the guerrilla war grew in intensity. It was estimated that more than 50 men were put to death by Burbridge's firing squads.

CHAPTER 3

Scattered Like a
Covey of Quail

Morgan's embattled cavalry spread out over Kentucky, some able to visit family and friends, while others sought food and shelter from Confederate sympathizers or from people who had to be persuaded to cooperate.

Jerome was one of a handful of cavalrymen who remained with Captain Gabriel Slaughter "Gabe" Alexander, 35, a Mercer County native. Alexander had been with Company C of the First Kentucky Infantry before joining the Second Kentucky Cavalry under Morgan.

Meanwhile, in another theater of the war, Bullitt County native Henry Clay Magruder, 20, was building a reputation. He fought in the Tennessee battle of Shiloh, was with Morgan and was a veteran of scores of skirmishes. Magruder, 5-foot-6, with shoulder-length hair and a stocky build, was the son of Dennis S. Masden and Amy Magruder of Bullitt County. Amy was the daughter of Ezekiel Magruder of Maryland and Nancy Miller of Pennsylvania.

On April 29, 1847, Amy married John Shelton Masden, Dennis Masden's first-cousin. *Three Years in the Saddle*,[1] mentioned earlier, said Magruder was 15 when he learned he was a bastard child, but he expressed only love for his mother in the opening pages of the book, not blaming her for his "fatalistic approach to life and hatred of mankind." Henry Magruder lived with his uncle William M. Magruder and aunt Elizabeth Ann (Samuels) in his late teens. When he was 19, Magruder joined the Confederate Army at Camp Charity in Nelson County, where Colonel John "Jack" Allen, a

Morgan officer from adjacent Spencer County, was recruiting. When Allen's command was moved to Bowling Green, Magruder had to select the company into which he would be mustered. At that time, an honor guard was being organized for General Simon Bolivar Buckner. An enlisted man from each of Kentucky's counties was to serve in "Buckner's Guides" and Magruder became "the member from Bullitt."[2]

When Buckner pulled out for Fort Donelson, he left his fancy-riding honor guard in Bowling Green, where General Albert Sidney Johnston observed them in action. He watched Magruder and his comrades picking up dollars from the ground at full gallop, plus springing from their horses on the run and vaulting back into the saddle without slowing the speeds of the animals. Johnston had the unit attached to him as bodyguards, saying he would also use them as "scouts, spies and guides."

When Johnston fell in the battle of Shiloh, Magruder was again a detached soldier and hardened by the bitter fighting. "I was sent the night of the first day (at Shiloh) with dispatches for General Breckinridge, whose headquarters were near the river, in sight of the gunboats," Magruder dictated to Talbott.

"My way led directly across the battle-field, and that night I shall never forget. It was dark and raining. I could hear the groans of the wounded all around me, and often my horse would stumble over some unseen object, and a low, piteous groan would tell me it was some stricken soldier or the dull, dead sound of my horse's foot would tell me it was a dead one, whether Rebel or Yankee I could not tell, nor did I care." Magruder left it to the torch details to remove the dead and help the wounded from the field, but in the darkness he flipped the bodies to empty their "fob and pockets." He claimed to have collected $1,200 that night. The next morning, Magruder said he obtained $2,000 in gold from a young Negro boy who told him he'd taken it from the dead general's (Johnston's) tent. "I gave him a ball through the brain and that gold was mine," Magruder said.[3]

After Shiloh, Magruder needed a new command and he chose to join Morgan. He fought numerous skirmishes through northern Tennessee and southern Kentucky as he and others sought Morgan's whereabouts. The band made its way to Bardstown, then to Bloomfield, where the community's many Southern sympathizers provided food and shelter for the Rebs and forage for their horses.

Magruder heard that Morgan had been fighting around Harrodsburg and, commanding a small unit, left in that direction.[4] Before Magruder had reached the vicinity of Harrodsburg, members of Morgan's Cavalry who had fought at Cynthiana were encountered and Magruder received the intelligence he had sought, but the breakup of Morgan's force was not the news he'd hoped to get.

He turned his mount and led his men back toward Bloomfield, just 32 miles southeast of the federal headquarters at Louisville.[5] Jerome Clarke had also found the Nelson County area hospitable to Confederate soldiers and, when he hooked up with Captain "Gabe" Alexander, became acquainted with Magruder. Alexander gathered 40 Confederate cavalrymen, including Jerome and Magruder, and led them south to the Cumberland River and into Tennessee.

To the squad, Jerome became known as "Rome" or "Rome-ee." Magruder was sometimes referred to as "Mack" or "Captain Mack." Magruder did not endear himself to the residents of Monroe County that borders the Kentucky-Tennessee line during the southern trek. Colonel C.W. Biggers wrote to Governor Thomas E. Bramlett, June 16, 1864, asking for ammunition so a force could be raised to fight guerrillas.

"Magruder is now in our county with 25 men only, scouring and stealing about," Biggers wrote, adding that he could chase Magruder and his band from Monroe County in two days if the governor would supply guns and ammunition. The letter complained of horses and cattle being stolen in several Kentucky counties along the border with Tennessee.

Magruder claimed that in order to help local farmers, he would find the culprits responsible.[6] After determining the place where stolen cattle would likely be taken across the Cumberland River, Magruder staked out the spot and waited. He saw 44-year-old Holman Rice Foster and two other men with a canoe and heard comments to indicate they were planning a raid. Magruder was accused of becoming the judge and jury, gunning them down. Foster's family claimed Magruder ambushed the three men and it appeared they were correct, although later, Magruder denied that he killed the three.[7] Foster served as coroner of Barren County two terms and was a major in the state militia, which gave Magruder a motive for killing him.

After a month of skirmishes, Alexander's losses were severe. Besides the killed and wounded, many of his men had been captured, prompting Alexander to direct the remainder back toward north-central Kentucky. A long ride for the Rebs ended at Silver Springs in Marion County, July 27, 1864. There, Alexander's men met a scout of federals who opened fire immediately. Alexander was shot in the head and died instantly.

The demoralized command was taken over by Lieutenant Dick Mitchell of Springfield.[8] As the detached ex–Morgan cavalry members and others continued to circulate across the state, the idea of using black soldiers to hunt them gained momentum in Louisville and Washington.

LOUISVILLE, Ky.,
July 28, 1864.
(Received 12 P.M.)

Hon. E.M. STANTON:

General Burbridge has earnestly asked for authority to mount two colored regiments, the horses to be seized from citizens of known disloyalty. General Thomas has reported to you fully, favorably on the application. It is most important that this authority should be given, and promptly.

These regiments, composed of men almost raised, as it were, on horseback, of uncompromising loyalty, and having an intimate knowledge of the topography of the country, would prove a powerful instrumentality in ridding the State of those guerrilla bands of robbers and murderers which now infest and oppress almost every part of it. Besides, their presence in the different counties engaged in this popular service would exert the happiest influence in favor of the Government policy of employing colored troops.

J. HOLT[9]

Federal patrols had fanned out and were looking for unattached Rebels in areas where they'd been seen before, such as Bloomfield, Taylorsville, nine miles north of Bloomfield, and Bardstown, eleven miles southwest of the Confederate oasis. Mitchell's squad received word that Jessee was packing up to leave the state, but when a rendezvous was made with Jessee, he denied the report and said his orders were to remain in Kentucky.[10]

Jerome and others found "citizens clothes" and melded into some of the safe abodes. Jerome chose Nelson County, where he boarded for some three weeks.[11] His stay was uneventful until he overheard some women at a meeting saying that he was one of Morgan's men, a Rebel in their midst who might represent danger if Union patrols came looking for him. He asked his landlord for advice and was told Magruder was in the area with a group of eight or ten men and maybe he should join them. There was little chance of Jerome being turned over to the federals, but he chose to leave. He looked for and found Magruder.[12]

Heavy rains in the latter days of August 1864 caused streams to run high and presented an obstacle to travel. Magruder's guerrilla command had grown to 30 men, but was forced to wait for the waters to recede before taking on new adventures. It was on a ride to Bloomfield by way of nearby Fairfield that the guerrillas encountered the pugnacious federal guerrilla hunter, Major James Henry Bridgewater from Hall's Gap in Lincoln County. He called his home guard force the "Hall's Gap Battalion" or sometimes the "Hall's Gap Tigers."

Rather than engaging Bridgewater's force, the guerrillas skirted them and took flight in a maneuver so successful they had time to stop for beverages and roll tenpins in Grayson Springs.[13] As members of the Magruder-Clarke consortium considered their next move, other guerrilla bands were operating nonstop across Kentucky.

Jacob Coffman "Jake" Bennett's gang raided Burkesville June 10, 1864, forcing men of the Union's 13th Kentucky to flee. A story in the *Louisville Daily Democrat,* June 18, 1864 said:

"Burkesville is situated on the Cumberland river (*sic*), and has prob-

Former Confederate officer Dick Mitchell of Springfield, Ky., rode with Jerome Clarke on numerous raids and was among the guerrillas who made Bloomfield his headquarters. Bloomfield resident Grace Green Snider recited a poem to the author about Mitchell in 1971. "Dick Mitchell got his horse shot, expecting to be killed. But (Zay) Coulter killed a Yankee and the horse's place did fill. Dick Mitchell jumped the Yankee's horse and away he then did ride. He rode right into Bloomfield with his men all by his side. They drank up all the lagers and danced around the town. The plumes the girls put in his hat swung almost to the ground" (courtesy Snider-Ballard Collection).

ably been visited by the guerrillas oftener than any other town in the State." The same story said Bennett's gang broke open the stores in Burkesville and took everything of value. Bennett was born March 17, 1840, in the Island community, a part of Muhlenburg County that later became McLean County. Jake was the fourth of six children born to Washington and Indiana (Coffman) Bennett. He served with the Confederate army, joining Company H, 8th Kentucky Infantry. One of his claims to fame was playing a major role in planning the tunneling out of the Ohio State Prison at Columbus with General John Hunt Morgan, Captain Thomas Hines and others.

Major James H. Bridgewater established a reputation as a fearless Rebel guerrilla hunter and led his Kentuckians successfully against William Quantrill and others. Bridgewater made many enemies because of the behavior of his force in the disregard of the rights of citizens (image courtesy of Patti Hesterly and David Gambrel).

Jessee was leading as many as 200 men through Shelby, Spencer and Nelson Counties, reportedly with intentions to soon join General Nathan Bedford Forrest, who was believed headed for Kentucky. News reports said that other than stealing horses, Jessee's men committed no depredations during their leisurely ride, but added recruits in every town. The column went on to capture Bardstown, where the force was divided, with part going into Meade County and the rest to do damage to the Louisville and Nashville Railroad.[14] Four men robbed people on the streets of Bloomfield, June 18, 1864, boasting that they were Union deserters. Considering where they had chosen to rob, the story was easy to believe.[15]

Trains were intercepted at Pleasureville and had to

back up to Louisville until the guerrillas, who placed obstructions on the tracks and opened fire on the train crews, could be routed. Citizens were not particularly eager to battle the guerrilla bands. G.W. Caplinger wrote to Governor Bramlette that he had only been able to recruit eight men in Shelby County in his effort to gather a company, but that 50 men were reported at the command of a captain in Mount Eden, where Spencer, Shelby and Anderson Counties come together.[16]

The story was the same throughout the state. Citizens could not be persuaded to fight without the promise of arms and ammunition and the federal commanders could not supply them. The guerrillas were so active along the Ohio River during the summer of 1864 that hardly a day went by that the Louisville newspapers did not have a report, whether accurate or not, of their activities. The reports called guerrilla leaders "notorious outlaws."

Six guerrillas boarded the steamer *Tarascon* when it docked at Lewisport July 10, 1864. Saying they were under the command of Captain Tom Henry, a former man of Morgan from Union County, the six claimed they only wanted something to drink. They met a federal soldier from Company B of the 44th Indiana Volunteers and demanded he have a drink with them. When they toasted the health of Confederate President Jeff Davis, the Yankee declined, but soon was persuaded that it wasn't worth the consequences not to lift his glass. Because he drank with them, and to the health of Davis, the Rebs caused him no harm. When the women aboard refused to grant the guerrillas a "Southern air and a Southern song," they left the boat and waved farewell.[17]

Owen Garrett led a guerrilla band composed of men from Meade, Hardin and Bullitt Counties that was frequently seen in the West Point area. Bill Porter also directed irregulars in raids along the Ohio River. On July 29, 1864, state troops and Anderson County home guardsmen investigated a report of a guerrilla encampment on the Salt River in Spencer County. The force found an abandoned camp and broke up into squads, searching for signs of the Rebs. Twenty of the loyalists rode into Taylorsville, Spencer County's seat of government, unaware that eleven of Jessee's men were leaving town after having a drink at a local tavern. The Rebs saw the 20 coming across the Salt River covered bridge and retreated only long enough to wheel and charge. The firing occurred across the street from the courthouse and the result was the death of one of Jessee's men, Albertus Redman of Anderson County, and the wounding of another man.

Besides the gunfire generated by Jessee's men, some townspeople were also shooting at the home guard, including an unidentified woman "very conspicuous in the use of a revolver," said a report Aug. 1, 1864, in the *Tri-Weekly Commonwealth*. The *Louisville Daily Journal*'s coverage of the event said it wasn't true that townspeople fired on the home guard.

Conflicting reports were not uncommon as the newspapers of the time clamored for scoops. Reports of death and violence poured into the newspapers daily. The body of a man about 22 years old, 5-foot-9 and a half with dark hair and eyes, was found beside the road at Bloomfield. He'd been shot five times. There was a pair of broken handcuffs in his pocket and one wrist exhibited evidence that he'd been shackled.[18]

Guerrillas invaded Bagdad in Shelby County Aug. 6, 1864, seized telegraph operator G.H. Radford, stole his money and telegraph key and burned the telegraph office. Radford was released unharmed.[19] John Martin, W.D. Schoolfield and Dr. J.R. Foy of the Second Kentucky Cavalry, CSA were arrested further north in Owen County Aug. 2, 1864, and charged with leading guerrillas. The members of Company B, 4th Kentucky Cavalry, CSA were taken to Louisville, then to Lexington for confinement.[20] The Lexington Military Prison was an old warehouse near the Central Kentucky Railroad. It was described by a Kentucky Unionist in a James M. Prichard article about General Order 59 as a "loathsome prison," containing the refuse of both armies. It was where guerrillas and Confederate regulars were confined along with political prisoners, Union deserters and bounty jumpers.

In Mount Washington, only 16 miles southeast of Louisville, Thomas Pratt, George Day and J.F. Blankenbaker were seized as suspected guerrillas and confined.[21] Getting plenty of press from the Louisville papers was Thomas Carlin Dupoyster, a 21-year-old Reb from Ballard County whose brother, Joseph, fought for the Union. Dupoyster was a Confederate soldier in Company A, 2nd Kentucky Regiment and served at Fort Donelson, where he was captured.

He was imprisoned at Camp Douglas in Chicago where his mother, Elizabeth (Nichols) Dupoyster, visited him in 1862. It proved to be the last time she would see him. She drowned on the way home when the boat in which she was riding overturned.[21] Dupoyster escaped Fort Donelson and joined Woodward's Cavalry, but became a free agent of the war as did Jerome Clarke and many others after Morgan's defeat at Cynthiana. On Sept. 12, 1864, the *Louisville Daily Democrat* listed the Dupoyster gang, although not identifying the source. They were: Captain Dupoyster, Ben Wiggington, Tim Wiggington, Ern Simmons, Lib Garrett, Owen Garrett, Polk Burch, A.C. Combs, Henry Thompson, John Thompson, Jim Norris, William Hubbard, Damphrey Hays, Clay Hays, Tom Kelly and Frank Strand.

The Ohio River community of Henderson was reported to be "almost deserted" by mid–August 1864 as refugees, fearing roving bands of guerrillas, fled to Louisville and cities farther north. Residents of Union and Daviess Counties were also in fear of their safety and many had fled as well.[22]

Fighting occurred any place Union patrols and Rebel guerrillas crossed paths. Gunfire could be heard at any hour of the day or night and Kentuckians were terrified to hear approaching horses or gunfire in the distance. It was not possible to know what answer would be the best should a voice in the night ask, "Is this the house of loyal people?"

Guerrillas and federals fought along Simpson Creek in Spencer County Aug. 17, 1864, and although several were reported killed on both sides, other details were absent.[23]

Guerrilla leader "Black" Dave Martin became active in Shelby County, his band throwing a train off the Louisville and Frankfort tracks in Bagdad Aug. 25, 1864. "Black Dave" was of dark complexion, but was Caucasian.

The following day, Martin led 25 men into Shelbyville, but they were beaten back by sharpshooting citizens firing from a blockhouse in the town square. The fire from the blockhouse killed three and wounded five.

On Aug. 30, 1864, federal troops and home guardsmen were fired on by Rebel guerrillas as they entered Taylorsville through a covered bridge. The guerrillas made it so hot for the blueclads, they were forced to take shelter in the courthouse. No casualties were reported.[24]

CHAPTER 4

The Battle Flag Flies High

Bloomfield was a quiet village, traversed by the usually docile waters of meandering Simpson Creek. It was centered on hilly terrain through which passed a north-south, mostly-dirt turnpike. The turnpike north would take a traveler to Taylorsville and hence to Louisville. To the south of town was a crossroads, one leading to Springfield and the other to Bardstown. The towns of Fairfield and High Grove were west of Bloomfield and Chaplin to the east.

Bloomfield was a community of fewer than 450 inhabitants in the early 1860s. It was a Rebel town and it was said that of the total population, there were only four Union sympathizers.[1] It was a town of such Southern proclivity that the arrival of federal soldiers did not need to be announced because people only needed to watch those considered unloyal heading for hiding places. A doctor who feared punishment for his pro–Confederate politics hid in the hayloft to avoid a federal patrol and another outspoken Reb climbed a mulberry tree, going in the house for supper only after darkness fell and the Union boys departed.[2] One faithful federal in Bloomfield was John Allen Terrell, a 40-year-old dry goods merchant. Another was a former clerk in the store, Felix Grundy Stidger of nearby Taylorsville, who spied for the Union against the Confederate underground known as the "Copperheads." The identities of the other two Yanks were a matter of conjecture.

Bloomfield played a special role during the Civil War, becoming a haven for Rebel guerrillas. So close to Louisville, it also became a hunting ground for federal patrols, decoy guerrillas and home guardsmen who sought to kill or capture the irregulars. Still the guerrillas returned, despite the danger of confrontation, which they viewed as a challenge. Flying majestically from a pole in the middle of town was the welcome banner for Rebel soldiers, the battle flag of the Confederate States of America.[3] The flag of rebellion should have been expected in the town that claimed to have furnished the first Kentucky volunteers for the Confederate army.[4]

Bloomfield scribe Dr. A.H. Merrifield said the Rebel guerrillas had a significant role to play in the town during the Civil War. "They would change their base of operations as often as the wind would change. When least expected they would dash into the town at any hour of the day or night. They were always more welcome than Yankees not withstanding they were bad enough. The approach of the Yankees always brought apprehension as well as consternation to the citizens of the old town. I suppose I was troubled as much as anyone, my farm midway and an equal distance from the two pikes, Chaplin and Springfield. Wishing to avoid Bloomfield when the Yankees were there the guerrillas would invaribly strike through the country from one pike to the other frequently stopping at my house at the hour of midnight. Supper had to be prepared for them and their horses fed. Notwithstanding they were looked upon as desperadoes and cut-throats I much preferred seeing a guerrilla any time than a Federal. They professed to have been friends to the South although their mode of warfare was not conducted on a line with that of the regular army. Yet with all their cruelty and no fear of death they (were) always met with an open welcome. They seemed to love Bloomfield and were willing to shed their blood in her defense."

Nelson County native Henry Turner, 20 in 1864, rode with Jerome and Magruder. Turner had been with the Confederate Army's Company G, Eighth Kentucky, Cluke's Cavalry. Others in the usually close alliance with Jerome and Magruder were Bill Maraman of Bullitt County, who was 17 in 1864, and Bill Marion, 33, who wore a full, scraggly beard and mustache. Marion was actually Stanley Young, of Nelson County, born in 1831, the son of Virginian St. Clair Young and Kentuckian Amelia Hammond. During the September term of court in 1850 Young was shot and killed at the Jameson boarding house in Corydon, Harrison County, Indiana, by William Charles Marsh, father-in-law of his son, William Singleton Young. Family troubles had boiled over until the two were bitter enemies. At the dinner table that day the quarrel was renewed and Young threw a fork at Marsh, then Marsh drew a revolver and shot him dead.

Stanley Young was 19 when he witnessed the killing of his father. He vowed revenge, which was fueled by Marsh being acquitted by a court that ruled he fired in self defense. Nearly eight years later on May 26, 1858, in Brandenburg, Young learned Marsh was talking to some other men on the street. He made his way to the second floor of a hotel and crawled out onto a porch directly above Marsh. He killed the man who had taken the life of his father by shooting him in the top of his head.[5]

Young was never arrested or brought to trial for his crime. While on the run from the law, he decided his family had suffered enough by his actions and he sought to cloak his identity by becoming "Bill Marion." It was Jerome Clarke, Henry Magruder, Bill Marion, Dick Mitchell, Samual Oscar "One-Arm" Berry, Jr. and James Warren "Jim" Davis who initially made up the core of a redoubtable guerrilla band.

Berry was born in November 1836 in Clay County, Mo., and at the age of nine was orphaned. He was accepted by the Shakers near Harrodsburg in 1845 along with his brother, William Wallace Berry, 7; and his brother

Thomas F. Berry, 6, was adopted by the Shakers in 1847. Berry lost his right arm just above the wrist when it became entangled in machinery while he was working in Lexington before the war. Davis, 32, from Woodford County, had ridden with several guerrillas, including Jerome, Magruder and Berry, after escaping from military prison in Louisville. He suffered from epilepsy and sometimes had to be rescued from a seizure by his comrades. Davis was treated regularly by Dr. Isaac McClaskey, who lived a few miles north of Bloomfield and was the personal physician of many other guerrillas as well.

Confederate Orderly Sergeant Samual Oscar "One Arm" Berry (left) with Rebel Cavalryman Marcellus Jerome Clarke. Berry, a former Mercer County school teacher, lost his right arm just above the wrist in a machinery accident in Lexington, Ky., prior to the war. Berry was generally known as a peacemaker among the irregulars, but Clarke became menacing, especially after the sobriquet "Sue Mundy" was attached to him (courtesy Warren Larue).

Davis, who painted himself at times to look like a native American in war paint, also carried a bugle with him. He would occasionally announce his comings and goings with blasts from the instrument and sometimes to the chagrin of his associates.[6] On one occasion, he sounded a charge and led a band of guerrillas several miles before giving up the ruse. Magruder's stoic ruthlessness became known far and wide. The Bloomfield merchant, John Terrell, who was 41 in 1864, said of Magruder:

> I know Henry C. Magruder. I saw him very frequently in the streets and on the road leading to Bloomfield, dressed generally in a fancy suit, sometimes in a velvet jacket and pants, high boots, large spurs, and riding fine horses and accoutered with several large sized pistols. Sometimes he wore a large ostrich feather in his hat. I have seen him in a suit of red clothes, made of red cloth or flannel. The party he was with rarely exceeded 25, from that to 60, but sometime he was with two or three.

There were other bases of operations for various guerrilla bands throughout Kentucky.

Dupoyster's clique was frequently seen in and around the Ohio River town of Brandenburg. A letter published in the *Nashville Daily Times and True Union*, Sept. 2, 1864, told a story of brutality that was attributed to Dupoyster and his men. "On Tuesday evening, the 23rd (of August, 1864), Captain Deposter (*sic*), with twenty-two of his guerrilla band, went to the house of David Henry, and, after cursing and abusing him and his family, demanded all the arms and money about the house."

The story said that after the guerrillas destroyed the guns by smashing them against trees, they took jewelry and shawls from Henry's daughter, as well as Henry's shirts, then one of his men by the name of Bryant shot Henry through the left breast. Dupoyster then slapped Henry's daughter as she sought to comfort her dying father and threatened to kill both the daughter and Henry's wife if they did not stop their wailing. After examining Henry's wound and taking his pulse, Dupoyster declared the "damned old abolitionist had got about enough." He then "arrested" Henry's youngest son and declared there were three other men in the neighborhood he would kill before nightfall. His men seized William Brown and Neal Neafus, but Dupoyster was talked out of killing them by Jonathan B. Shacklett, whose word that they were innocent of being Yankee sympathizers was accepted.[7] The guerrillas were on the move in September 1864, seldom knowing what lay ahead in the next bend of the road. It was just happenstance that John Smith, a Negro soldier of the Union army, had been home visiting and was riding toward his unit in Louisville when he met them. Smith was hanged, without fanfare or justice, by the side of the road. The names of those responsible were not learned.

While many of his former cavalrymen continued to fight on their own hook, Morgan paid the supreme price for the Confederacy with his life. Morgan was shot in the back Sept. 4, 1864 in Greeneville, Tennessee. News of their leader's death filtered back to the guerrillas, reinforcing what loyalty they retained for the weakening Confederate army. They had no lack of loyalty to Morgan.

On Thursday, Sept. 8, 1864, the Magruder gang stopped at the home of 50-year-old Luke Samuels, two miles from Lebanon Junction, which was 27 miles south of Louisville. Magruder asked Samuels about a fine horse he had owned. Samuels told Magruder the horse had been sent away and he would not be able to get it back. Magruder told Samuels that when he returned in a few days, the horse had better be there.

The guerrillas returned four days later, but Samuels again said it was impossible for him to get the horse back. Magruder, becoming enraged, spotted Samuels' 21-year-old son, Isaac, in the yard and knotted a rope around his neck. The elder Samuels' pleas that the boy's life be spared fell on deaf ears and the guerrillas strung him up. Samuels reminded Magruder that he and his son were schoolmates and he begged loudly for the boy's life. As his punishment for not having the horse as ordered, the elder Samuels was bludgeoned on the head with a heavy Navy Colt revolver, leaving him unconscious.[8]

Soon after the guerrillas left, Isaac Samuels' sister, Lucinda, 32, came out of hiding, cut the rope and lowered her brother to the ground. Both Isaac and the elder Samuels recovered from their injuries. The guerrillas rode to a camp just south of Lebanon Junction where they stayed until the following morning, planning a raid and adding more men to their ranks.

CHAPTER 5

Workin' on the Railroad

Jerome Clarke, Henry Magruder, Sam Berry and at least a dozen other Rebel irregulars were early risers Sept. 12, 1864. By 6 A.M., they were seven miles south of Lebanon and six miles from New Haven on the Bardstown Branch Railroad.

The guerrillas stacked large stones and several worn-out ties on the rails in a cut with steep banks on both sides. The work was done with dispatch and the guerrillas took their positions. A postwar military court-martial transcript shows John Morgan, no known relation to the Confederate general, was returning home to Marion County from his studies in Louisville.

He was sitting in a left-side passenger seat reading a book as the train entered the cut. There were 47 Irish railroad laborers also among the passengers. Morgan looked out and saw men on the hillside with guns, and when they started shooting, all the shots were aimed at the train's engine. One of the laborers was wounded, but everyone else escaped injury. Then came the unmistakable signal that the engineer had spotted the obstruction as he hit the brakes and the frozen wheels began squealing as they scraped the cold steel, producing showers of sparks.

It was too late to stop the locomotive, which plunged from the tracks with its tender and came to a halt. The guerrillas quickly moved to the cars. "Get down!" someone shouted and most of the passengers dove for the floor, although Morgan didn't have time to oblige. Magruder and Clarke were in his car so fast, he could only raise his hands where he sat. Magruder, dressed in Confederate gray with four pistols buckled around him and one in each hand, was like a man possessed. "God damn you, get out!" he yelled. Morgan moved quickly, but others hesitated, which earned them another prompt from Magruder, whose dark eyes were gleaming like a demon's.[1]

"What do you mean, you God-damned, sons-of-bitches! Get out of here!"

This rare photograph shows (left to right) Henry Magruder, Jerome Clarke and "One-Arm" Sam Berry. A reverse image, because the original was a tintype, probably accounts for the appearance that Berry had a complete right arm below the elbow. Testimony in guerrilla courts-martial proved it was Berry's right arm that had been severed between the wrist and elbow prior to the war. Magruder is wearing a fur and Jerome had taken a fur from a woman during a raid on Springfield, Ky. in November 1864 (courtesy Frank Walker).

As Magruder and Jerome were forcing the passengers from the car, some were sneaking valued items to an elderly woman who was letting them know she would take care of them.[2] She kept $4,000 worth of valuables and cash in her bag, refusing to allow any of the guerrillas to touch it. None had the nerve to challenge her as she left the train and walked to Lebanon. Morgan had managed to smuggle her a ring and some of his cash as they left the car, but lost $35 plus his hat and coat to a guerrilla who confronted him. Morgan and other male passengers were trying to scamper up one of the embankments, but were halted by the guerrillas. Four Union soldiers and a lieutenant were among the passengers, but offered no resistance.

Magruder ordered some of the male passengers to unhitch the baggage car and after the baggage and mail were rifled, he forced them to burn the car, baggage and all. Magruder was carrying a mail bag containing the plunder, which included cash, watches, breast pins, rings and other articles of jewelry.[3] He ordered the Yankee soldiers and the officer to accompany them to a point beyond the tracks. Within a half-hour the five came back to the train, saying they'd been paroled. Once the fire was roaring, Magruder told the passengers he and his men had to meet Jessee in Bardstown and they left.

The woman who had walked to Lebanon boarded the uptrain to Louisville with her treasure, that was turned over to authorities. On Monday, Sept. 12, 1864, Jerome Clarke, Henry Magruder and the gang struck again, on the same rail line and at nearly the same place.

CHAPTER 6

Guerrillas, Guerrillas Everywhere

The guerrilla bands that roamed Kentucky in the latter months of the Civil war were not homogeneous. While Jerome Clarke, Henry Magruder and Sam Berry were usually associates, there were times when the groups of guerrillas intertwined. Solon Francis "Sol" Thompson of Lebanon, a 24-year-old ex–Morgan officer, was usually a leader rather than a follower. He had taught at St. Mary College in his native Marion County before the war. Captain James Pratt of Mount Washington also had a following, and seemed to be held in a degree of esteem by others.

In southern Kentucky and along the Kentucky-Tennessee border, Champ Ferguson and Captain Littleton Richardson ruled the roost. Champ's reputation was that of a brutal Reb who finished off wounded federals on the battlefield. Ferguson, O.P. Hamilton, William Bledsoe and others teamed with Richardson to form a guerrilla band of infamous note. Richardson was captured March 5, 1864, and Union Captain George P. Stone reported Richardson was killed by his 37th Kentucky Mounted Infantry at Cave City while trying to escape.

Ferguson, a Clinton County native who later called Sparta, Tennessee, his home, was an angry Southerner and leader of a company of men who were similarly dangerous. Ferguson claimed his wife and daughter were whipped and abused by his neighbors, who were sympathetic to the Yankee cause, so he started killing the neighbors and anyone else with loyalist inclinations.[1] It was unknown exactly how many people Ferguson killed, but among them were his mortal enemy Elam Huddleston and one of

Huddlestone's men. Ferguson killed them with a knife after crashing through the door of Huddlestone's cabin. Stories of Ferguson's brutal knife tortures and killings were legend.[2] Ferguson also killed a federal lieutenant colonel as the officer lay wounded in a southwest Virginia hospital. Ferguson claimed the officer had killed a prisoner, a Southern major, who was a friend of his. The folklore of the Cumberlands was that eleven of the men Ferguson killed were those who had abused his wife and daughter. Ferguson met his end at the end of a rope Oct. 20, 1865, for the murders of at least 53 people. One who was labeled a "bushwhacker" by John Hunt Morgan officer Basil Duke was "Tinker" Dave Beaty, a Tennessee mountain man who fashioned himself a loyalist and commanded a large following.

The guerrilla career of Dupoyster ended in Taylorsville, Sept. 12, 1864. James McCrocklin of Spencer County was a Southern sympathizer who was especially obliging to the needs of Captain Pratt and his followers. It was known that Dupoyster and Pratt did not get along and perhaps therein lay the motive for Eliab Garrett of Dupoyster's band to kill McCrocklin. But the *Louisville Daily Democrat* of Sept. 14, 1864, said McCrocklin had sold a lot of stock in Louisville, indicating robbery was the more likely motive. Garrett was seized by Pratt and Dick Hedges of Pratt's command and jailed in Taylorsville.[3] Dupoyster rode into Taylorsville seeking the release of Garrett, but was unsuccessful and here the story has different versions.

The *Democrat* reported that Pratt shot Dupoyster and when he attempted to rise, Pratt shot him again and when he got up and ran, Pratt shot him dead in the doorway of Kurtz's Hotel. *Louisville Daily Journal* of Sept. 16, 1864, reported it was Hedges who shot Dupoyster. Whoever did it, Dupoyster was dead and Garrett escaped, according to both newspapers. The *Journal* said Hedges and Dupoyster had accosted each other, then drank together at a saloon, giving the appearance that the animosity had ended. But, according to the *Journal*, when the two started out of Taylorsville together, Hedges shot Duposyter, the bullet breaking Dupoyster's arm and sending him tumbling from the saddle. As Dupoyster ran, a second shot missed, but a third proved fatal, the *Journal* said. Hedges returned to the saloon and found the guerrilla Dick Metz. They went together to where Dupoyster lay and stripped his body of everything they wanted. Metz got his hat, according to the *Journal*.

CHAPTER 7

The Creation of Sue Mundy

The Nicholasville to Harrodsburg stage moved slowly down the grade leading to the Shaker Run Creek covered bridge on the outskirts of Pleasant Hill in the village known as Shawneetown. The beautifully kept farm with its large dwelling houses and other buildings was more often referred to as Shaker Village. The Shakers got their name from the gyrations of their ritual dance, but the modesty of their virtuous living included a separation of the sexes, so the dancing was not intended to be flirtatious or an enticement for courtship. The Shakers did not have children of their own, but reared orphans and accepted other children and adults into the sect.

It was Friday, Oct. 7, 1864. Driver Billy Wilkinson, spotting mounted men at the far end of the bridge, applied the brake and reined in the team. A 6-foot-6, black-haired guerrilla appeared to be the spokesman for the group. It was Isaiah Coulter, a native of Anderson County who was also known to his friends as "Big Zay." Jerome Clarke was there along with Benjamin Franklin Foreman, 27, an Anderson County native who had enlisted in Company I, Second Kentucky Infantry and later was a cavalryman. Coulter, Foreman and Jerome rode up to the stage where Coulter ordered the driver to throw down the mail.

Jerome told Wilkinson to unhitch one of the stage horses so he could try it out, which he did by leaping on bareback and riding down the road, his long hair flowing out behind him. He returned, declaring the animal unfit for a riding horse.[1]

While Berry talked with the ladies on board, a guard was kept on a group of travelers who had been forced off the road and robbed prior to

52

the stage's arrival. Among those under guard were two federal soldiers, John C. Robinson, 41, who had been traveling with his wife, Rebecca, 38, and Richard Hightower. Robinson was with Company D and Hightower Company C, both of the 11th Kentucky Cavalry.

The detainees were forced to stay behind a stone fence while the stage was being robbed. The exception was Robinson, who was summoned and forced to open the contents of three bags of mail that were surrendered by Wilkinson. Foreman told the stage driver he would have to return to Nicholasville because the five were going to "use the road" that night and he shouldn't return until 3 A.M. He also said they would burn every coach if guards were put on them.[2]

The women on the stage were not bothered by the guerrillas, but the men were robbed. Wilkinson lost $25. Wilkinson was to say later that Jerome Clarke was in command of the guerrillas, but went by the name of "Lieutenant Flowers." There may have been confusion over Tom Flowers, who could have been the fifth guerrilla present.[3] From the stage robbery, the guerrillas and their two captives rode into Harrodsburg, some five and a half miles distant. After robbing people on the road as well as the tollgate keeper, they dashed into town and headed straight for the Savings Bank.

Cashier J.W. Cardwell saw them coming and hastened inside, locking and barring the windows and doors, leaving his wife Sue standing on the street. The guerrillas fired into the doors and threatened to set fire to the building if the doors were not opened. Jerome, his long, brown hair fluttering as his hat lay back, tied by a string to a buttonhole of his jacket, repeated the order to Berry several times to apply a torch to the bank.[4] He finally threatened to report Berry to Colonel George Jessee if he did not comply with the order. Harrodsburg's Assistant Assessor, Dr. J.L. Smedley, heard the gunfire and hurried up to the bank, where he saw Sue Cardwell just opposite the bank door being robbed of her watch by a guerrilla. Beriah Magoffin, a former Kentucky governor, was also on the street and engaged Jerome in conversation. Jerome asked Magoffin to use his influence to get the bank opened so the home guard's weapons could be removed.

Smedley strolled up to Berry, who appeared intoxicated and quite excited. He introduced Magoffin to a long-haired guerrilla he referred to as "Captain Flowers."[5] Berry knew most of the people in town, including

Smedley. "Now Dr. Smedley, you are a abolitionist," Berry said. "I am not an abolitionist, but I am called so by Rebels and copperhead parties generally," Smedley replied. "Doctor, there are arms in there and I want to get them out," Berry insisted. Smedley told Berry there were no arms inside except what belonged to private citizens, but Berry insisted and said he wanted the door opened whether there were arms in the bank or not. "Doctor, I wish you would go and tell Cardwell to open the door," Magoffin said. Smedley begged Magoffin to differ with Berry because he assumed there were other motives besides wanting the guns. Berry said he would take off his guns if he could go inside and speak to Cardwell.

Another acquaintance of Berry, Bowman and Company store clerk Thomas Stagg, was moseying up to where Berry sat on his horse by the bank door. Stagg heard Berry talking to Sue Cardwell. "Miss, you shall have your watch. I will go and get it for you. You shall have your watch. My name is Berry. You shall have your watch." As Berry was being the gallant guerrilla and retrieving Mrs. Cardwell's watch, Stagg met several men and asked if they were going to fight the intruders. They said it would be of no use because the guerrillas were likely an advance guard of Jessee's men. Not everyone in town felt the same because two blocks away, near a blacksmith's shop, a half dozen men with guns were assembling. Outside the bank, Stagg walked up to Berry and the one-armed man spoke first.

"How are you, Tom?" Berry asked. "Will you shake hands with a damned son-of-a-bitch?" "Certainly I will," Stagg said, and Berry laid his pistol in front of him and reached out his left hand to shake with Stagg. Berry had a knot tied in the rein of his bridle and it was hung over the stump of his right arm. "The last time you saw me, Tom, I was a gentleman. Now I am a damned thief, murderer, liar and robber," Berry said.[6] As the guerrillas began riding up and down the street, Stagg headed off in the direction of another gathering of citizens he'd spotted. Church bells began to ring and the guerrillas suddenly realized the town was being called to arms and they had worn out their welcome. Berry had one more thing to say to Smedley. "Doctor, if you shoot at us I have two prisoners and if you make an attack on us I will kill them both," he said.

Several men with guns began to get organized as the guerrillas left the bank and headed down the street toward Morgan's Tavern. They didn't stop at the tavern, but rode up and down Main Street, perhaps in defiance of the threat against them. The armed citizens had lined up along a fence by the Engine House and a man named Comstock squeezed off a shot with his Smith and Wesson rifle at Berry, who was in front of the Baptist church. Berry gave a "whoop" and fell over on the side of his horse "like an Indian," Stagg observed.[7] The citizens retreated to the U.S. Military Asylum and formed a line there. Stagg had a pistol and the rest shotguns and muskets. Finding the opportunity, Hightower was able to slip away, but the guerrillas still had Robinson in tow as they headed up a hill toward Morgan's Stable.

The citizens fired on the guerrillas, who rode up to Mack Grier's corner, a curve where the Perryville and Mackville roads fork. The guerrillas and their captive took the Perryville road. The citizens stayed in pursuit on foot, although some who were not armed, like Ben Hardin, gave up the hunt. He took cover in the Asylum. Berry and Stagg exchanged gunfire at 50 yards' distance and neither was hurt, but Jerome's large chestnut horse was hit and went down.

Berry whirled his mount and rode alongside Robinson, but it wasn't clear whether Berry or Jerome fired first.[8] The federal soldier was hit and tumbled from his horse, although one foot remained in a stirrup. Jerome shook Robinson's foot free and mounted the horse, then turned and fired at

Jerome Clarke (left) wore his fringed jacket in this pose with Samual Oscar "One-Arm" Berry. Henry Tinsley of Bloomfield, Ky. made the fancy jackets and other clothing for the guerrillas, including all-red outfits that were meant to show that no quarter would be given. Tinsley's "public house" was in downtown Bloomfield and when federal patrols were not in town, the guerrillas were often visiting Tinsley's (courtesy of the Miles-Peck Collection).

Robinson, as did the other guerrillas. The citizens came forward and found Robinson dead, the result of a half dozen bullet wounds. He'd also suffered buckshot wounds in his shoulders that were fired by the citizens, but an examination revealed the buckshot would not have killed him. As the guerillas began returning to Bloomfield, they were about to have their loyalty to the people questioned.

On Monday night, Oct. 10, 1864, McKay and Wilson's store safe in Bloomfield was robbed by unknown thieves. A total of $6,000 was taken, including $3,000 that was being held for citizens who believed the safe was theft-proof. Ben Wilson, Ludwell McKay's partner in the business, sent a note to the McKay house a little after midnight, saying that the keys had been taken from him by a party of men. McKay had gone to Louisville and the note was delivered to a guest at his house, Samuel S. Hamilton of the Samuels community of Nelson County. Hamilton wasn't sure what to do, so he sought public room keeper Henry Tinsley and the two went down to the store. They found the door open, the safe empty and papers strewn about on the floor.

Hamilton said that Berry, Mitchell and Jerome Clarke had been in town about 4 P.M., directly across the street from the store when it closed. He saw Magruder and 17 to 20 others ride toward Chaplin but didn't know if Magruder had returned. Wilson could not or would not identify the thieves.[9] The question of who had committed the robbery was important, because if the guerrillas were responsible, it proved that some didn't mind biting the hands that had been feeding them.

Tuesday, Oct. 11, 1864, readers of the *Louisville Daily Journal* got the George Prentice version of the Shawneetown stage robbery. Prentice reported the story accurately at first. He included the previously unreported details of how stage contractor James Saffell was thrown from his buggy as he unknowingly approached the scene of the robbery, and had the accident trying to avoid the guerrillas. He hid behind a stone fence until the excitement subsided. Prentice also was fairly accurate in his report on the Harrodsburg raid, but it was in the same story that Prentice created the character "Sue Munday."

> One of the peculiarities of this band of cutthroats is the officer second in command, recognized by the men as Lieutenant Flowers. The officer in question is a young woman, and her right name is Sue Munday. She dresses in male attire, generally sporting a full Confederate uniform. Upon her head she

wears a jaunty plumed hat, beneath which escapes a wealth of dark-brown hair, falling around and down her shoulders in luxuriant curls.

She is possessed of a comely form, has a dark, piercing eye, is a bold rider, and a daring leader. Prior to connecting herself to Berry's gang of outlaws, she was associated with the notorious scoundrel Captain Alexander, who met his doom — a tragic death — a short time ago in Southern Kentucky. Lieutenant Flowers, or Sue Munday, is a practised [*sic*] robber, and many ladies, who have been so unfortunate as to meet her on the highway, can testify with what sang-froid she presents a pistol and commands "stand and deliver."

Her name is becoming widely known, and, to the ladies, it is always associated with horror. On Friday evening she robbed a young lady of Harrodsburg of her watch and chain. If the citizens had not so unceremoniously expelled the thieving band from the town, in all probability this she-devil in pantaloons would have paid her respects to all of the ladies of the place, and robbed them of their jewelry and valuables. She is a dangerous character, and, for the sake of the fair ladies of Kentucky, we sincerely hope that she may soon be captured and placed in a position that will prevent her from repeating her unlady-like exploits.

CHAPTER 8

The Fatal Rumor

Edward Darnaby Massie was a family man, a Christian, a farmer, a public servant and someone who believed that the United States could survive as long as it was not divided.[1] Although Massie supported the federal government, he was a slaveholder, as were many other Kentuckians who claimed loyalty to the Union. Massie and his wife, Martha (Coots), were the parents of five boys and seven girls.

Massie was elected to the Kentucky House of Representatives in August 1859, and when the debate began in the General Assembly two years later over the position of the Commonwealth in the Civil War, Massie rejected taking sides. He voted against a request by Governor Magoffin to arm a force that would expel invaders from Kentucky soil. His voting record showed that Massie favored a neutral position for the state, but when neutrality was violated, his loyalty to the Union was expressed.

When his term was up, Massie volunteered in August 1862 for a 60-day hitch with the Kentucky State Troops. Shortly after Confederate General Braxton Bragg's withdrawal from Kentucky, Massie and other state guardsmen returned home, remaining on call, but continuing their farming pursuits.

There had been a heavy frost the morning of Oct. 9, 1864, killing the corn blades.[2] It was brisk again Monday morning, Oct. 10, 1864. The 45-year-old Massie was having breakfast with his family as riders were moving up the road leading to his isolated farm in Spencer County near the Spencer-Shelby County line, 34 miles east-southeast of Louisville. Some of the intruders were dressed in Confederate gray while others wore clothing common among the citizens.

Massie saw them coming and rushed upstairs to fetch his rifle and pistols. Once the guerrillas reached the house, the usual threats were made. If Massie didn't come out and give up his arms, the house would be burned. Gunpowder was spread around the house and a fire was struck.

Some ignition to the house had occurred when Massie brought out his weapons and surrendered. The 18 riders pressed close to Massie and while there is no record of what was said, the brief discussion would have likely involved the report circulating that Massie had cast the deciding vote to keep Kentucky from seceding. The report was false because there was no such deciding vote by any individual in the legislature.

They forced Massie backward, pressing ever closer with their horses. Eight-year-old William and six-year-old Ella, the youngest of the Massie children except for four-year-old Celestine, suddenly broke past their mother and ran to their father's side.[3] William stood defiantly on one side of his father and Ella on the other, each tightly gripping one of their father's hands as he backed into a trellised gate leading into the flower garden.

Ben Foreman led the guerrillas, but it is unclear who opened fire first.[4] Balls struck Massie just above both knees, then in his right side and finally in his forehead. It snuffed the consciousness of a mind that had been filled with so much of Kentucky, so much love for his wife and children and so much determination to see his country survive. A neighborhood youth who had been forced to show the guerrillas the way to Massie's house came forward to grieve with the family.

"Foreman has killed my best friend on Earth," the youth said to Massie's family as the guerrillas were leaving. He told Massie's son, Israel: "I had to lead them here. Please don't blame me." Israel Massie said later that Foreman and the others were sent to his father's home as part of a plot planned by the former lawmaker's bitter, secessionist enemies.

Also in the group of guerrillas were: Henry Parker, Tom Flowers, Ben's brother Samuel Foreman, Weeden M. Hardesty and his brother, William H. Hardesty, Alexander Hunter, his brother, Eliphalet "Babe" Hunter Jr. and Larry Dorset, alias Bragg.[5]

Oct. 11, 1864, the Rev. Benjamin Franklin Hungerford, a Spencer and

Shelby County Baptist circuit preacher wrote in his diary: "Have just heard of the cold-blooded murder of one of my neighbors, Mr. Edward Massie. He was murdered yesterday morning by a band of eighteen guerrillas. Shot down in the presence of his family who was not able to render him any assistance. But justice will not always sleep. Preached his funeral from first Samuel, 20th chapter, third verse. Family deeply afflicted. May God in mercy sustain them." The Bible verse was: "And David sware moreover, and said, Thy father certainly knoweth that I have found grace in thine eyes; and he saith, Let not Jonathan know this, lest he be grieved: but truly as the Lord liveth, and as thy soul liveth, there is but a step between me and death."

Edward Darnaby Massie, a former member of the Kentucky General Assembly, was murdered by guerrillas at his home in northeastern Spencer County, Ky. The guerrillas were acting on a false rumor that Massie cast the deciding vote that prevented Kentucky from becoming a Confederate state. Massie was also a member of the Home Guard, giving the Confederate irregulars an additional incentive to take his life (courtesy Mary Charles Stout).

Three days later, the same band of guerrillas returned to the Massie farm and stole two horses and saddles. They continued robbing people and stealing horses in the Mount Eden area for several days and even robbed blind storekeeper John R. Buckner.[6] It was a short time after the killing of Massie that Burbridge fired off a telegram to Captain E.W. Easley of Pleasureville. The message informed the captain that three Confederates were being sent from Lexington by train and that they were to be executed for the killing of Massie. William E. Waller, Monroe Wellman and Hugh Harrod didn't know Massie from Adam.

8. The Fatal Rumor

Fate was at work for the three Confederates and one hour before the scheduled executions, Easley received a telegram from President Lincoln.

Easley saw the word "deferred" and was elated, saying he would rather have gone into battle against any force than execute those men.

Thirty years later, Easley was looking over his wartime papers and made a dramatic discovery. The telegram from Lincoln asked that the execution of Waller be deferred. Wellman and Harrod were supposed to have been shot.

CHAPTER 9

No Mercy for the Messenger

On Oct. 14, 1864, Jerome Clarke, Berry and five others rode into Bruner's Town just southeast of Louisville, relieving area citizens of their valuables whenever they met them en route. Magruder was on a trip southward and missed the excursion that was so near Louisville's Union garrison. Bruner's Town got its name from Abraham Bruner, who successfully petitioned Jefferson County Fiscal Court in May 1797 to establish the town of Jefferson on a 122-acre tract he'd obtained three years earlier. After Bruner's Town, the settlement became known as Jefferson Town, then Jeffersontown.

Abraham Fink lost a fine horse and all his money to the guerrillas that day, but Hugh Wilson, a Union solder from Mount Vernon, Ill., lost much more. Wilson was a courier, carrying the mail from Jeffersontown to the Totten Hospital at the head of Broadway in Louisville. He was halted at gunpoint, taken prisoner and watched as the guerrillas rifled the mail, removing money whenever they found it. They took control of the village.

Jerome went into the Davis House Inn and had his canteen filled with whisky. As he walked back into the street, Berry had a surprise for him. Sitting on a horse that Berry had obtained from a resident of the same street was a "Negro boy," fully armed and looking slightly bewildered.[1] Berry introduced him as the new "lookout." The temporary recruit watched the horses as the guerrillas roamed about town, robbing citizens and stores. Wilson, the captured soldier, was left tied to a post in front of a saddle shop.

Every now and then, when someone would pass by, especially other blacks he knew, the horse watcher would draw one of the heavy revolvers bestowed upon him and demand "all your cash." After tiring of their escapade, the guerrillas sent the lookout on his way and rode southeastward with Wilson. A short distance out of town, the group turned down Heady Road and made their way into a ravine on the Joseph Leatherman farm.[2] Wilson was untied and told to step down from his horse, then, each guerrilla drew his revolver and fired.

Wilson crumpled to the ground with five bullets in his body, then one of the guerrillas leaped off his horse and twice plunged a knife into Wilson's heart. Blood from Wilson's wounds nearly obliterated a letter in his pocket. But the words, "My dear husband ..." and "... send love to pa," were still visible when federal troops went to retrieve the body.[3]

The Oct. 17, 1864, *Journal* reported the raid and murder. In the story, Prentice changed the spelling of his character's surname from Munday to Mundy. He said that Berry and Sue Mundy were at the head of the guerrilla band and reported that a rider, James Simpson, was stopped and robbed of $27 on the road to Jeffersontown. Prentice said Simpson noticed Sue Mundy's pistol was empty but fresh powder stains showed it had been fired. "While the traveler (Simpson) was being robbed, this she-devil was engaged in loading her revolver," Prentice wrote. "She pointed the muzzle at the breast of Mr. S., and smiled with fiendish satisfaction at his embarrassment, as she capped the tube of each barrel of the cylinder." Simpson was allowed to leave, whereupon he rode to Jeffersontown and reported there were eight men in the group, including a captive soldier (Wilson). Prentice admitted the evidence that Sue Mundy killed Wilson was circumstantial, but alleged that the murder was committed by one hand, "that of Sue Mundy, the outlaw woman, the wild and daring leader of the band."[4]

Since the murder of Massie by the irregulars under Foreman, the Union military command in Louisville was considering retaliatory measures for such cold-blooded acts.

It took Burbridge a few days to act after Wilson's shooting, but on Oct. 24, 1864, he directed Captain Rowland E. Hackett and 50 men of the 26th Kentucky, Company A, to the Exchange Barricks in Louisville, where they retrieved four prisoners. The prisoners were placed in a one-horse spring wagon along with a local minister and directed by Hackett toward Jeffersontown. About 2 P.M., the procession stopped at the foot of a hill not far from where Wilson was killed. The four men — Lindsey Duke Buckner, Wilson P. Lilly, William C. Blincoe and the Rev. Sherwood Hatley, a 70-year-old chaplain — were forced to march to the top of the hill.

Union soldier Hugh Wilson of Mount Vernon, Illinois, was a mail carrier who was in the Louisville suburban community of Jeffersontown at an unfortunate time. He was robbed by guerrillas, who took his money and all the cash they could find in the mail. Wilson lost more than money that day as he was taken out of town and shot dead. George Prentice accused "Sue Mundy" of killing Wilson, but Jerome Clarke was never charged with the crime. Wilson's grave is in the Union section of Louisville's Cave Hill Cemetery (photograph by Thomas Shelby Watson).

Hackett, 35, a former recruiter, read a sentence of death for each man. They were not suspects in the killing of Wilson, nor had they been tried for any crimes, including guerrilla activity. It was Burbridge's General Order No. 59 that would claim their lives. The minister who accompanied the condemned men talked with them for 30 minutes. They all knelt in prayer, then arose to be lined up one foot apart and at their own request, were blindfolded. Sixteen Union soldiers marched forward to form a line 15 feet from the prisoners. The order to fire came quickly and balls crashed into their heads and hearts and they were dead.

Buckner was from Company H, 1st Kentucky Cavalry, C.S.A., Lilly from Company G, 1st Missouri Infantry, C.S.A. Hatley said he was not a soldier and hadn't handled a gun in 40 years. Blincoe was a Confederate private. Bruner's Town residents pulled their shades and the streets were empty. Their shame was salient.

On June 12, 1904, nearly 40 years after the executions at

Jeffersontown, the Albert Sidney Johnston Chapter of the Daughters of the Confederacy dedicated a monument to the memory of the four men. Hundreds of people gathered and as the final strains of "One Sweetly Solemn Thought" by a Confederate choir faded, the Rev. E.I. Powell stepped forward and read from a letter Buckner had written as he waited to die. Buckner wrote to his sister that he would soon be shot, but for what cause he did not know.

Powell condemned Burbridge, yet he hoped God would have mercy on his soul. "Let us have only a cloak to hide him in, for we would not mention his name. The bitterness of our indignation is a testimony that there is no honor in infamy."

The inscription on the monument called the four slain men "martyrs" and said they were "deprived of the glory of death on the field of battle. They were executed by Stephen G. Burbridge, who ordered them shot without offense and without trial." Relatives of Buckner and Blincoe had their bodies moved to family burial sites. Lilly and Hatley were allowed to rest in peace at the monument site.[5]

CHAPTER 10

The Warrior Wardrobe

As activity by the guerrillas and guerrilla hunters increased, so did the outcry from Kentuckians for protection. Prized horses were hidden in thickets in efforts to keep them from being taken by any combatant. Families hid greenbacks in all sorts of places from hollowed-out books to straw beds, where they were added to the stuffing.[1]

Burbridge's General Order 59 had also stated that guerrillas would no longer be taken prisoners of war. They were to be shot on sight or, if captured, executed on the spot. The guerrillas appeared unaffected by the order and designed wardrobes to make them even more conspicuous. Clarke and Magruder went to see Tinsley, who besides running a public house and keeping bar was an accomplished tailor. They wanted to begin work on their new image.

It took Tinsley several days to produce velvet jackets and pants for the irregulars. The jackets were trimmed in lace cord of gold and other colors. Tinsley made Clarke a jacket of light cloth and gold lace. Magruder's was black with gold lace. He also made velvet suits for Magruder and Tom Henry. Davis, Maraman and Warford also had jackets made. Marion had Tinsley make him a black, knee-length frock coat and a blue one with state guard buttons. The guerrillas also wore high-topped boots, many of them made by Andy Cleary, a sandy-haired Irishman from Great Britain whose shop was in Fairfield near Bloomfield.[2]

They wore black hats with ostrich or chicken feathers protruding. Marion decorated his hat with various colored ribbons, feathers and polk leaves in season. Some of the jackets were red flannel and some of the guerrillas asked for red jackets and pants, an outfit that told foes no quarter would be given.[3] They literally dressed fit to kill. Tinsley had been able to keep a peaceful relationship with the guerrillas because most of them paid for their new clothes.

With communications in those days quite limited, the truth sometimes became embellished rumor and led to deadly consequences. One day Tinsley saw Berry and a young guerrilla named King White in front of his public room at Bloomfield. In view of information he'd recently received, Tinsley was less than enthusiastic about their arrival. He'd been told the two had threatened to wear out a pistol on his head and cowhide him but the reason wasn't clear to him.[4] Reluctantly, Tinsley went to the public room and White asked what he owed. Tinsley told him eleven dollars for a suit of clothes and eating there several times with Berry and others. White said he'd been told that Tinsley needed to collect $150 from him for a coat and other considerations. Tinsley denied making such a claim and said whoever came up with that was "a scoundrel and liar."

Berry came rushing in and said the coat in question had been obtained for Jerome Clarke, so Tinsley suggested Berry pay for it. The story began to make little sense and Tinsley's teenage son, William, put his hand on his pistol expecting, as Tinsley would say later, "a difficulty." That prompted Berry to shove a pistol against the teen's breast saying if the boy drew a weapon, he would blow his brains out.[5] The elder Tinsley slipped out to get his shotgun, dodging lead as Berry opened fire. Berry and White retreated to the street as the tailor's son began shooting. One bullet hit Berry and another struck Berry's horse.

Berry and White rode eastward toward Chaplin and when Berry's mount went down, they rode double on White's horse. Tinsley knew that as soon as the word got out of a rift with the guerrillas, there would be serious repercussions. He went to some neighbors who knew Berry more intimately and they all rode out to find the wounded guerrilla and make peace.[6] Berry was taken to Horace Edrington's in Anderson County where he remained inactive for about two weeks.[7]

The details of Berry's wounding came from Tinsley some months after it supposedly happened and could have been a ruse. Tinsley may have feared he would be punished by the government for making guerrilla clothing and sought to show he was doing such work under duress. There is no doubt Tinsley's son would have been hunted down and killed by Berry's fellow guerrillas and there was no report of that happening. The date of the alleged run-in with the Tinsleys was not disclosed in courts-martial testimony nor did the newspapers report such an incident. If it happened and no reprisal followed, it would have been because the guerrillas considered it a fair fight and peace had been restored.

Meanwhile, another attempt was being made to recruit new Rebel soldiers and round up those involved in guerrilla warfare and return them south to rejoin regular Confederate forces. This time, Spencer County native Colonel Jack Allen was in charge of the effort and under orders by the Confederate War Department to raise a brigade of cavalry. Allen was headquartered in a rolling, peaceful Nelson County valley that was called "Camp Charity." Morgan and his Lexington Rifles had used the same site as a camp in September 1861, almost three years earlier. The camp had earned its name from the friendliness of the people in the area toward Confederate soldiers. They had refused payment for the food they provided. So much good food was prepared for the southern warriors by the Charles Dawson family at the eastern edge of the valley that the family's cabin became known as "Dawson Hungry Lodge."

Magruder continued to recruit for the Confederate Army and one sojourn into Bardstown got the attention of Prentice. He reported in the Oct. 3, 1864, *Louisville Journal*:

> When Magruder was at Bardstown with his guerrillas, he remarked that he was hunting up drafted men to take them away with him, and wished some friend would let him know who they were. A young traitor, overhearing the remark, ran out of a store and placed a full list in his hand. Let that young Rebel miscreant be identified and punished. His neck is too long.

Allen hoped that as many as 2,800 men would gather for the move south, but only 120 reported. Many of James Pratt's band in Bullitt County refused to go without their leader. Pratt was too injured to make the trip. His horse had recently run into a tree and Pratt was knocked out of the saddle. Jerome, Magruder, Coulter and Mitchell were among those expressing a willingness to ride toward Dixie. In fact, Jerome had 45 green recruits with him that he'd rounded up in the Bloomfield-Taylorsville area. Before the trek south began, Jerome's recruits refused to go and ran away. Allen, Magruder and others went to see Jessee, but Jessee, the officer in command of a large remnant of Morgan's cavalry, would not make the attempt.[7] Berry was unable to ride due to his wound, and with the defections, only 40 or fewer men left with proper intentions of returning to regular soldiering. Prentice reported the southern trek Oct. 19, 1864, and half heart-edly praised Allen: "Allen says that he has grown tired of a partisan strife and we give him credit for desiring to secure some protection to the people of Kentucky by using his influence to effect the withdrawal of outlaw bands from the state."

The group continued without incident until they reached the Green River. Two federal soldiers managed to be in the wrong place at the wrong time and were captured. Allen ordered that they be paroled. At Ray's Cross Roads in Metcalfe County, the group passed a small grocery where a man dressed in blue fired into them, wounding one and killing the soldier's horse. Return fire killed the Yankee and a brief investigation determined he was a deserter.[8]

With a guide, the Rebels reached the Cumberland River at Turkey-neck Bend in Cumberland County, where they crossed with their horses. They camped on the other side until daylight, then visited houses in the area for breakfast. After continuing southward along the Cumberland for some distance, the soldiers made camp and, due to Allen's illness, remained for a week. Intelligence was gathered that a federal force was in Glasgow and Allen sent a party to investigate. It was learned a brigade of Union troops had just left, so the Rebs went to a Glasgow hotel and ate break-fast. They then plundered the stores, selecting clothing and boots to fit their fancy.[9]

During late morning, word was obtained from the driver of an arriv-ing stage that a large force of Union cavalry was headed to Glasgow from Burkesville. The Rebs left quickly, passed through Tompkinsville in the afternoon and returned to the Cumberland River country where they remained two weeks. With little progress being made at returning south, Magruder, Jerome and five others were given permission by Allen to return to north central Kentucky and recruit.

The significance of Jerome, Magruder and others' making an effort to resume regular soldiering is evidence that they were more interested in helping secure a victory for the South than pursuing the rewards of irreg-ular fighting. Had they successfully returned to regular Confederate units, it would have been difficult to convict them of acting as guerrillas and eas-ier to prove they were Partisan Rangers.

CHAPTER 11

Rome Meets Mollie

Jerome heard and confirmed with a visit that Butler Remey Thomas and his wife, Louisa (Porter), were dyed in the wool Southerners. Butler and Louisa had ten children, and the older boys Alfred Porter Thomas, 22; Ben Hardin Thomas, 20; and John Henry Thomas, 19 — became fully involved with the guerrillas from scouting to riding with them on raids.[1]

During a federal patrol's stop at the Thomas house in search of a guerrilla thought to be hiding there, Louisa Thomas, a "large, fleshy woman," was in bed and had the guerrilla hide under her. She raised up on her elbows to prevent the guerrilla from being seen and no doubt to allow him room to breathe.[2]

Also among the Thomas children were the twins, Martha Thomas and Mary Porter "Mollie" Thomas, born Aug. 30, 1848. It was 16-year-old Mollie Thomas who captured the attention of 20-year-old Jerome Clarke. They may have met at one of the parties the Thomas family threw for the guerrillas and girls of Southern proclivity who held the young Rebs in high esteem. The Thomas boys were accused of riding throughout the region, claiming to be cattle buyers and occasionally purchasing a few head of fat cattle in an effort to prove the claim.

Soon after each visit to a farm that had decent horseflesh, the guerrillas showed up and traded their jaded mounts for fresh ones.[3]

District Provost Marshal T.H. Hickman, in a communication with Brig. Gen. Edward Hobson, called the Thomas neighborhood of Nelson County the headquarters of guerrillas. "It is where the wounded guerrillas are taken and concealed," he wrote.[4] The Thomas place wasn't far from Chaplin, and the winding, weathered horse trails of the time isolated it securely from Union patrols. The road that passed the Thomas house wound down hilly terrain to the Chaplin River, providing an escape route should it be needed. It was purely Confederate territory and a network of Rebs to the bone made certain there would be no surprise attacks.

While Jerome, Magruder and Berry generally rode together, other former Morganites continued to stake their own territory. James Pratt's band made Bullitt County home and was often seen in Mount Washington. So were Henry Turner, Dick Hedges, James Metz and Bill Gray, four on which the federals would spring a trap Oct. 25, 1864. Gray was a suspect in the bushwhacking of a Louisville policeman earlier in the year. Captain Edward H. Green of Company E, the 11th Kentucky Cavalry, led 40 men out of Louisville Oct. 22, 1864, in search of guerrillas.

The federals passed through Middletown, Jeffersontown and Fisherville just east of Louisville, but encountered no guerrillas. They camped two miles from Plum Creek in Spencer County, then saddled up at 2 A.M. the next morning and rode rapidly into Taylorsville, dashing in

When Jerome Clarke met Mollie Thomas, one of the twin daughters of Butler Remey Thomas and Louisa (Porter) Thomas, she and her sister Martha were 16. The meeting likely occurred after the August 30, 1864, birthday of the girls. During the war, a union officer reported to his superiors: "The Thomas neighborhood is guerrilla headquarters," and added that it was where wounded Rebels were taken so they could recover in a safe place. Dr. Isaac McClaskey, another supporter of the Confederate cause who treated wounded guerrillas, lived just a few miles distant. *Top:* Mollie Thomas at 16. *Bottom:* Mollie Thomas a few years later (courtesy Thomas-Russell Family Archives).

The Butler Remey and Louisa (Porter) Thomas house near Chaplin, Ky., was a reconnoitering headquarters for Southern guerrillas during the war and one of Jerome Clarke's favorite stopping places. He visited "Mollie" Thomas there often. The location of the Thomas place offered a long frontage to the main road and a trail in the rear that led to the Chaplin River and several escape routes if needed (photograph by Thomas Shelby Watson).

at daylight. Green was told two of the four men he sought had left only minutes earlier.

The patrol camped at Shelbyville, 28 miles east of Louisville, Sunday, Oct. 23, 1864, and Green left word that he was headed back to Louisville, having given up the hunt. Instead, the trap was set as Green's men again camped near Plum Creek, not far from Mount Washington, which was just 16 miles southeast of Louisville. The next morning, Green split the patrol, with a captain leading 20 of the men in one direction while he led the balance in another.

Just before daylight on Tuesday morning, Oct. 25, 1864, Green's men galloped into Mount Washington, picketed the town and placed an ambush on the main road. Two of the four men who had been the object of the search and another Rebel came leisurely riding in and one of

Green's men opened fire before they were close enough to become perfect targets.

As the guerrillas turned to flee, all of Green's men behind the ambush bunker opened fire and the guerrillas tumbled from their horses. Billy Harrison received a mortal wound. He tried to run but bled profusely and died a short distance from town. Metz received a flesh wound. The sun was just beginning to spread light across the land, but Metz and Gray still had enough darkness to cover their escape. The three lost their horses to the federals and Gray also lost his coat.

Green found letters in the coat from Gray's friends in Louisville advising him to give up his way of life and return to the regular army. The guerrillas gained the house of a friend and received treatment for their injuries. The horses and coat became trophies of the Yankees, who returned to Louisville.[5] Also on Oct. 25, 1864, lesser known guerrilla Bill Marshall and his men raided the Robert Graham farm at Peak's Mill in Fayette County, and Graham was killed.

CHAPTER 12

In Search of Fast Horses

Convinced that central Kentucky had the best horseflesh in the world, Jerome and Berry joined Davis, Ben Foreman and Billy Hughes in a jaunt to press new mounts.[1] Davis was particularly familiar with the horse farms in his home territory of Woodford County, so they decided to concentrate their hunt there. It was Oct. 27, 1864, when guerrillas arrived at the training stable of Woodburn Farm, the home of some of Kentucky's foremost thoroughbred horses. The British flag was flying in front of the main house that was occupied by the family of Robert Spreul Crawford Aitcheson Alexander. He felt that since the British sympathized with the Confederacy in the war, the flag would help protect him from raids, but it wasn't effective.

Alexander had just finished dinner and was getting to his feet and wiping his mouth with a napkin when an elderly black woman came rushing in, sounding an alarm that someone was after his horses. Alexander wasn't concerned because he'd heard such reports before and it was usually a false alarm, plus he had several men on the farm with weapons at their disposal. So, he laughed.[2]

Then a young man who worked with the horses came running in with a more convincing report. "There are some people at the stable taking your horses!" he yelled. Then, when a field hand rode in on a plow horse to report what was happening, Alexander became a believer. He turned to one of the men who had been his guests for dinner and implored him to go and get the farm hands and have them report mounted and armed. Alexander began removing guns from a cabinet. Meanwhile, the guerrillas had rounded up valuable horseflesh and were headed west.

74

Among the horses taken was the famous thoroughbred "Asteroid," who had just been returned to the farm from the fall racing meet at Lexington. Alexander considered him the best racehorse in the United States. The guerrillas also fled with other thoroughbreds that were two-year-old offspring of the celebrated stallion, "Lexington."

"I suppose we had a half a dozen in the party (to chase the guerrillas) ... all intent upon getting the horses," Alexander testified after the war. "As I went across the place, I saw that they had gone up a sort of lane, I followed them by Mr. Nichols' (farm). I was not certain that I was on the right road at first, but we met a Negro woman that told me that they had passed there and I followed them on. The tracks turned toward Frankfort." Alexander then confirmed he'd been on the right trail.

After going a few hundred yards, I came to some men driving some horses and asked them if they had seen any men passing through there with some horses. They said "yes," that they had stopped and robbed them. I said "come on, go with us." One fellow said "if you will give me a pistol, I will go." I told one of my men to give him a pistol. The other fellow had thrown his pistol over the fence when they came up to them so that he had [retrieved] his pistol. They were, I think, residents of Frankfort. When we got to a blacksmith's shop about nine miles from Frankfort, [we] came in sight of some people standing still in the road. It was a larger party than were usually together and I was satisfied it was the party we were in pursuit of.

Some of my men commenced hollering at once. They were gratified to come in sight of them. I told them to hold their tongues. As soon as we observed the party we made way for them as fast as we could. Some of my men tried to get across the corner of a field. I passed on with three others. Two men got in advance of me. One of my own men and one of this party from Frankfort began firing at random. I suppose they fired some four or five shots. I hollered to them not to fire, [I] did not want to fire if it was possible to get the horses without it. I was after the horses.

Alexander broke off from the main party of pursuers and chased a man he saw going up a neighbor's lane but it was one of his neighbor's men and he rejoined the chase.

When I got into the lane again, these men who had taken the horses had stopped in the road and were firing on the pursuing party.... My horses, never having been accustomed to firing, were jumping around and the men, I suppose, were somewhat scared. As I galloped up, I hollered out to my men to dismount and fire, but they did not hear me and before I got up to the front, the men that had the horses had turned and gone around the lane.

The chase continued along a winding lane for some distance, halting briefly when Alexander found one of his horses.

We stopped long enough to tether this horse then passed on. About 300 yards farther, the lane turns to the right. Upon coming to the corner, we saw three horses loose and a man dismounted standing by them. We supposed that this man was one of those who had taken the horses. Calling to him, I ordered him to advance to us. First he would not come, but upon me presenting my carbine at him, ordering him to come, he came up slowly. When within 50 yards of us I recognized him as one of my neighbors and asked him what he was doing in possession of stolen horses. He replied that he had stopped these horses in the lane having found them loose. We inquired if he had seen anybody riding in that direction. He answered that he had not. The search continued toward the Kentucky River where shots were exchanged with a man whose horse had given out.

When we got to the river, we found that the party that had taken our horses had passed [crossed] the river about 20 minutes before. While deliberating as to what we should do, some for going on, some for turning back, I saw a man come down from the top of the hill towards the river. About the time we had made up our minds to go home, this man began talking and making a great fuss and saying that he had our race horses, "come across and get them," [and] all such expressions. And after a while, [the man] began firing his pistol at us across the river. When he had fired several times, my gardener, one of the men that was with me, and who was a hot-headed Irishman, wanted to fire upon that man.

Alexander didn't try to stop the Irishman from returning fire.

The gardener missed after firing two or three shots, but gained the interest of a second guerrilla in gunplay. After he had fired several shots, a second man came down from the hill and several shots were fired whether by the second or first man, I don't know. As I had a little carbine with plenty of ammunition, I was the only one that was really well armed and after about six or eight shots had been fired I thought I would try my gun and I got down from my horse and went to a fence which was close by where I could rest [the carbine] and fired perhaps three or four times. I found that they did not appear to mind my shots at all, which surprised me a little.[3]

Other firing took place. A man came down from the top of the hill and I fired at him and I supposed hit him. We then got on our horses and left.

"Asteroid" was recovered, but the circumstances of the recovery are somewhat clouded.

The Nov. 2, 1864, *Louisville Journal* reported:

Asteroid—We learn that Mr. Alexander has recovered his fine horse Asteroid ... stolen from his stables last week by Sue Mundy's gang of guerillas. Two gentlemen met two of the scoundrels lagging behind the main portion of the band in the vicinity of Bloomfield, and, presenting their revolvers at their breasts, forced them to relinquish the horse.

Other newspapers offered varying versions of the recovery of Asteroid, in later years sometimes confusing the October 1864 raid with one that occurred in 1865. Perhaps the most widely told story was that Maj. Warren Viley and Colonel Zachariah Henry, friends of Alexander, recovered Asteroid by finding two guerrillas in Nelson County, one aboard the famous horse, and negotiating with them.

"After a ride of forty miles or so (into Nelson County), through a region infested with murderous bushwhackers, they came upon two guerrillas, one of them riding Asteroid," Dan M. Bowmar wrote in the 1960 *Giants of the Turf.*

In answer to Major Viley's salutation they drew their guns and it looked as if the long chase would have a tragic ending. The rescuers began a parley with the fellow on Asteroid, telling him the animal was a pet colt and asking him to relinquish it. The guerrilla stoutly refused, declaring the horse to be the best he ever rode, but finally, not knowing the colt's value, agreed to release it for $250, on condition that Viley would later furnish him with another horse that would be as good a saddler. Viley wrote the check and received Asteroid safe and sound. They were given an ovation upon their return to Versailles.

Another version of the story quoted the guerrilla aboard "Asteroid" as saying: "That's a very good story, boys, but that's no three-year-old. He has carried me 60 miles, and is the best horse I ever threw a leg over."

The story that the two friends of Alexander bought "Asteroid" back from the guerrillas for $250 does not seem impossible to believe, but it's a challenge to accept a version that two Alexander friends, dressed as guerrillas, made the rendezvous, struck the deal, then wrote a check for the return of the horse.[4]

Alexander could not identify any of the guerrillas because he didn't see them up close. Henry Granison, one of Alexander's slaves, who was forced to accompany the guerrillas, saw their faces and testified after the war that Jim Davis was one of them. He didn't offer a guess as to the identities of the others, except he noticed they had pokeberries in their hats.

Granison was ordered to go along and take care of a colt, which he rode. When the guerrillas met some stock drovers and took a grey mare, Granison then rode the grey and led the colt. They also took a pistol and an overcoat from the drovers and gave the coat to Granison. When an opportunity presented itself three hours after the raid, as the guerrillas turned onto a dirt road leading to Frankfort, Granison escaped and returned to Woodburn with a sorrell, a filly and a bay colt following.

Graniston said the guerrillas thought Alexander's men were "Union men" and stopped and held a position against them.

Prentice published a story on the Alexander horse raid, but was a day behind in his reporting. The guerrillas had struck at Nantura, another famous horse farm in Woodford County, on Nov. 1, 1864. They wore Union overcoats and as they filed past, the farm hands paid them little attention. John Harper met the riders at the gate and demanded to know their business. "To press horses," was the reply. "By what authority?" Harper asked.

Jerome Clarke rode forward, holding a large revolver.

"Here is our authority and we mean business," Jerome is quoted as saying.[5] John Harper retreated into the house and gunfire came pouring out. Two guerrillas were unsaddled but there was no immediate retreat and a steady fire was trained on the portions of the house where the shooting was coming from.

In the intense battle, Adam Harper, John's brother, was gravely wounded in the breast and died a few hours later. The guerrillas retreated. On Nov. 2, 1864, eight captive Southern soldiers were transferred from Lexington to Frankfort to be executed in retaliation for Adam Harper's death. At twilight, S. Thomas Hunt, Thomas Lafferty of Lexington, John Jones, a Texan, and Elijah Horton were escorted to the corner of a field owned by Lucy Hunt of south Frankfort.[6]

Lafferty, "an old man and political prisoner,"[7] was able to slip his irons from his ankles. He turned and ran, but was riddled with bullets as he sought to scale a fence. Lafferty had freed himself as the Rev. B.B. Sayre was offering a prayer and fled when he heard, "Amen."[8] The firing squad then killed the others. The bodies of the four were buried without coffins, a little under ground.[9] It was reported that when Hunt was being shackled for removal to Frankfort and his awaiting fate, he told his fellow prisoners, "If it is for my country I die, it is all right."

The next day, four other prisoners were marched from Frankfort to

Pleasureville and lined up near the depot. William Long of Maysville, William Tithe of Williamstown, William D. Darbro of Owen County and R.W. Yates of Hart County became victims of Burbridge's retaliation order. They were shot because two blacks they'd never met were killed by guerrillas several days earlier.

Long would not wear a blindfold, nor would he kneel. He told the firing squad; "Shoot, cowards, I am not afraid to die for my cause."[10]

CHAPTER 13

Trial by the Gun

It was the sabbath in Bloomfield, Oct. 30, 1864, the day of prayers, which were especially needed for five local people. Three slaves, Elijah Dugan, Alfred Harrington and John Sutherland, had been taken into custody the previous night while holed up in a barn along with three white men. All were quite fearful, but not of each other.

The whites were John Violet, 22, one of his brothers, and a local whose surname was Gist. John Violet's brothers were James, 20; George, 18; and W.K., 16. Records are imprecise as to which brother was involved along with John. They were being held in custody at the Nancy Thomas place after they were found armed and hiding out in a barn on the Foster farm.[1]

Some of the Rebel guerrillas wanted to kill them, but Colonel Stone said it might bring trouble. A decision was made by some citizens to take the five to the Bardstown jail. Henry Russell, Eli Snider, William Milton, John Henry Thomas and Milton Greer began the escort as some of the guerrillas ordered dinner at Tinsley's, and the matter appeared settled.[2]

School teacher–surveyor James F. Moore was looking out the window of his hotel and saw a crowd at the other end of town which attracted his attention. The citizens had apparently persuaded the guerrillas not to shoot the prisoners, but Jerome and Berry rode up to Moore's hotel about dinner time and were "very much excited," Moore noted.

They had heard of the Negroes being taken to Bardstown and "they talked about following them and killing them and said they would do it. They finally jumped on their horses and put out after them," Moore recalled.[3] Tinsley was to say later that Jerome and Berry accused the Violets of robbing stores and blaming it on the guerrillas. He said the Negroes had been robbing under the cover of disguises and darkness while representing themselves as Sue Mundy, Magruder and Berry.

Among those in pursuit were Jerome, Berry, Jim Davis, Holmes Tindel, John Mackey, Harvey Warford, Tom Flowers, Ben Foreman, Jack Parkhurst, Dick Taylor and King White. They caught up with the guards and prisoners some two and a half miles south of Bloomfield on the road to Bardstown.

John Green and others had gone up to James Greer's house, about 140 yards off the road, to fetch some water. Green was just returning to the place where the prisoners and their guards were resting when the guerrillas arrived. Jerome ordered the Negroes over the fence and into the road where he gunned down two of them. Jerome dismounted and Russell tried to prevent him from firing again by pinning Jerome's arms while pushing him back against a fence, but another guerrilla drew his gun and Russell was forced to release Jerome, who had nearly struggled loose anyway.

Warford then shot one of the Negroes who still exhibited signs of life. Green testified later that a guerrilla told him if the Negroes went to jail, they would be put in the army against them. Mitch Russell followed the guerrillas out of concern for his father, Henry, who was in command of the prisoner transfer.

"Father told them to get over the fence (and escape) and Clarke attempted to shoot father with his pistol," Mitch Russell recalled. "Berry ran in and grabbed him (Jerome Clarke)."[4] In the confusion, the third Negro and the three white men escaped. One of the white men suffered a hand wound. Foreman handed John Violet over to Berry, who allowed him to escape.[5]

The horrendous acts of guerrillas spread terror across the land and many citizens trying go about their usual business found themselves witnessing the cruelest acts imaginable. On Nov. 2, 1864, Elijah Jones, a farmer from Edmonson County, was reading a newspaper at the Rocky Hill Station of the Louisville and Nashville Railroad, just above the Edmonson-Warren County line. It was around two o'clock in the afternoon. Jones heard someone say, "Here come some soldiers." He looked out and saw some men ride up to a railroad car. There was a pistol shot and in moments, the car was on fire.[6]

A one-footed black man named Lewis was shot in the car before the fire was started. It was not known if he died before the car was consumed by flames. While Magruder was charged with the murder, it could not be proven he did it.[7] As Jones and other citizens were standing by a store, one of the guerrillas rode up.

"What in the hell are you all doing there?" he asked.

The storekeeper said he was just selling goods to customers and friends, to which the guerrilla replied, "That will do to tell." Then the guerrilla asked how long it would be until the cars came in and he was told it would be about an hour. He turned to the men at the burning car and yelled, "Hurry up there, boys." Two boarding cars on a siding and their contents were destroyed.[8] Jones attempted to slip away, but he was stopped, searched and ordered to stay put. Jones had no valuables, but others did, and were relieved of them.[9]

Storekeeper William Durham was watching the activity when one of the guerrillas rode up and asked him for the time. The man then dismounted and emptied Durham's cash drawer. Three other guerrillas then entered the store, followed by the appearance of a "small, light-haired" man on a horse who rode up and ordered those inside to leave the building.

It will perhaps never be known why William Fox, a young federal soldier, walked to Rocky Hill Station that afternoon as a cloud of smoke, billowing into the sky, warned of something seriously awry. Durham saw Fox pass the front door of his store, walking in the direction of Brownsville. He also saw the first guerrilla, who had left the store under orders, begin firing. Fox's mother, who had come to the station to see her son on his way back to the Army, began screaming that "they" had killed her son. Jones heard as many as ten shots and saw Fox raise his hands and walk toward a fence, where he fell on his right side.

The man who shot him first, a tall, thin man with very dark, long hair, rolled Fox over on his back, stooped over him, picked the young soldier up by his collar and with a pistol he held in his left hand, shot him one more time in the head. One witness thought the last shot was behind an ear and the ball came out in the front. Another thought the entry wound was over an eye. Fox lived about two and a half hours.

About nine o'clock the night of Nov. 2, 1864, guerrillas arrived at the residence of Phillip and Catherine Raymer in Edmonson County. Philip was at Nolin that night, also in Edmonson County.[10] Phillip, 21, was a federal private in Company A, 12th Kentucky Mounted Volunteers. He and Catherine were married Aug. 13, 1862. The 18-year-old Catherine was defenseless against the intruders. They broke in the doors and ransacked the house but found no money. One of the guerrillas picked up Catherine and carried her into the yard. Afterward, she told military authorities she'd been raped. Magruder was accused of the attack, but his guilt could not be proven.[11] The Jake Bennett gang was not ruled out as suspects in both the Rocky Hill Station raid and the attack on Catherine Raymer, but on March 24, 1865, General Palmer received a letter in which a witness said it was Bennett, and not Magruder, at Rocky Hill.

Months after the attack on Catherine Raymer she recanted the story that she was raped. "One of them picked me up and carried me off, you know what it means, he threatened to kill me if I didn't. He was choking me. He choked me until I was all but out of breath. He didn't bother me, just asked me what men folks there was." She said he lay on top of her but made no move toward her clothing or his. "I screamed and cried and he got up and gave orders to go. He attempted to, I tell you, but he didn't complete his business." Asked why she wouldn't confirm what she told her family and the military, that she was raped, Catherine Raymer replied: "Why, it sort of embarrasses me and I hate to tell it."[12]

The killing of the Negroes south of Bloomfield on Oct. 30, 1864, cost more Confederate prisoners their lives. On Nov. 7, 1864, James Hopkins, John W. Sipple and Samuel Stagdale were executed at Bloomfield. It was not only the executions that were bothering Kentuckians in the latter months of 1864. On Nov. 5, 1864, Governor Thomas E. Bramlette fired off a letter to Maj. General D.W. Lindsey, inspector general of Kentucky, expressing grave concern over Burbridge's hostility toward state militia and other state authority. Bramlette ordered that muster-out rolls be prepared to pay off the militia and disband them. "Better take the chances of defending as we have by the citizens than endanger our national cause by collision (with federal forces)," the governor noted.

Also on Nov. 5, 1864, the game of catch-as-catch-can continued in Bloomfield and on that Saturday, Captain Joseph J. Borrell led a detachment of 30 men of Company K, the 37th Kentucky Mounted Infantry into town, where some 15 guerrillas were gathered. The Union troops arrived with guns ablaze and captured three of the irregulars, while the rest escaped. Two days later Major Martin sent his report to Louisville.

BARDSTOWN, Ky., November 7, 1864.

CAPTAIN: I have the honor to report to you that on the 5th instant as one of my companies entered Bloomfield, under command of Captain Borrell, they surprised a lot of guerrillas at that place, fifteen in number, who were having their horses shod, and had been pillaging the town. Three guerrillas were captured and 2 badly wounded, said to be mortally; the 2 wounded ones made their escape.

On the following day the captain started the three to me at this place, and about five miles, he states, from Bloomfield they tried to escape, and all of them were killed by the guards. Their remains were carried to Bloomfield the following day (or on the 6th instant) by citizens, who gave their names as follows: Tindle, Parkhurst, alias Jack Rabet (Rabbitt), and Warford. The notorious Sue Mundy and Berry are said to be the ones who were wounded and made their escape. Sue's fine pipe fell a trophy to my men, and various other articles. Berry is now reported dead; that he died the day after the fight at Fairfield. I have sent men there for information. My rations ran out two days ago, and I have been forced to subsist off of the citizens; sent for rations yesterday. There is no battery here for the telegraph office. Nothing more of importance.

Will go farther south soon. I am, respectfully, yours,

SAMUEL MARTIN,
Major, Commanding Forces.

Berry was not dead, as official reports would soon prove. Why would Confederate guerrillas "pillage" Bloomfield? Could it be Martin was prone to exaggeration? Or were the irregulars developing a new attitude in which they no longer felt any particular allegiance to the town or its residents? It may also have been that not all bands of guerrillas or guerrilla leaders held allegiance to anyone or any place.

Nelson County Sheriff James Wood and Bloomfield merchant John A. Terrell, who was serving as state deputy provost marshal for Nelson County, sent an attachment with the report on the incident. They listed the captives as: Holmes Tindle, 22, a 6-foot, sandy-haired native of Anderson County with red whiskers and gray eyes; Harvey Warford, 22, of Nelson County, 5' 10", light hair, gray eyes; and John Parkhurst, 30, of Louisville, 5' 8", dark eyes and hair, married with two children. Parkhurst was also listed as a former member of Morgan's command.[13] The next day was Sunday. The three were taken to the place where the Negroes had been killed Oct. 30 and shot by order of Borrell, who claimed in his report to Louisville military headquarters that they were shot trying to escape.[13]

Borrell soon began to think about possible rewards for the guerrillas and made the request Nov. 7, 1864, in a dispatch to Louisville. In addition to Tinnell, Warford and Parkhurst, Borrell wanted to know how much he was to receive for killing "One Armed Jesse Berry." There were no rewards on the heads of those his men killed and there was no such person as "One Armed Jesse Berry."[14] Borrell was obviously thinking of Sam Berry, who, as stated, was not killed.

Prentice was worried that mention of Sue Mundy's pipe would lead to the discovery that his character was not female. He wrote in the *Louisville Daily Journal,* Nov. 9, 1864:

It appears that some ambitious youth aspires to the reputation as made in a few brief months by Sue Mundy, the notorious outlaw woman and the leader of a desperate cut-throat gang. Not having nerve to rob and murder wholesale this beardless youth would associate his name with the terror by assuming the title of Sue Mundy.

We have no doubt the cowardly knave would grace the petticoats better than Miss Sue does herself, but when he makes pretensions to bolder acts, the cheat is so very apparent that even the most unsuspecting are not deceived. The name of the young aspirant is Clark. A few days ago, he doffed pantaloons and donned crinoline and flowing skirts and thus attired entered the camp of Major Bristow at Bloomfield. Clark has connected himself with a small cut-throat gang and is acknowledged their leader. We would advise Mr. Clark [sic] to abandon this field or, if he will persist in traveling the road to the gallows, let him sail under his own name and stand on his own reputation.

CHAPTER 14

A Visit to Mackville

When the guerrillas left camp off the Bloomfield-Chaplin Road on a morning in early November, Magruder remained behind, saying he felt a bit poorly. Jerome and others were out scouting the region when a Rebel sympathizer came riding into camp with news that there were federals in Bloomfield. Magruder forgot his ails and was quickly in the saddle and on the hunt.

As he arrived in town, Magruder spotted two bluecoats feeding their horses near the Masonic Lodge. He fired on them and they ran into the lodge and locked the doors. They returned Magruder's fire from an upstairs window as he rode back toward camp.[1] This may have been Saturday, Nov. 12, 1864, because there was trouble in Bloomfield that day. The Bloomfield Baptist Church records include for that date: "No meeting on account of soldiers' presence having had a slight skirmish this morning. E.C. Tichenor, clerk."

Magruder decided to wait for the rest of the men to return to camp before going to Bloomfield again and in three days, on Nov. 16, 1864, with Jerome and 13 others, he rode back to town. The two soldiers were still in Bloomfield, as were several other men of the 37th Kentucky Infantry commanded by Major Samuel Martin. The guerrillas rode in from the east on the Chaplin road, firing at the boys in blue.

Some of the federals put up a brisk fire from the lodge and shot guerrilla Bob Miller out of the saddle. The Rebs kept right on riding through town, stopping only briefly on the outskirts to rob a Union soldier who was watering his horse. They took his horse and equipment but let him live. The guerrillas rode on and Martin's men gathered up their wounded prisoner for a wagon trip to Louisville, but Miller didn't live long enough to get there.

The guerrillas consumed quantities of whiskey after the modest skirmish. After the federals left Bloomfield, Jerome, Marion, Davis, Berry and others returned to town and torched the Masonic Lodge. Davis got credit for striking the match, according to local tradition. Magruder recalled later that it was Jerome and Marion who burned the lodge while intoxicated.

Once the fire was going, the guerrillas were satisfied and rode out in the direction of Taylorsville. The citizens put out the fire, saving most of the structure.[2]

While Jerome and his closer allies were into something almost daily, there were guerrilla raids being carried out across the state by a myriad of other irregulars as well. On Nov. 14, 1864, Salvisa in Mercer County was raided by some 20 guerrillas. They hit William Palmer's store immediately and made off with $400, a shotgun and Palmer's "full-blooded horse."[3]

Wood Forest lost more than $500 worth of goods of all description. There was no report on identities of those responsible. And on Nov. 14, 1864, Assistant Adjutant-General J.S. Butler, at the headquarters of the First Division, Military District of Kentucky in Lexington, authorized state troops in the bluegrass region to protect Versailles, at the risk of being considered horse thieves. The message was:

Captain GOIN,
State Troops, Versailles, Ky.:
   You will take such a number of horses from the citizens of Versailles and vicinity as will enable you to scout the country 'round Versailles and protect the town from Rebels.
   These horses will be well used and returned to the owners when done with by your scouts. Mr. Ward will assist you in procuring horses. Scout the country well and keep it clear of guerrillas.
   By order of Brigadier-General McLean:

J.S. BUTLER,
Assistant Adjutant-General.[4]

Another dispatch indicated the guerrillas were going to have their hands full. It was from the headquarters of the Army of the Ohio, then in Pukaski, Tennessee. It was also dated Nov. 14, 1864.

Thomas E. Bramlette,
Governor of Kentucky:

GOVERNOR: I have just received your letter of October 12, relative to the organization of troops for the protection of Kentucky and asking that the Fourteenth Kentucky Infantry be sent to the State. I am glad to inform you that the regiment has been ordered back, with three others, and I have no doubt will be able to do service in the way you suggest. I have referred your letter to Major-General Stoneman, who now acts in my stead as commander of the department. Please confer with him on the subject.

I am, Governor, very respectfully, your obedient servant,

J.M. SCHOFIELD,
Major-General.[5]

CHAPTER 15

An Eye for an Eye

The weather was fair and cool most of November 1864, which proved inviting for guerrillas to be on the trail as well as the Union patrols who searched for them. An exception was Nov. 8, 1864. Spencer County farmer John Lilly wrote in his diary:

"Rained incessantly all day and the (Salt) river rose and prevented those on this side from voting for the president and vice president of the U.S." Despite the high water on that election day in 1864, Abraham Lincoln and Andrew Johnson were reelected. Lincoln won despite opposition to his direction of the Union Army in its conduct of war. Neither before nor after the election had the president issued an order for Burbridge to halt the executions of Southern soldiers.

Two were shot Nov. 6, 1864, at Munfordville because guerrillas had killed a Union soldier. Four were executed at Midway Nov. 9, 1864, in retaliation for the death of Adam Harper. For the killing of "Union men" a mile above Henderson, three were shot Nov. 13, 1864, by a firing squad composed of black soldiers. On Nov. 15, 1864, two Rebel prisoners were hanged near the Fairground in Lexington. On Nov. 19, 1864, eight Southern prisoners were killed by firing squad at Munfordville and six were executed at Oceola in Green County.

Burbridge claimed no prisoner was executed without being tried "by a regular court." There are no records, reports or newspaper stories to indicate that any of Burbridge's victims received a trial or even a hearing. On Nov. 16, 1864, Lincoln declared the nation would conduct a day of thanksgiving and prayer in eight days. The next day, Thursday, Nov. 17, 1864, another name would be available for the prayer list.

A cold rain had been falling, as Magruder, Sol Thompson, Henry Metcalf and about nine others rode on Muldraugh's Hill, part of a string of knobs generally northeast of Elizabethtown. The guerrillas wore oilcloth overcoats and had blankets around them.[1] The 34-year-old Metcalf, 6-foot-2 and 214 pounds, was a private in Confederate Company A, 3rd Regiment, Kentucky Cavalry from Muhlenburg County, while Thompson, 5' 9", and a native of Marion County, served in Confederate Company K, 8th Kentucky Volunteer Regiment. Both were former members of Morgan's cavalry.

Late in the evening, near sundown, Thompson and Magruder saw Thomas Franklin "Frank" Crady on the road near his home between Hodgenville and Shepherdsville. It was apparent they'd been looking for the Union soldier. In fact, they rode up to the residence of J.H. Sherard and asked where Crady lived. The declining visibility may have caused the guerrillas to miss the fact that Sherard, of the U.S. 19th Kentucky, was wearing his Army blouse.

They quickly determined that the 24-year-old Crady was in the road ahead. A few words were exchanged before Thompson shot him three times. In a few minutes, when it was evident Crady was still alive, Thompson told Magruder to get down and finish him off. Magruder poked the barrel of a pistol into Crady's head, under a cheek, and fired. Crady, a corporal from Company K, 26th Kentucky Volunteer Infantry, died about 3 A.M. the morning of Nov. 18, 1864. After Sherard had helped carry Crady into his house, he and another local dedicated loyalist, Richard Hall, hightailed it to avoid becoming the guerrillas' next victims.[2]

The site of the shooting wasn't far from Magruder's home at Samuels Old Place in Bullitt County. There would be some who later swore Magruder wasn't even close when Crady was shot in the head, but William Allen, a resident of the area, witnessed the shooting. He said Thompson stopped Crady in the road and robbed him of his money. The 5-foot-7 Crady was then told to get off his horse and hand over the horse's halter, but the soldier struggled with the halter. Allen said Thompson got off his horse and began beating and kicking Crady, then shot him three times. He verified that the mortal wound was inflicted by Magruder.[3]

The guerrillas moved on toward Hodgenville, robbing at every opportunity.

CHAPTER 16

The Ride of Death

On Sunday, Nov. 20, 1864, Magruder and Jerome found federal soldier Samuel Williams at the residence of William Hanley, some eight miles from Campbellsville in Taylor County. They shot him dead.[1] A "Negro" was then "pressed" into action as a guide to get the guerrillas to Campbellsville. They arrived about 4 P.M. and began plundering the stores.

The *Louisville Daily Journal* account of the raid, published Nov. 29, 1864, added: "There happened to be present two soldiers of Captain Crandall's company, the 13th Kentucky, who were shot down instantly, one of them after having surrendered himself, and neither making the slightest resistance. One of them, Mr. Blankenship, has since died, and there is no hope for the recovery of the other."

The stores of Captain Samuel Marksbury Crandall, Gowdy, Turner & Company and Chandler & Mourning were entered. About $75 was taken from the former and nothing from the latter. Citizens were relieved of pocketbooks and watches to the tune of $2,000. The raid was cut short when a dozen discharged Union soldiers of the 2nd Kentucky Battery, on their way home from Louisville, raced into town. With mostly bluster, since only about half of the federals were armed, they were able to get the guerrillas on the run.

They captured a carbine and a blanket and thought they seriously wounded the robber who dropped them. When a band of 25 guerrillas left Bloomfield for Springfield, Nov. 25, 1864, they were led by Dick Mitchell and "Big Zay" Coulter.[2] Richard Berry "Dick" Mitchell, 25, of Washington County was the son of parents who had the same surname before they were married. James R. Mitchell was wed to Nancy Rankin Mitchell. Dick Mitchell had been a sergeant in Company A, 3rd Kentucky

(Morgan's) Cavalry, Gano's Regiment. The 21-year-old Coulter was a mountain of a man. He was the son of Rowan Coulter of Washington County and Sabra Morgan of Anderson County.

The guerrillas were within a half-mile of Springfield when Irish laborer James Grans was met, pistol-whipped and relieved of $17. The tollgate keeper nearby lost $50, and others using the road also found the toll to be much higher than usual. Washington County Sheriff Charles F. Bosley was sitting in the back room of Jacob "Peck" Perkins combination residence and drug store in Mackville the night of Nov. 25, 1864. He'd been talking with Perkins and another local resident, Squire Mitchell. They heard shots and Mitchell jumped up exclaiming, "What does that mean?" "There are some drunken soldiers," Perkins said, and he offered to go outside and calm them down. "Never mind," said the sheriff, who was not aware of the futility he would propose, "I will settle them and make them behave themselves." Walker, Perkins' clerk, was in the front room and exclaimed, "They are guerrillas!" Bosley looked around and said, "I reckon not." Walker replied, "Yes they are. I know them."[3] The back-room boys had moseyed toward the front as the guerrillas came in the back door.

"You God damn sons of bitches," a guerrilla yelled. "Come out of there, God damn you!" Nobody wanted to be the first to go out, so they stood motionless. Sam Berry, wearing a federal soldier's hat, blue-black overcoat and cape, appeared to be captain that night. "You God damn fools. Do you think you can resent 25 soldiers?" Berry bellowed.[4]

Perkins then came out and was robbed of his pocketbook and a roll of some kind of tickets. He had a pistol in his right-hand side pocket that belonged to a friend; it went undetected. They took what money Walker and Bosley had. Bosley said later it was between $100 and $103. They took whatever they wanted from the store, cursed Perkins and accused him of writing a pamphlet against the guerrillas. Perkins said he didn't know what they were talking about.

At an opportune moment, Perkins tossed the previously undetected gun under a bed. Magruder found it and pressed it cocked to Bosley's head. When Perkins begged for Bosley's life, Magruder shoved the barrel into Perkins' right side. "You God damn son-of-a-bitch, I intend to kill you anyhow," he said.

Perkins begged Coulter, who was behind the counter, for his life, and Coulter told Magruder, "You God damn son-of-a-bitch, put that pistol away, God damn you." Magruder put the pistol in his pocket and went to the front part of the house.

There is no indication from available records what demeanor the guerrillas maintained during such interaction. Were they serious with one another? Was there competition for leadership? Did their senses of humor, no matter how bizarre, play a role in their actions? It seems more likely there was a code of camaraderie that, most times, overshadowed petty differences.

The guerrillas broke open a wardrobe upstairs at the Perkins place and took jewelry and silver worth about $800 from a trunk. Perkins said later he knew Coulter and Berry of the group. He said Berry had robbed him on two other occasions. During one of the other visits, with Jerome and Coulter along, Berry kicked his foot through a showcase and took albums and numerous knives. On the other occasion, Jerome allegedly pistol-whipped a man named Derr who was caught loading a gun. Dates of the two robberies are imprecise, but appeared to have occurred in September and November 1864.

It was, however, a group of 18 Confederate guerrillas who arrived in Mackville Nov. 25, 1864, dismounted and were led into Perkins' store by Berry. The one-armed man then ordered Bosley and the other men to go into the front room. Coulter took Bosley's pocketbook and Perkins' whisky, after making him taste it first, as Berry was going through the sheriff's saddlebags. Bosley asked Berry to leave the books and papers and he did, but kept Bosley's pistols and the saddlebags.

Those losses were meager compared to the ones that would follow in rapid succession.

Upon arrival at Daniel Green's house, a mile from Mackville, they found Green's 21-year-old son, Samuel, home on furlough from Company I, First Kentucky Volunteer (Wolford's) Cavalry, who had arrived about an hour earlier. He was standing in the yard, wearing his federal overcoat, when his body was riddled with bullets.

James Devine was down the road in his wagon going over to see his neighbor, John Foster, who had served in the Union Army two years earlier, but was discharged for physical disabilities. At the time of his discharge, Foster was a corporal in Company I, the First Kentucky Volunteer Cavalry.

Coulter rode up with a dozen or more of the gang with him, took Devine's pocketbook containing $14.50 at gunpoint and was about to take his lead horse when Berry arrived. "How are you, Devine?" Berry asked. Berry shook hands with Devine and asked what he was doing there. While conversing with Devine, Berry told the others to "let his horse alone." Devine had grown up with Berry and had known him when Berry taught school. They continued down the road toward David Foster's, where John Foster lived.

William E. Riley and his wife were at Foster's and Riley had vivid memories of what happened: "When they got near the fence, they hallooed for us to come to the fence, but before I got halfway to the fence, some five or six were in the yard. They called on us to hand out our pocketbooks. His (John Foster's) was searched, found to be empty and tossed on the ground." Foster drove Riley's dog around the house and when he returned a man met him and started talking to him. Suddenly, Foster was shot dead, the bullet crashing through his nose and into his skull. The ball did not come out, Devine discovered. Foster's wife stood at the fence, screaming.

Riley told the man who shot Foster that Foster was a discharged soldier. The gunman replied, "They treat us that way; we have to do the same."[5] Riley said Foster's killer was a "small, 5-foot-6, heavy-set man." When it was over, Devine went home and sat by the fire. There was nothing else he could do.[6]

On Nov. 26, 1864, the same band of guerrillas, some wearing red sashes, was active again. William Yeager looked out at dawn's early light and saw the riders coming down the road. Isaac Butner, a private in Company F, the Fourth Kentucky Volunteer Infantry, had spent the night at Yeager's. Butner, 38, stepped into the yard, wearing his Union overcoat, to determine who the riders were. They began firing and Butner started running. He ran through a field, ignoring orders to halt. About 250 yards from the house, as Butner was running up a branch, he was shot. A bullet in the forehead came out near the right ear.[7]

Berry, who did not pursue Butner, took a pair of pistols from Yeager. Butner's body was searched and his money and a watch taken. It was not clear why Butner was back in his home territory that day. He was not related to Yeager but was a neighbor and lived close by.

Another neighbor, William Yates, was robbed of his pocketbook containing $14 and a "parcel of money in a drawer" by Coulter. The tall guerrilla also took goods out of the house. Yates saw Berry out front and became brave enough to ask the others not to take his daughter's horse because she'd lost her husband in the war. They took it anyway. The horse was valued at $150.

Then Yates heard firing in the direction of Stith Thomas Hall's place just over the hill and the voice of a woman screaming. Hall was a lieutenant colonel of the home guard or, as it was also called, the Kentucky State Militia. The home of Tom and Martha (Noe) Hall was surrounded by the guerrillas. Tom, 29, told his pregnant wife to take the children — William, 7; J.M., 5; Nancy, 4; and Sarah, 2 — and go upstairs. Hall fired at the guerrillas until he'd spent the loads in three weapons. He then walked upstairs and asked Martha to go down and beg for his life.[8]

Martha Hall went downstairs, met the guerrillas at the door and began begging as requested by her husband. She was told to get out of the way or she would have her brains blown out. Tom then appeared at the door and said that he would give himself up and not to shoot him. One of the guerrillas squared himself in the saddle and shot Tom Hall in the left side. Hall slapped his hand on the wound, leaned over and exclaimed, "Lord have mercy." The same man fired again and the bullet crashed into Hall's head, killing him. He dropped at Martha's feet and the guerrillas fired four more rounds into his body as Martha screamed hysterically.[9]

The shot that killed Hall went into his forehead and came out the top of his head. Another shot went into his chin and the rest into his torso.

Sam Berry stood in the door after Hall was dead and asked Martha three times what her husband's name was. She didn't tell him, but one of her little sons did. The guerrillas dragged Hall's body into the yard and threw him out full length on his face. Martha said later the man who killed her husband was light complexioned and over moderate height, but it was not Berry, and Coulter was at the Yates place when the gunfire was heard. It could have been Jerome Clarke.

They took all the weapons and without compunction, burned children's clothing, blankets and several personal items of the family.[10]

Jerome, Tom Flowers and others stopped in a hotel at Taylorsville November 29, 1864, to have dinner. Afterwards, the guerrillas rode toward Chaplin, where Flowers and another guerrilla were in front of the others as an advance guard. Suddenly, Flowers, who was drunk, fired his pistol, apparently as a joke to frighten the others. A guerrilla known as "Georgia" was not amused.

Georgia and Flowers had words over the incident and the argument became heated. Flowers drew his pistol and killed Georgia, prompting a serious reaction from the other guerrillas. They threatened to kill Flowers, but settled on dismounting him.

CHAPTER 17

The Springfield Raid

Charles B. Butner was sitting at his desk in his Springfield law office Dec. 3, 1864, when he heard horses on the street outside, moving "pretty fast." He saw a band of a dozen guerrillas and one was carrying a black flag, the sign that no quarter would be given.

They came back up the street, stopped outside and began hallooing for the citizens to come out. They fired their guns in the air to enforce the demand.[1] Davis was captain on the raid, supported by Jerome, Magruder, Sam Berry, Henry Metcalf, Dick Mitchell, Sam Jones, Zay Coulter, Henry Turner, Tom Henry and perhaps two others.

They wore Confederate uniforms and roundabouts trimmed in yellow or red lace with small brass buttons. One wore a dark, beaver cloth overcoat and others wore jeans and overcoats. It was a cold day and Davis had socks over his boots that came up to his knees.

The guerrillas immediately rounded up the citizens and forced them into the public square where they were told to remain. One guerrilla rode his horse into a large foyer of a house and fired into the ceiling. It didn't take Jerome long to confiscate a woman's furs and he wore them as he rode about Springfield.

People in the town had lately been talking about defending themselves should such a raid occur. They had considered construction of a blockhouse from which they could fire through portholes. They had not taken time to act on ideas for defense, in part because of concern the town might be burned by attackers if they could not be chased off. Shots were fired into some of the stores to discourage resistance. Such was the case at Gideon Josephus Bosley's grocery.

After three shots poured through his front window, Bosley fled out the back door and took cover in a house. He heard someone across the street yell, "There goes a damn yankee with a gun in his hand!" But the guerrilla wasn't talking about Bosley. It was 41-year-old wagonmaker Thornton Washington Lee, who wasn't about to give up Springfield, his home for 12 years, without a fight. He had loaded an old musket and made his way up an alley, crossed a garden and rested his gun against a stable. Lee got off a shot in the direction of Jerome and Davis, who were sitting on their horses on the sidewalk.[2] Davis had a minor knuckle wound, but Jerome wasn't hit.

One of the guerrillas came riding hard around the blacksmith shop yelling, "Shoot the damned rascal!" Lee ran for all he was worth as Jerome and Davis opened fire on him. They fired four rounds and three of them struck Lee, who grabbed a fence to steady himself. Lee continued into the Clemons residence and hid in a pantry. The guerrilla giving chase jumped his horse over the garden fence, arrived at the house where Lee was hiding and went inside. There was gunfire heard and a moment later the guerrilla emerged carrying Lee's musket and a pistol and declaring, "By God, I sent him up twice." The pistol had been fired three times, indicating Lee went down fighting. Lee was shot once in each temple.[3] Lee's killer was described as full-faced and fleshy, weighing 180 to 200 pounds. The description was a fit for Magruder, but Jones said the day after the raid that he killed Lee and had Lee's pistol.[4] Witnesses said young Turner seemed very sorry about the death of Lee and appeared to be weeping.[5]

A short time after Lee's murder, a guerrilla rode up to the home of 28-year-old shoemaker John Urias Wetherton. It was just an empty lot and small house away from the residence where Lee was killed. When he saw the rider, Wetherton headed for the back door, but before he reached it, he was shot in the side.

Neighbors went for a doctor and as he cared for Wetherton, the doctor asked him who had shot him. Wetherton named no one, but said he was shot "for nothing." He said he was going out the back door and the man who shot him was coming in the front. He lived but a short while and it was believed the doctor gave Wetherton his last rites because a priest could not be found in time.[6] Jesse Marattay was in his drug store when Wetherton's wife came running in, hollering that her husband had been killed and she wanted "some men" to come to the house. Turner asked which Wetherton had been shot, and when told, approved some men going to the house. Wetherton was from Bardstown and had lived just a short time in Springfield. Turner was also from Bardstown. The mid-morning raid continued for about an hour.

Stock trader Grandison Robertson had stuck most of his money into a keg at the drug store just before a guerrilla rode up and demanded his pocketbook. He asked if he could go home just a few doors away, but the gunman told him to walk to the public square or he would "blow your damned brains out." Robertson went to the square and was placed in a line of at least eight other men who had also been forced to give up their pocketbooks. Robertson had grown up with Dick Mitchell, so when he appealed, Mitchell agreed to escort Robertson and Hugh McElroy to their homes. Mitchell went back to Robertson's a short time later to get a glass of water. McElroy was worn out from an encounter with Tom Henry and Magruder, who had robbed his bank. He didn't have the key to a drawer in the counter and one guerrilla picked up a bench and attempted to break the drawer open. McElroy showed them how to open the drawer by pushing on it slightly and no key was necessary. Three pocketbooks dropped out. They contained $150 in greenbacks and $600 in Confederate scrip. Then, McElroy was forced to open the safe. The vault inside wasn't locked and they took $16 in silver belonging to one man and $50 in silver and $60 in bills that were the property of a local woman.

They took bank stocks and certificates that were later found torn and scattered along the road about a half mile from town. A silver pitcher and tumblers that belonged to the church were taken. They threw the pitcher back when it was discovered it belonged to the church, but kept the tumblers. Two of the tumblers were afterward given back as well.

The plates were not taken. The guerrillas, some wearing feathers in their hats, found their strange sense of humor sometimes rubbing off on robbery victims. One said, "I have been delivered of my money." When a guerrilla went to Jesse Marattay and demanded money, Jess said he didn't have any. The robber replied, "Give me 50 cents then. I haven't got any money today." A young man who said he was to be married that night was told to hand over his ring, but claimed he couldn't get it off his finger. They held his finger up to a doorsill and were ready to shoot it off when he discovered he could get the ring off after all.

There were some guerrillas whose rudeness and insouciance never seemed to wane. Combined with a lack of education or training in propriety, their excessive drinking exacerbated their fatuous comments. Bullying or frightening their victims was also part of their arsenal. Several women were looking for a doctor for Wetherton, when a guerrilla was overheard saying: "God damn you, we expected to send you after the doctor before we got here." A woman was going for a priest for Wetherton and a guerrilla remarked they wanted a priest "immediately" to pray for them. Butler was one of the men who went to the Wetherton house where he examined the victim's wounds. "The bullet entered just above his left hip and passed through to the skin near the right nipple. I could feel the ball," he said of Wetherton's death wound.

Davis found a better mount but would not leave his roan horse when Robertson refused to take it as a gift. Davis also threatened to return and burn Springfield if anyone fired a shot during their departure. The Springfield raid ended in the late morning and the guerrillas headed for Perryville, 15 miles to the east. Prentice reported that "Sue Mundy's Gang" took $2,000 in money and property from Springfield and said the guerrillas were led by Sue Mundy and Dick Mitchell. On Dec. 2, 1864, S.S. Fry wrote to Captain J.S. Butler, the assistant adjutant general, that he had just received a letter from "a most reliable Union man in Washington County." The letter gave an account of the "most horred (*sic*) outrages committed by a gang of guerrillas upon the people in that county," Fry wrote.[7]

"They have killed in a few days past some fourteen quiet, inoffensive citizens, among them one discharged soldier." Fry told Butler he had 150 of the 13th Kentucky Cavalry, sent back by Burbridge, and if there were no specific orders for them, he wanted a portion of the 13th to be used for guerrilla hunting.[8]

CHAPTER 18

Deathly Cold on Salt River

From Springfield, the dozen guerrillas rode seven miles east–southeast to the village of Texas and two more miles in the same direction to Pottsville. They were just six miles west of Perryville. Word preceded them and the people of Perryville feared for their lives as rumors put the force at a hundred guerrillas, approaching by way of Mackville.[1] The estimate of the band's size was highly inflated, but the tale of their approach wasn't far from accurate. Mackville was a few miles north of the road being used by the irregulars.

Residents were so afraid, many stayed up all night to keep watch. The only problem was they didn't have guns enough to defend themselves.[2] Sunday, Dec. 4, 1864, Jerome led the guerrillas into Perryville, where people on the street were robbed. A federal soldier named Lawson was shot and killed while handing over his pocketbook and the guerrilla who shot him claimed it was an accident. The guerrillas rode up to storefronts and ordered the merchants to bring out the contents of their money drawers. Berry rode his horse into Green's Drug Store to get faster service from the merchant.[3] The raid was over in 20 minutes and the gang moved on to the little communities of Nevada and Cornishville. Federal Captain James Marion Fidler and another officer soon arrived from Lebanon and attempted to track the guerrillas, who headed in the direction of Bloomfield, where they could melt away into the countryside.[4]

On Dec. 8, 1864, Prentice's *Journal* reported on other guerrilla activity.

Jesse — Train Captured — Jesse [CSA Colonel George Jessee] is becoming quite troublesome again. He is now in command of a large mounted force, and almost every day makes a demonstration on the Frankfort Railroad. Yesterday [Dec. 7, 1864], he captured a freight train near Bagdad [Shelby County] and destroyed it. The passenger train from Lexington had not arrived in the city [Louisville] up to twelve o'clock last night. It was telegraphed to remain at Frankfort until the road should be cleared of the outlaws and the trip rendered safe. It would prove a great blessing if some measures were taken to drive Jesse and his gang from the State.

Fear of guerrillas prompted citizens of Harrodsburg to petition the federal government for arms. Nat Gaither was one of a half-dozen Harrodsburg residents who signed a Dec. 7, 1864, letter to Union General D.W. Lindsey. It said in part:

My dear sir.

This will be handed you by Captain Lawson who has 71 men regularly mustered in to the state service and who desires to have arms to protect our town from the thieving bands now infesting our county.... Our banks are in danger. Coulter's gang have sworn they will burn our town and we are in danger of life and limb and the Capts [sic] Co. must have the guns.... These gangs are the enemies of all mankind, have no principles, fight for no cause and they ought to be exterminated.

Such requests came from all parts of the state and the military was generally slow to respond, although select decoy guerrillas and guerrilla hunters were hired and equipped.

With the start of December, Kentucky's weather changed drastically. It rained on Dec. 6, 1864, but within three days, winter-like weather took a fierce grip on the state. Benjamin Dunlavy wrote in the East Family Journal at the Shaker Village of Pleasant Hill, Dec. 8, 1864:

"Mercury at 14 above. We previously had about two weeks of pleasant weather." Spencer County farmer Tom Lilly wrote in his day book Dec. 9, 1864: "Snow fell fast this evening on the frozen ground to the depth of four or five inches." Also on Dec. 9, 1864, Dunlavy's journal entry confirmed the snowfall was fairly general across north central and east central Kentucky. He entered this in his Journal: "Mercury at 13. It snowed about 4 inches this P.M. The first (of) any note this winter." Dunlavy said the temperature dipped to 6 degrees above zero by noon on Dec. 11, 1864, after standing at 20 degrees in the morning. It was still 6-above that night. On Dec. 12, 1864, it was 2-below in the morning, according to Dunlavy.

Despite the stinging cold, the guerrillas returned to the trail. The Shelby-Spencer County circuit preacher, Rev. Benjamin Franklin Hungerford, noted in his diary Dec. 12, 1864: "Have just heard that guerillas (*sic*) last night hung two of my neighbors, believing that they had money they would not give them, but they did not kill them. O Mores, O Tempore! When will this cruel war end: No law, no justice, no security for life! I can understand how Job felt when he said, 'Oh, that the Lord would hide me in the grave until his wrath be past.'"

Also on the same Monday, Dec. 12, 1864, Sam Berry, Henry Magruder, Jim Davis, Bill Maraman and a young Rebel named John Butts, from the Van Buren community on Salt River in Spencer County near the Spencer-Anderson County line, rode into Taylorsville. Spencer County Jailer Samuel Snider had just taken breakfast to four slaves, two men and two women, who had been arrested and accused of stealing and attempting to burn property.[5]

Another version of why the arrests were made said that after a house burned, Miss Humes' ex-slave, Frances, carried away the major part of what was left from the fire. Frances was repeatedly hanged by some local men in an effort to make her tell where the items were taken. On the verge of being strangled by the rope, she said clothing had been given to a former slave named John Russell.[6]

Just as the guerrillas were entering town, one of the male prisoners asked Snider if he would go across the street and get him some cigars. Snider obliged, and as he returned with the cigars, he was met in the street by Magruder and Davis, who, holding Snider at gunpoint, said they wanted the jail unlocked. One of the guerrillas told the jailer he'd heard there were some "damned smoked Yankees in there." They forced Snider back to the building and upstairs where the jailer surrendered the prisoners.

In addition to Frances Bell and John Russell, the other prisoners were Belle Cooper and George Tansley. Berry was on his horse talking with citizens John Froman and Thomas Kirk, who were trying to discourage violence. Berry protested taking the prisoners from the jail and said he would have nothing to do with killing them. A short time later, Berry told Froman and Kirk: "Gentlemen, I have done all that I can for those Negroes without endangering my own life. And I will not do that for the sake of a Negro. I can do nothing more than make them take these Negroes from town as far as I can. But my life is in danger and I have been threatened." Berry told Froman if the citizens had left them alone when they came into town, they would have had nothing to do with the Negroes.[6] It was said some little boys on the street told the guerrillas about the prisoners. Berry, dressed in a red, hooded outfit under his black hat that was pinned up on one side with a silver, half-moon broach, rode over to the jail as the prisoners were being brought downstairs.

"I hear there are some God damn niggers put in this jail for burning down barns," Berry said.[7] The prisoners were marched less than a half mile and after crossing the Salt River covered bridge, each was forced to get on a horse behind a guerrilla. Russell got up behind Berry. Soon, Butts caught up and joined the solemn parade as it headed eastward, upriver.

"Uncle, I believe they are going to kill the last damned one of you," Berry told Russell. "Let me off then," Russell replied. Berry said he could not let Russell off the horse because the captain would punish him and might kill him.[8]

The other guerrillas and their passengers moved a short distance ahead of Berry and Russell along the frozen ground by the river. Suddenly, Russell decided to make a run for it. He jumped off the horse and dashed through a field. Berry followed and as Russell jumped over a fence, he fired four shots. One of the projectiles found its target, striking Russell in the left hip. Russell looked back, saw Berry jump his horse over the fence, then fell with his head downhill on the frozen tundra, partially playing possum, but wounded badly enough that he would not be able to outrun Berry. When he raised himself up, Berry was gone.[9]

Berry's apparent benevolence was to be upstaged that day by Davis and it was perhaps a major reason many of the guerrillas lost confidence in the man with the bugle. Davis had Belle Cooper riding behind him and after a prolonged period in the bitter cold, he rode to the nearby residence of recent refugees Robert and Ann Blanton, a quarter mile from the Watson-Froman mill pond. Davis and Belle warmed themselves that morning and Davis asked Ann Blanton to allow the young ex-slave to remain there until she could make an escape. Davis said he would pay her board. Robert Blanton was not home for consultation, so Ann made the decision alone to try to save Belle's life.[10] She decided, at the risk of her own safety, to allow Belle to spend the night.

Soon gunshots were heard down by the mill pond. Tansley was shot just above the eye and his body stuffed under the ice covering the pond. Frances Bell, the smallest of the slaves, was riding behind Maraman, one of the smaller guerrillas. Maraman told her that he would let her down and she could run across the frozen river and escape. Maraman thought the ice would break, but when Frances successfully dashed across, he went after her, brought her back and shot her dead. He found a place where he could break the ice and shove her body into the river.[11]

Early that evening, Ann Blanton was visited by two or more guerrillas. She didn't know, or was afraid to say, who took Belle Cooper from her house and shot her at the mill pond.[12] Belle was shot three times, including once in the side.[13]

The Watsons, ancestors of the author, assisted the Cooper family in building coffins and burying the dead.

CHAPTER 19

A Guerrilla Christmas

Brigadier General John Bell Hood was at the head of the Army of Tennessee on Dec. 15, 1864, moving northward toward Nashville with the ultimate intention of drawing Brigadier General William Tecumseh Sherman out of Georgia. The Battle of Nashville followed, resulting in Brigadier General George Henry Thomas' routing of Hood's army. Hood retreated to Tupelo, Miss., and resigned his command.

The Rebel army could have used the former Morgan troops in the closing months of the war, but few returned to duty. On Dec. 16, 1864, Magruder led a group of guerrillas to New Haven on the Lebanon Branch Railroad, where they burned a railroad bridge over the Rolling Fork of the Salt River. The act cut off rail communication between Louisville and Lebanon. The raid was reported in the Dec. 18, 1864, *Louisville Journal* and there was an addendum: "Magruder and his gang of thieves deserve the halter, and we hope that they will soon get their deserts."

On Dec. 21, 1864, 34 guerrillas under Bill Davison, Zay Coulter, King White and Henry Cox boarded the riverboat *Morning Star* at Lewisport. Coulter shot and killed William Campbell, a Union soldier, as robberies were being carried out. Davison also robbed the safe. The boat's steward and two Union soldiers dove into the Ohio River and while the soldiers escaped, the steward drowned. "Where are the Yankees?," asked White as he roamed the boat. "We need to kill some more damned Yankees." The guerrillas stayed on board and robbed every passenger until the boat reached Hawesville, some 20 miles away.[1]

Christmas Day, 1864, fell on Sunday. It was cold in Kentucky with the temperature hovering around the freezing mark.[2] It was on that holy day that Sam Berry allegedly committed a rape in Spencer County. Military authorities said the victim was Susan Lee, a former slave.³ It was a Christmas to remember at the Van Buren Church of Christ along the Salt River in Spencer County.

Diary keeper William Thomas "Salt River Tom" Love made note of it:

> As the brethren began to congregate, to their surprise and amazement, Tom Flowers and John Mackey, two guerrillas of evil repute, came walking in with their cavalry spurs on and heavily armed. Flowers demanded [to know] the purpose of the gathering. Brother Green Milton briefly stated the object of the meeting. Synchronously, Jim Campbell came riding by with a bag of meal. "A Sabbath profaner," said Flowers, and going out, he flourished his pistol and ordered Campbell into the church. Campbell was interrogated about his bag of meal and Flowers chastised him for hauling on Sunday. "Throw it on the fence or the ground and get in that meeting house," Flowers demanded.
>
> Mackey, by order of Flowers, went up one side of the street and down the other, and forced the citizens to come to the meetin' and every one he saw had to come in. He compelled them to come in until the house was filled with guests. "A song," said Flowers. Green Milton announced a song and soon the entire congregation were singing the melodious hymn: "Joy to the world, the Lord has come!" Green started the song and dropped to base [*sic*] as Flowers took the lead and the congregation carried all the parts.

Love said the Davis girls were in particularly good voice.

> Green, a little shaky and agitated, read with fear and trembling and Lemuel Davis chanted an orison [a prayer] that he had but little rememberance [*sic*] of afterward. Flowers asked the priviledge [*sic*] of making a few remarks. He said, "Friends, this reminds me of better days, days when that mother, who is far away in Alabama, use to take her then darling boy to the old camp meetings where he could hear the soul entrancing songs of Zion that purified the heart and sent a thrilling sensation to my soul. This cruel war has coated and molded me in a casket of sin and driven me far from a mother's tender love." Flowers then dismissed the audience and no one complained. The congregation sang a hymn and filed out of the church.

On the day after Christmas, 1864, three federal officers in advance of a command moving toward Morganfield in Union County confronted four Confederate officers.⁴ The Confederates were not guerrillas, but had been cut off from General Hylan Benton Lyon's command. The Union officers were quick on the trigger, killing three of the Rebs and wounding the fourth. The dead were: George Henry, brother of guerrilla Tom Henry; Captain George Stedman of Frankfort; and Lieutenant George Woolfolk of Hopkins County. The wounded man's identity was not learned.

On Dec. 29, 1864, a cold and overcast Thursday, the Rev. J.M.P. Kearny of Springfield was on the road in Washington County when he met a guerrilla band that included Henry Magruder, Bill Marion, Jim Davis and Dick Mitchell. Magruder, Marion and Davis were dressed in their give-no-quarter red flannel suits.[5] Davis was showing evidence of a recent foot wound. There were three others reportedly from Pratt's command.

Kearny was about a half mile from the residence of Tom Blandford, the father-in-law of a discharged Union soldier, First Lieutenant Charles E. Spalding.[6] A veteran of Chickamauga and Missionary Ridge, Spalding was 18 when he entered the Union Army in 1861. He began as an orderly sergeant in Company G, the 10th Kentucky Infantry. The son of Theodore B. Spalding had become ill and was forced to return home. He was married in July 1864. Kearny was quizzed by the guerrillas as to his identity and intentions.

"I told them I was a clergyman and was on my way to see a colored woman who was sick," Kearny was to say later in recalling the meeting.[7]

The guerrillas rode ahead of Kearny and straight into the yard of the Blandford house. Dr. J.C. Pash had spent the night at the Blandfords' and after breakfast in the early morning, he bade all farewell and a young daughter of Blandford opened the door for Pash to leave. Pash walked into the teeth of a guerrilla charge as he left the house. Pash got on his horse but was immediately told by a guerrilla that he wanted him and the horse. When he told the guerrilla he was a doctor, there on "professional business," Pash was ordered to leave.[8]

As the guerrillas fired, Spalding ran into an adjacent field, perhaps to draw the fire away from his wife and family. Marion led the charge and may have been the first to shoot Spalding. Magruder, Davis and the rest swarmed around the fallen soldier and continued firing. A black girl ran inside and told Fanny Spalding that there was firing in the field and she saw Charles Spalding fall to the ground. Magruder rode to the house, identified himself and told Fanny Spalding he'd just killed Charles.[9] She threw up her hands and sobbed, "They've killed my husband."

Dr. Pash had left when the firing started, but returned when it stopped and examined the body. He determined that Spalding had been shot seven times. There were two wounds in the front part of his chest and one in each side, an arm, the back and the forehead over his right eye. The guerrillas had stormed into the house, ripped up beds, torn open trunks and stolen whatever pleased their fancies. They took coats and pants and a set of Fanny Spalding's furs. Fanny looked on helplessly as the six discussed their haul. Mitchell had Spalding's pistol, but Marion told him to give it to Magruder, who was only armed with three revolvers. They scavenged for an hour and finally Marion became restless and ordered the others to "Come on! Come on!"[9] They left the Manton area, crossed the Washington-Nelson County line into Nelson, and headed for the Botland community to get their horses shod.

CHAPTER 20

The Edward Caldwell Affair

Snow began falling across central Kentucky during the afternoon of Dec. 28, 1864, and continued into the night. The winter remained hard through New Year's Day, 1865, which was sunny and cold.[1] It was on the first day of 1865 that the guerrilla who had become known as "the butcher of Lawrence" entered Kentucky.

A Confederate commander of scouts, Captain William Clarke Quantrill crossed the Mississippi River and led 45 men into a state where he was not being hunted for wholesale murder and destruction. Quantrill became infamous for the Aug. 23, 1863, raid on Lawrence, Kansas, in which 166 men and boys plus 17 Union Army recruits were killed.[2] It was said that in a four-hour period, Quantrill and his force of 294 men left 80 widows and 250 orphans. Lawrence was left in flames and damage was estimated at $2 million, an even greater sum in those days than today.[3]

As Quantrill and his scouts began a slow trek out of western Kentucky, they had a gunfight with three Union soldiers who had taken shelter in a house near Hopkinsville. It was there that Quantrill's Lieutenant James Little was gravely wounded and died the next day.

Meanwhile, Jerome and the Kentucky guerrillas remained at the ready and were stalking in Bullitt County. It was drizzling rain and cold Jan. 5, 1865, as five guerrillas looked for the best place to cross Long Lick Creek, three miles from Shepherdsville. The creek was running high on its trek toward the Salt River.[4]

Snow had fallen on December 29 and January 2, but the rain was promoting a slow thaw. Jerome, Magruder, Maraman, Metcalf and a fifth guerrilla not recognized by the civilians who saw him were dressed in layers to fend off the rain and cold. The outer layer consisted of federal blue overcoats. Jerome wore his red velvet jacket. Magruder's was black and Maraman's gray. Each was tinseled in yellow. Metcalf and Maraman wore tall riding boots.[5] Magruder, on a bay horse, wore a low black hat pinned up on each side, a tassel of yellow and black and a feather. Jerome rode a bay and Maraman a gray.[6] They were headed for the home of Benjamin Franklin Caldwell and Margaret Hoagland Caldwell. Their son, Edward Curtis Caldwell, 27, was a sergeant in Company D, 15th Kentucky Volunteer Infantry. Margaret Caldwell had recently telegraphed Edward, telling him that his father was dying. Edward, granted a 30-day furlough, had not been home for three years and as he came within sight of the house, 120 yards distant, his father died.[7]

The guerrillas arrived at the Caldwell house, dismounted and burst inside with pistols drawn. True to their modus operandi, the guerrillas used surprise and terror to discourage an immediate response. "Surrender, every damned son of a bitch of you," someone yelled. The guerrillas rounded up three men who had been chopping wood and ushered everyone inside where they sat down.

Edward Caldwell, his brothers George, Samuel and J.W., H.D. Cowherd and Alfred Canton obeyed an order that followed. "Every man stand." The guerrillas started tearing through bedding and breaking open bureau drawers, searching for guns, money or anything that looked worth stealing. They grabbed up the family's overcoats and took Edward's smoking tobacco and pipe. The name "Sue Mundy" was used by the guerrillas when referring to Clarke.[7] Edward Caldwell gave them his pistol and penknife, then they demanded Edward go with his brother George to get a mare out of the stable. Margaret Caldwell pleaded for Edward's life, grabbing Maraman's arm twice, then passing out. She was caught before hitting the floor, was revived and immediately resumed screaming and begging.[8] The family knew Maraman and Magruder, but that didn't seem to matter to the guerrillas.

Edward reassured his mother nobody was going to be killed as he walked to the stable some 40 yards from the house with George Caldwell and Alfred Canton. J.W. Caldwell also walked to the stable, where he was told to bridle and saddle George Caldwell's mare. He said he couldn't, so the guerrillas did it. When the guerrillas mounted to leave, Jerome left his horse and mounted George Caldwell's bay.

111

Edward was ordered to get on a horse, but said he wouldn't do it. "Step out here, Mr. Caldwell, I want to see you a moment," one of the guerrillas said.[9] They began circling their prey with their horses and moving in closer. "Bill Maraman, you are not going to kill me, are you?" asked Edward Caldwell. "Not while I am here," Maraman replied.[10]

Magruder's revolver was within four or five inches of Edward Caldwell's head when he fired, the blast blowing off the soldier's eyebrows as the lead crashed into his forehead. The others then fired separately, sending two bullets into Caldwell's stomach, one through his neck and one in each hip.[11] As Caldwell fell dead into the mud, the guerrillas dismounted and searched the pockets of his blouse and soldier pants. They took a book in his pocket that contained the photographs of three young ladies. He had between $300 and $400 when he came home, according to his mother. She said Edward paid $39 for his father's coffin. The balance was in his pocket and taken by the guerrillas. Edward Caldwell had planned to return to the Union Army that Thursday night, but the guerrillas made sure that wouldn't happen. "They shot him down like a hog in the mud," Caldwell's mother was to say later.

After the war, Magruder said that he and Tom Henry, rather than Henry Metcalf, killed Edward Caldwell. The claim was dismissed by Union authorities and seen perhaps as an effort by Magruder to get Metcalf off the hook and save him from the hangman. Before leaving the area, the guerrillas rode to Peter Kulmer's house on the south side of Long Run, dismounted and broke his door down. Jerome, Magruder, Maraman and Metcalf demanded his pistols and money. He got the key from his wife and unlocked the drawer containing the pistols and money. One took the pistols and another the money.

They asked if there was any more money. He said "no," but was accused of lying and they threw everything in the floor looking for cash. They found a couple of bullet molds and some bullets and said there was bound to be more pistols because some of the bullets were for pistols that were not found.[11]

"Fetch me a rope and we'll hang him," Metcalf said. "No, we won't hang him. I will go and shoot him five times," Magruder interjected.

Peter Kulmer recalled the incident in these words:

They went into the other room and Magruder was standing beside me and snapped three times at me, but his pistol did not fire and then, after he snapped a second time, my wife said, "If you are going to kill him, you had better kill me first." He snapped another time and then quit and told me to get my horse out of the stable for them. We walked out, two of them on each side of me, and they made me take a couple of horses out and take the saddles off their horses and put them on mine and then told me to put the other two horses in the stable and take good care of them and if they were not there when they came back, they would kill me sure. I took the horses as though to put them in the stable and went around the stable and got away from them. They went into the house again and when they were going they called me. I heard them, but I did not answer. Then my wife called me and I still did not answer. So they started off and I did not see them anymore after that.

Edward Caldwell's mother abandoned the farm and moved away following the death of her son and the violence she had experienced.[12]

The guerrillas weren't through for the night after killing Caldwell. They rode down to Wilson Creek, Magruder's old home neighborhood in Bullitt County near the Bullitt-Nelson County line. Near the Mount Carmell Church, they found discharged federal Private Henry Milligan and ended his life as well. Milligan had been with Company E, 37th Kentucky Volunteer Infantry.

CHAPTER 21

Trouble at the Junction

January 1865 was a busy month for guerrillas in Kentucky with Walker Taylor and his band active in western counties, Quantrill's guerrillas moving eastward into central Kentucky and the gang of Jerome, Magruder and associates raising constant hell in north-central parts of the state, just to mention a few of the active groups.

Tennie Glasscock of Bloomfield wrote to Governor Bramlette Jan. 2, 1865, asking for help. She explained that her husband, a local doctor, was forced to flee for his life after two guerrillas dressed as federal officers tricked him into admitting he was a good Union man. She acknowledged the area was mainly Southern sympathizers and suggested some of them or their property be taken hostage to trade for Dr. Glasscock's release (should he be captured) and safety. She said a threat by the governor to carry out such a plan might be all that would be required.

"It would probably never require to be executed, especially if (James) Bridgewater should be named as executioner for his name is a terror through this community," Tennie Glasscock wrote. Tennie was forced to leave, however, when the guerrillas threatened to "wipe his (the doctor's) habitation from the face of the Earth."

John Butts, the young Confederate soldier who had associated with guerrillas now and again, was at home near Van Buren Jan. 5, 1865. He'd been ice skating on the frozen Salt River with family members when his mother called them to dinner.

He had just sat down to eat when a voice outside said, "John Butts, come out here. We want to see you." Butts stepped out onto the porch and was gunned down by Ed Terrell and his men.

"Another damned Rebel gone to hell," Terrell proclaimed.[1]

Edwin Terrell was born in 1845, the son of storekeeper Richard Coleman Terrell, 25, and Martha Baker, 18. When but eight years old, Edwin lost his mother to typhoid fever and the following year, his father left on a trip to Indiana and never returned. Ed was reared by his grandfather, Robert J.R. Baker of Harrisonville, a Shelby County hog farmer who held many slaves in bondage and whipped them regularly. It was the kind of brutal environment to which young Ed Terrell became accustomed.[2] Ed joined the Confederate army in 1862 at the age of 17, but deserted in just over a week. He joined the Union army the following year in Glasgow.[3]

Terrell's men, according to a paymaster's file for May 1865 in the National Archives, were: First Lieutenant John Thompson, 2nd Lieutenant Horace Allen, and the rest, with the rank of scout, were Scott Anshutz, William Bloom, Albert Bowman, Gilbert M. Brooks, Andrew Cook, Joseph Cook, William Cook, Levi Cotton, Sylvester Cheatham, Franklin Dougherty, Robert Edwards, Talton Embry, Warren Hackett, Thomas Johnson, John Johnson, Benjamin Kirkpatrick, John Langford, John Middleton, Albert Ross, John Rogers, Benjamin Stevens, Henry Smith, Elias Stohl, Charles Taylor, Joseph Taylor, George Trumbo, Anderson Terrell and Thomas Wilson.[4]

Many of Terrell's men were from the Mount Eden area where Spencer, Shelby and Anderson counties come together. Others were from Larue County, the birthplace of President Abraham Lincoln.[5] On the day after Edward Caldwell's killing, Jerome, Magruder, Maraman and Metcalf rode to Pitts Point near the Ohio River, then to the Louisville and Nashville railroad station at Lebanon Junction.

Ann Engle had gone to "the junction" with her 18-year-old brother, Union Private James Engle of Company E, 15th Kentucky Volunteer Infantry, who was returning to duty. With him was Private Charles F. Barnett of the same outfit. They were dressed in blue uniforms that day as they arrived at the small Bullitt County station where they planned to catch the train to Louisville.

On the way to the junction, Jerome stopped and was busy chopping down a telegraph pole when someone pointed out two soldiers, running in an open field. Engle and Barnett had seen the riders coming and hoped to reach the far side of the field before they could be spotted.

Jerome, dressed in red, and Magruder in a blue overcoat, raced after them yelling, "halt" and calling them "God damned Yankee sons of bitches." The two stopped and were forced to walk back toward the station. They were separated, with Engle driven to one side of the station and Barnett to the other, where they were shot. Bill Maraman and Henry Metcalf accompanied Jerome and Magruder.

Harvey K. Wells was keeping the hotel adjacent to the Mayfield Tavern and had just sat down for dinner at 2 P.M. when a young man named Hunter came running into the dining room and said the guerrillas were coming.[6] Wells continued eating as gunshots rang outside. He could see two riders through the window and a man falling to the ground. Maraman had ridden up and shot Engle in the head with one ball and three other bullets struck the soldier in the back. Almost simultaneously, a bullet crashed through the back of Barnett's head and lodged in his forehead. Other shots took effect as well.

Jerome kicked a barroom door open, smashed open a door leading into the dining room and with a pistol in each hand demanded to know the whereabouts of the telegraph operator. Jerome learned that the telegraph office was upstairs, but when he went to see the operator, no one was there.

Wells stopped eating and Jerome jammed a pistol in the hotelman's face, but Wells insisted he did not know where the operator had gone. Jerome took Wells' and Hunter's pocketbooks, removed the cash and returned the pocketbooks, saying he didn't want "private property." As Jerome and Magruder started upstairs to the telegraph office, Wells asked them to use the doorknobs and please not to kick any more doors open. Magruder assured him he would honor the request, but he kicked the stove over in the telegraph office and hot coals spilled onto the floor.

When they came back down, Wells asked if he could put the fire out as the building was in danger of burning. "Well," said Magruder. "Go and put it out."[7] The guerrillas set two railroad cars of a construction train on fire, ran the engine into a wood train and burned a car loaded with hay that was standing on a siding.[8]

As the fire was burning, they searched the Mayfield house nearby, discovered and killed Private Joseph L. Barnett, 29, and Private Jacob F. Winstead, 21, also of the 15th Kentucky. Barnett was with Company D and Winstead with Company E. They too had come to catch the train to

Union soldiers who caught the train to Louisville at the Lebanon Junction station in Bullitt County just southwest of Louisville became easy targets for the guerrillas. Jerome Clarke, Henry Magruder, Bill Maraman and Henry Metcalf were there to kill four soldiers Jan. 6, 1865. Charles F. "Doc" Barnett, Joseph L. Barnett and James W. Engle were buried side-by-side at the Cave Hill Cemetery in Louisville. Jacob Winstead was also a victim of the guerrillas at the train station that day, but his marker is not shown in this picture of a section of Union burials (photograph by Thomas Shelby Watson).

Louisville, as did William Hill, who was to obtain his discharge from the Union Army.

Hill, also with the 15th Kentucky Vounteer Infantry, escaped death by hiding at the Mayfield house.[9] Several times during the raid, his comrades referred to Jerome when they shouted the name "Sue Mundy."[10]

James D. Hill, a farmer who witnessed what was happening, said later that Maraman called "Sue Mundy" once or twice and the man to whom he referred, answered to the name. Hill was sure it was Maraman who yelled the name "Sue Mundy," because Maraman was his cousin and he recognized his voice. The guerrillas left after about an hour of producing pure hell at the junction.

It appeared that so many people now knew that Sue Mundy was not a female that Prentice would surely be forced to admit the farce. He made an effort in the Jan. 10, 1865, *Louisville Journal*.

Sue Mundy — We have it from good authority is not a female, as is generally believed, but is in reality Jerome Clark [*sic*], a son of Hector M. Clark of Simpson County, Ky., and cousin to Hon. Beverly L. Clark, also cousin to Tandy Clark, now in the state Prison for robbing the mails.

He is about 22 years of age, of medium female stature, small feet and hands, face beardless and quite handsome, voice soft and feminine — all together making a counterfeit so perfect that even John Morgan, on a certain occasion, mistook him for a female. He belonged to Morgan's command, and was with him on his raid through Ohio.

His first experiment at deception in female attire was played off upon his commanding General. He was neatly dressed in Bloomer costume, wore a fancy military cap, containing a wig of female hair, which in long tresses flowed down carelessly over his shoulders. Thus attired, he was introduced to his chieftain by some of his comrades in arms as Miss Sue Mundy, who, under the irresistable [*sic*] promptings of patriotism, was earnestly solicitous to obtain a position in his command favorable to the development of her highly intended sympathies and prowess in behalf of the Rebellion.

Morgan, struck with the beauty and heroic bearing of Miss Mundy, at once consented to enroll her, and give her a desirable position. But on inquiring particularly in reference to her name, she replied, "Jerome Clark, sir." When the merriment resulting from his successful experiment had subsided, Morgan remarked, "All right boys, we will have use for Sue Mundy." It followed that Clark, in the character of Sue Mundy, rendered invaluable service to John Morgan.[11]

There were no witnesses to such a meeting between Jerome and Morgan and it appeared Prentice was once again calling upon his vivid imagination. Also, Prentice wasn't very good at guessing Jerome's age. He was 20, not 22.

One of Jerome's compatriots, "Big Zay" Coulter, was indeed 22 when, on Jan. 11, 1865, in Hawesville, he decided to get married. Emma Fulkerson was blessed with physical beauty and Coulter decided he must have her. The only problem was, Emma already had a husband, a discharged Union soldier who remained in Louisville for fear of guerrillas.

Nevertheless, Zay went to the clerk's office in the Hancock County Courthouse and obtained a marriage license so he and Emma could be wed. The $100 bond was posted by fellow guerrilla Will Davison. Written on the marriage bond by a deputy clerk was: "This bond and the license were obtained by force of arms."[12] Zay threatened a preacher and the ceremony was conducted at Emma's house. The Anderson County guerrilla lived with Emma an estimated three or four days, then gave her $500 in gold and left.[13]

Southern Kentucky guerrillas Captain Jacob Coffman "Jake" Bennett and George H. "Beanie" Short led their followers through Cumberland County, and during one raid took some $15,000 worth of cash and goods from storekeepers and other citizens. They fled into Tennessee but returned a few days later and killed Solomon Long, a discharged soldier from the 5th Kentucky Cavalry. Long's service had ended after he lost a leg, the result of battle.

The citizens decided to fight back and acquired Captain Burr Huddleston as their leader. W.S. "Shanghai" Cloyd, a discharged Union soldier of the 15th Kentucky Cavalry, joined him along with ten other men. The band rode into Monroe County Jan. 13, 1865, and found their prey at the residence of Dr. Samuel Moore. It was around midnight and the wanted men were found drunk and asleep.

Huddleston entered with his Navy revolver in hand and with his first shot killed Short, then guerrilla William Raney. With a shotgun, Huddleston claimed the life of Short's lieutenant William Ashlock. He captured two horses and five Navy revolvers. The Jan. 30, 1865, *Louisville Journal* reported:

"Huddleston now wears Beanie's coat. It is a fine, Rebel gray coat, lined with red flannel, and was worn by him (Short) when on a murdering scout with the red side out."[14]

CHAPTER 22

A Battle in Bardstown

It was Jan. 16, 1865. Rain was falling as Jerome, Magruder, Henry Turner, Pat Ball, James Pratt, Bill Maraman, Billy Hughes, Sam Jones, Sam Berry and others stopped at Dr. George Washington Foreman's house in Nelson County.[1] They passed a half-gallon of whisky around and soon decided to go to Bardstown and find some federals to harass. Foreman was given a dollar for the whisky.

Ball and Turner were the last to leave, Ball telling the doctor he did not want to go to Bardstown because he had an uneasy feeling. There were 20 in the group as they reached Bardstown, and after setting fire to the railroad depot, the guerrillas moved closer to the center of town.[2]

"Into the jaws of the Yanks rode the brave twenty," Magruder recalled later. "With a yell, we dashed into town, but not a federal to be seen."[3] Shortly, four federal soldiers were seen leaving a house and walking leisurely down the street. The liquored-up guerrillas charged and the boys in blue dashed into the courthouse. A citizen told the irregulars there were 25 Union soldiers inside.[4] The citizen was wrong in the estimate as 30 federals came running out of the courthouse with guns ablaze.

The guerillas fell back a half-mile and the federals advanced slowly, then stopped. The guerrillas dismounted and prepared to fight infantry style, only to discover they had made a mistake.

Magruder recalled later:

While things were in this position, 25 cavalrymen who had approached the turnpike by a bridle path, appeared as if they had fallen from the clouds and came thundering on the charge.

I had no time to remount my men, and, ordering them to lay low and fire when the Yankees came abreast of them, Sam Berry and I rode slowly up the road, hoping they would follow us and come near enough for my boys to empty their saddles.

In this, I was disappointed. They saw the trap and started back. I wheeled, and the boys, anticipating the move, were all back in their saddles, so that when Berry and I reached them they joined us and we charged the cavalry, now retreating in turn. The federal infantry had been moved forward, and in perfect folly we rushed into the very fate we had prepared for the Yankees.

I and Berry were in advance of my squad some fifty yards. The boys in the rear saw the game in time to escape, but Berry and I got the full discharge of twenty-five Brindleback muskets. My horse fell dead under me, pierced by a dozen balls. Berry was severely wounded in the left shoulder and his horse mortally wounded. The noble animal, of the best blood of Kentucky, had strength enough to bear us both away.[5]

Pat Ball's premonition was correct, as he rode from the fight with a mortal wound. The son of Tennessee native Bennett B. Ball and Bullitt Countian Nancy Ann Dunn would have been 21 on Independence Day, 1865. He died three days after the Bardstown raid. Captain James Pratt took a ball in the bowels and was whisked away by his compatriots, who left him at the Wieshart residence four miles from town. He was discovered and taken back to Bardstown by the Union Army, where he lived but a short time.[6]

Rebecca Wootton, wife of Dr. Bemiss Bloomer Wootton of Fairfield and who received reliable information on the activities of the guerrillas, wrote in her diary: "Captain Pratt was moved by his men some four miles from town that night and the federals went out the next morning and brought him to town (Bardstown). He died the next evening." The *Louisville Daily Journal* reported Pratt died at five o'clock in the morning on Jan. 18, 1865. Magruder and Berry made their way to John Mackey's, about five miles from Bardstown, where the wounded horse fell dead in the road. Magruder "pressed" a horse and buggy for Berry and a horse for himself, continuing the flight to Bloomfield.[7]

Arriving in the Bloomfield vicinity, Magruder received word that a federal force had gathered at Taylorsville, nine miles north, with the intention of running him out of the country. "I had intended to leave; now I determined to stay," Magruder said later.[8] Berry was hidden at James Brewer's, about a mile out of Fairfield, and Dr. Wootton came every night

These two towns were visited consistently by Confederate guerrillas and Union forces searching for them during the last months of the war. Bloomfield and Taylorsville were havens for the Rebels because of the large number of Southern sympathizers in and around both. Louisville, basically a Union garrison, was conveniently close to the Confederate towns for patrols, but too close at times for the guerrillas. *Top:* Bloomfield long before streets were paved. *Bottom:* Taylorsville when trees lined the streets (Thomas Shelby Watson [public domain]).

at midnight to check on him. After Berry was able to sit up, he was spotted through the window by a Negro cook and had to be moved. He was taken to Thomas Walters', two miles north of Fairfield, across the county line in Spencer County, where he recovered.[9]

CHAPTER 23

Quantrill's Disguise

It was Saturday, Jan. 21, 1865, when Quantrill and his 36 guerrillas, wearing Union overcoats, stopped at a federal campsite of the 17th Kentucky Infantry at Hartford in Ohio County.

Quantrill used the alias "Captain Clark of the Fourth Missouri Cavalry," after his entry into Kentucky, according to William Elsey Connelley in his *Quantrill and the Border Wars.* John Newman Edwards said in his *Noted Guerrillas or the Warfare of the Border* that when he arrived at Hartford, Quantrill used the alias "Captain Jasper W. Benedict of A.J. Smith's Corps," stationed at Memphis, Tennessee.[1] The alias "Captain Clark" was the one Quantrill used in Kentucky, as Union Army dispatches proved. Quantrill was mustered into the Confederate Army in February 1862 as a captain of scouts. The earliest record of his payment by a Rebel quartermaster was Aug. 7, 1862.[2] Quantrill and his men were welcomed at the federal camp in Ohio County and became acquainted with three men who, unbeknownst to them, were in mortal danger.

Andrew Martin Barnett, 20, and Isaac H. Axton had been recruiting in the Hartford area for the Union army. Walter B. Lawton, 49, was also there. Lawton, a native of Campbell County, Va., enrolled in the Union Army in 1861 at Owensboro, but was discharged in December 1862 due to "a general weakness in his system" and rheumatism. Lawton had been a private in Company H, 3rd Kentucky Volunteer Cavalry. As his health improved, Lawton was eager to rejoin the Union army, and in the winter of 1865, he sold himself as a substitute. Barnett was a private in Company D, 26th Kentucky Volunteer Infantry.

After a rainy weekend, snow began falling early Monday, Jan. 23, 1865 and was accumulating when Quantrill and his men readied themselves to depart. Lawton, Barnett and Axton left with them, saying they feared guerrillas and felt safer traveling with the federal soldiers. Axton had been suspicious from the start and became very uneasy. He told Quantrill he was going to cut across the countryside and get his best revolver, his money and a better horse and meet them a little ways up the road.

Quantrill had no objection and as soon as Axton left, he sent three men to watch for his return. Axton went to Joe Barnett's, Andrew's father, and told him Joe and Lawton were in desperate danger. The elder Barnett called on a hired hand who was a former private in Company I, 3rd Kentucky Volunteer Cavalry, 26-year-old James Wisley Townsley, to go bring Andrew back. Townsley was intercepted by the men Quantrill had sent out and his fate was sealed. They cut the reins from his horse and knotted a piece around the horse's throat and let him strangle, then used the rest of the reins to hang

William Clarke Quantrill taught at his father's Canal Dover, Ohio, school as a teenager before journeying west to serve as a schoolmaster in one-room schoolhouses. He polished his horseback riding skills while living with a Delaware Native American tribe and became embroiled in the Kansas-Missouri border war. Quantrill developed a following and led a force into Lawrence, Kansas, that left Union soldiers and male inhabitants dead and the town in ashes. He entered Kentucky in 1865, where he met other Rebel guerrillas, including Jerome Clarke (Kentucky Historical Society).

Union Private Andrew Barnett, 20, was among many fooled by the blue overcoat disguises of Quantrill and his men and paid the supreme price. Barnett was with the 26th Kentucky Infantry, having enrolled in 1864 in his native Ohio County, Ky., where he died. A Union report said he had been beaten and shot. Harry D. Tinsley, in his "History of No Creek," said Frank James killed Barnett. The people of the area were so frightened they would not go with Andrew's father to get the body. "His frozen body was laid on the hearth ... of his parents' home to thaw," Tinsley wrote (courtesy Harry D. Tinsley).

Townsley from a tree limb. It was three miles from Hartford on the Hawesville Road.

Lawton was shot in the temple about ten miles from Hartford, which left his face burned with gunpowder. Quantrill and his followers referred to a bullet wound between the eyebrows as "the mark," or "putting the mark" on the enemy. The guerrillas took his uniform and strangled his horse in the same manner as Townsley's. Some 16 miles from Hartford, Barnett was beaten and shot to death.[3] His body was found in a small stream between the communities of Adaburg and Ralph.

CHAPTER 24

The Simpsonville Massacre

Camp Nelson was a Union base in southern Jessamine County about five miles south of Nicholasville. The camp covered 4,000 acres and had some 300 buildings and fortifications. The Union Army had located the camp between the natural defenses of the palisades that rise over 400 feet from the Kentucky River and Hickman Creek to the south, east and west.

The northern boundary of Camp Nelson was protected by a line of eight earthen fortifications and breastworks. Fort Bramlette was constructed on a hill south of the main complex where it overlooked the Kentucky River and Hickman Creek.[1] The camp was a training facility for Union soldiers and many of those who trained there were black, such as the 5th Regiment Cavalry, United States Colored Troops.

It was the men of the 5th regiment who were assigned the task of driving nearly a thousand head of cattle from Camp Nelson to Louisville so that the thousands of Union troops stationed in the city would have food during the coldest part of the winter. It wasn't particularly cold Jan. 22, 1865, when the cattle train halted four miles west of Shelbyville to bed down for the night. Light rain had been falling and remnants of a recent snowfall had disappeared.[2]

It turned colder overnight, however, and the rain changed to snow, accumulating to a depth of three inches. It was two degrees above zero the morning of Jan. 23, 1865, and the high for the day was not to exceed 12 above.[3] The drovers were under the command of a white officer who directed the cattle be turned into a lot. The soldiers constructed tents while the officers prepared to spend the night in a farmhouse.[4]

The *Shelby Record* of Feb. 21, 1913, continued the story:

Suddenly, there was a loud knocking on an outer door, and a white man, who said he was employed on the adjoining farm belonging to Squire Absalom Matthews, demanded admittance and a chance to speak to the captain. This was accorded him, and he told the captain that the cattle were ruining a field of unshocked corn belonging to Squire Matthews, a Union sympathizer. The captain asked what could be done. The man asked how many men he had and was told there were near one hundred, and that there were one thousand cattle.

The man, who was, in fact, a guerrilla spy, suggested that the captain go out [and] instruct his men to each turn out ten head of cattle and in that way there would be no confusion. He said, too, that he would take the matter in charge himself, but that he had no suitable boots in which to tramp through the snow. The officer then told the man to take his boots and superintend the work.

After getting the boots, the guerrilla spy, who had torn down the fence which separated the cattle from the cornfield, before he had his talk with the officer, left for parts unknown, presumably toward the Spencer County line, while the Negro soldiers got the cattle out of the corn.[5]

Meanwhile, some 17 miles southwest in Taylorsville, Marion, Berry and Turner arrived with major mischief in mind. Berry and Marion were quite inebriated.[6]

They arrived on the heels of a group of federal soldiers who had left town after a stay in which the courthouse was used as headquarters.[7] It was the fourth Sabbath of the month, Jan. 22, 1865, and church services were being conducted throughout the town. Spencer County Circuit Court Clerk Thomas J. Barker was attending services in the Presbyterian church at the corner of Main and Jefferson Streets. A light rain was falling as Berry dismounted, walked into the church and called Barker's name. Barker acknowledged his presence and Berry asked if Barker was the acting master of the Masonic Lodge. Barker confirmed that he held that title and Berry gave him a strong hint that if he wanted to preserve the regalia or any records from the courthouse, the time was nigh.[8] The regalia were removed to Barker's office and vital records were quickly carried out of the courthouse as well.

Marion ordered Turner to round up town blacks and the young guerrilla rode up and down the street, occasionally finding black citizens and sending them to the courthouse to become arsonists. When too few blacks could be found, local whites were also conscripted. Torches were soon applied to the courthouse, but when the fire burned too slowly to suit Marion, some of the black conscripts were sent into the cupola with torches. Marion threatened them with a rifle and said if they didn't do his bidding they would have him to fight. The fire began to roar and sparks from the cupola showered the area, endangering Mrs. Shaw's house and others. Citizens formed a fire brigade and Turner, standing picket at a town well 30 yards from the courthouse, pitched in to help prevent houses from catching, although a small office in the rear of the courthouse and the county jail caught fire.⁹ The guerrillas left at their leisure.

The next morning, at the Shelby County drovers' camp, the men of the cattle guard split up with about half going to the front of the herd and the rest bringing up the rear. The *Shelby Record* reported:

As they passed through Simpsonville, the captain stopped in a store to warm his almost frozen feet and buy a pair of boots. The cattle and the soldiers, in the meantime proceeded towards Louisville. Suddenly, while the officer was looking at the boots, someone ran into the store and shouted: "Here comes Coulter and his guerrillas."

The quality, price and size of the boots had no longer any interest for the officer, and he ran out of and down under the storeroom, where he remained in hiding until the attack was over.¹⁰

The guerrillas rode into the rear of the train, firing at will and sending the black soldiers scurrying. There was a presumption that the soldiers were shot down attempting to surrender.¹¹

There were at least 14 guerrillas: Magruder, Coulter, Berry, Maraman, Mitchell, Marion, Billy Hughes, Jimmy Jones, Ben Foreman, another Foreman (perhaps his brother Thomas), two Johnsons, William Merryfield, a Whitesides and possibly Jerome Clarke, although he later denied taking part in the attack.¹² The guerrillas had left the Alexander Thomas place in Spencer County at 8 A.M., reaching Simpsonville in two hours over ice and snow. Less than 20 minutes after their arrival, 19 of the Negro troops lay dead and about 20 wounded, some whose lives would yet be lost.¹³

Despite reports that the black troops offered no resistance, Henry Magruder had a different version of the story:

I sent Dick Mitchell toward Louisville to see what was coming in that direction. By this time the Negroes fired on him. He came back, and the Negroes, thinking him alone, came on. I formed and charged them with a yell. As we came in view, thundering down on them, they fired a few shots, and, throwing away their arms, ran in among the cattle. At the first fire, they killed my horse. I was mounted again in a moment, and went for them with a yell. They had no officers, or at least they did not show themselves. Well, to make a long story short, we just went in among the cattle and killed the Negroes wherever we could find them. I don't know how many I killed, but I got plenty of wool.[14]

Three of the black troops escaped injury in the attack. One played possum, lying flat on his face for an hour and a half, another was under the bed of a commissary wagon that overturned early in the attack, and a third fled from the front portion of the rear guard when the firing started. Reports said he fled to Bagdad, several miles to the northeast, divested himself of his uniform and began chopping firewood for a farmer to make it appear he was a farm hand.

Citizens took the wounded into Simpsonville for medical care and the dead were buried in a long trench near where they were massacred. Several days later, ambulances were sent out of Louisville, under guard, to fetch the wounded.[15]

"The ambulances brought in 18 wounded Negro soldiers, who were placed in a foundry down town, where they will be attended to until they can be removed to a hospital in New Albany, Indiana. Fourteen Negro soldiers were buried near the site where the guerrillas killed them," the *Louisville Daily Democrat* reported Jan. 28, 1865.

After the attack, the guerrillas robbed Albert McDowell's Simpsonville store and several citizens of some $1,200 in cash and merchandise, their horses already loaded down with weapons and ammunition taken from the dead and wounded soldiers.[16] Magruder claimed to have taken $300 from a government agent.[17]

There were 22 black soldiers of Company E, the 5th United States Colored Cavalry who died as a result of the guerrilla attack. They were: Sgt. Harrison Lampkins, 26; Sgt. Benjamin Lewis, 24; Corp. Lewis Moton, 28; Corp. Jerry Moton, 24; Farrier Walter Bailey, 28; Private Allen Coleman, 20; Private Frank Ford, 20; Private Anderson Gray, 30; Private James Hackley, 19; Private Henry Harrison, 18; Private Lewis Jones, 19; Private Marcellus McCall, 20; Private Samuel Moton, 18; Private David Parish, 23; Private Shelby Phelps, 20; Private Alexander Seals, 29; Private Albert Thompson, 45; Private Georg (*sic*) White, 19; Private Murthey Moton, 18; Private Isaac Hodgers, 19; Private Samuel Huff, 18, and Private Jacob Padock, 20.[18]

It was also Jan. 28, 1865, that the guerrilla Dick Taylor and a compatriot named Smith were killed near Lawrenceburg. Taylor and three companions had visited his father the night before, then robbed a tollgate keeper and several other residents in the community of Rough and Ready. Taylor's father had admonished his son and instructed him to return to regular service with the Confederate Army. Dick Taylor refused to listen, and with his gang, visited the residence of Edward Martin, some two to three miles from Lawrenceburg. The elder Taylor went into Lawrenceburg and reported his own son to federal officers.

Lieutenant Moore of the 54th Kentucky tracked Taylor and his men to Martin's, but Martin's family denied they had been there. A search resulted in the discovery of booty-laden horses in the barn. Pressed with the evidence, Martin then admitted the guerrillas had taken to the fields on foot. Taylor and Smith were tracked in the snow to a rail pile where they surrendered. As the other two guerrillas were being tracked, Moore put Taylor behind him on his horse and Smith behind a young federal soldier named Shouse. Taylor, using the ruse of adjusting his saddle blanket, became involved in a life and death struggle with Moore, which ended with Moore killing both Taylor and Smith.[19]

Because of his ruthlessness, the federal government hired Edwin Terrell to lead a select group to hunt down Rebel guerrillas in Kentucky near the close of the Civil War. Terrell was a native of Shelby County, Ky., who was reared by his grandfather after being orphaned as a youngster. Terrell joined the Confederate Army, then switched sides and led a band of decoy guerrillas for the Union Army. Terrell and his men were feared by citizens as much as Confederate irregulars (photograph from Thomas Shelby Watson).

Even with Jerome Clarke's denial that he took part in the attack on the cattle drive, a widow of one of the dead soldiers said in a document filed in Franklin that the Rebels were "under Sue Munday" (*sic*). Martha Lewis, wife of Sgt. Benjamin Lewis, asked for his benefits. Her application was made Aug. 20, 1866.

CHAPTER 25

Ed Terrell's
Debatable Condition

On Saturday, Jan. 28, 1865, Jerome Clarke was checking with a resident near Bloomfield to determine if reports were true that Ed Terrell and his Union decoy guerrillas were in town. His fellow guerrillas awaited the report. A woman who lived just off a turnpike road said 20 "citizens" had passed by, which confirmed to Jerome that Terrell was indeed in the neighborhood.

Before Jerome was back on the turnpike, Terrell and his men appeared and charged. Magruder opened fire in an effort to give his comrade a degree of cover. Jerome and Magruder opened a gate and took to the farms with the enemy in hot pursuit. The guerrillas halted long enough to rapid-fire at Terrell, briefly slowing the chase. As Terrell's men began flanking, Jerome and Magruder rode back to the turnpike, meeting Jim Henry, Dick Mitchell and Joshua Chase of their own band. They wheeled and charged Terrell and his men and drove them to a field. They were within a hundred yards of the wounded Berry's hiding place and as the riders halted, sitting on their mounts and reloading, one of the guerrillas went to move Berry to a safer place. Berry was taken to John Bedford Russell's in Spencer County near the Spencer-Nelson County line at Ashes Creek.[1]

One of the group with Terrell was a prisoner, Isaac Ludwick, a member of Pratt's following who was captured in Bloomfield.[2] Terrell directed his men to return to the turnpike and just as the group began to move, Terrell rode up to Ludwick and shot him dead. Jerome, Magruder and two others slowly followed Terrell, not chancing a close fight with the larger decoy force. But when "Big Zay" Coulter and ten more guerrillas came racing to meet them, the butternuts cheered and had enough manpower to pursue Terrell.[3] After a three-mile chase northward toward Taylorsville into Spencer County, Terrell took refuge in a barn on the Charles B. May place. Jerome, Ben Foreman and Coulter chased Terrell's men, and, with a yell, rode into them firing as they were dismounting.

Terrell opened fire with a carbine, wounding Coulter in the side, killing Foreman's horse and ripping three balls through Jerome's clothing. Magruder took shelter in an old house 150 yards away and began picking off the Terrell gang's horses. Terrell's men rushed out, mounted what horses they could find and rode for the woods with bullets whistling all around them. Terrell was under heavy fire but made it to Squire Heady's barn. Jerome and Magruder kept watch as several guerrillas chased Terrell's men in the direction of Mount Eden.

The remainder found that rushing the barn would not flush out Terrell, who made the bullets "ring like bees."[4] Coulter took a ramrod and pushed a silk handkerchief from the entry wound of Terrell's bullet in his side to the exit wound in his back. He removed the ramrod and had a comrade tie knots in both ends of the handkerchief. He then rode to his aunt's house in Anderson County. The son of Rowan and Sabra Morgan Coulter died Jan. 30, 1865, after contracting pneumonia.[5]

As the mercury dropped and darkness began arriving, the guerrillas decided they would try to capture Terrell another day. Terrell slipped out the rear of the barn and made his way back to Shelby County. During the fight, Jerome, Magruder and their associates captured some of the Terrell gang's horses. The saddlebags revealed that the Union decoys had spent plenty of time plundering. The bags contained spoons, cups, a lady's dress, a bolt of luster, knives and combs.

Magruder had a metallic coffin sent to Dr. Isaac McClaskey's, where the body of Ludwick was made ready and taken to his wife.[6] Jerome, Magruder and Davis moved Berry again, this time closer to Springfield at the residence of Lucinda Selecman, the widow of John Fisher Selecman.[7] The trio then rode back to Bloomfield and found several Yankees had made the Baptist church their headquarters. The guerrillas avoided a fight, picked up Berry again and moved him to within five miles of Bardstown, there leaving "a Negro boy" to serve as his nurse.[8]

Members of William Quantrill's Confederate guerrillas who arrived in Kentucky in 1865 included Allen Palmer (left) and Thomas Edward "Bud" Pence. It was Palmer's killing of a federal lieutenant in Hustonville that created a furor and resulted in the torture and death of a guerrilla who was innocent of the crime. "Bud" Pence and his brother, Alexander Doniphan "Donnie" Pence, settled in Nelson County after the Civil War. Donnie was sheriff of Nelson County, while Bud served as marshal of Taylorsville in adjacent Spencer County (courtesy Miles-Peck Collection).

Just after the three passed through Bloomfield, Marion and some seven or eight men came racing through with Terrell and 25 decoy guerrillas hot on their heels. They wound down Turkey Run Hill just north of town when Marion got off a shot, wounding Terrell in the shoulder. Terrell's men continued the chase and killed guerrilla Henry Cox. A doctor was summoned and Dr. Dunlap went out and examined Terrell's wound. He told the chief of the guerrilla hunters it would prove fatal. Terrell told the doctor he was "a damned liar."[9]

Just as Berry had been moved from place to place to avoid Terrell, now the wounded Terrell was trying to stay a step ahead of the guerrillas. He was taken to Dr. Tom Allen's, then to safe havens in Shelby, his home county.

Prentice, in the meanwhile, chastised the federals for their inability to capture "Sue Mundy," and filled empty white space in the Jan. 27, 1865, *Louisville Journal* with farcical diatribe:

Sue Mundy, at the head of a small band of guerrillas has been going to and fro through a few counties of the State, for several months, committing outrages and atrocities of the worst description. The theatre of her operations has not been a wide one; she has confined herself within a rather narrow circle. How very strange that she isn't caught. She has no reputation, and probably deserves none for military sagacity or tact, or any other kind of sagacity or tact. Nevertheless, she goes where she pleases, and does what she pleases, and none of our military leaders seem to have the ability, if they have the disposition, to lay their hands upon her.

We can't imagine what the matter is; surely they are not afraid of her. To permit this she-devil to pursue her horrid work successfully much longer, will be, even if the past is not, a military scandal and shame. Sue has now been ramping [a] full nine months. Surely, it is high time that she should be confined, if she is ever going to be.

Prentice, as mentioned, invented the character Sue Mundy Oct. 11, 1864, some four months, not nine months, earlier.

The *Louisville Daily Journal* also offered Jan. 27, 1865:

Some say that Sue Mundy is a man, and some say a woman. We don't suppose the sexes will quarrel for the distinction of owning her. If she were captured and it should become important to ascertain to which sex she belongs, should the committee consist of women or men?

We have this moment received a communication, assuring us that it has been settled that Sue is a compromise between a man and a woman — a hermaphrodite. Sue, whether of the masculine, feminine, or neuter gender — whether he, she or it — is certainly a gramittical [*sic*] puzzle. Which of our grammer [*sic*] schools can parse Sue Mundy?

Prentice, on Jan. 10, 1865, had confirmed that Sue Mundy was Jerome Clarke, "the son of Hector M. Clark."

CHAPTER 26

Battle on the Little South Fork

Quantrill and his Union masqueraders moved southeastward and on Sunday, Jan. 29, 1865, rode into Hustonville where several federal soldiers were camped. It was four above zero.[1]

Quantrill told his men to look about the town and procure the best horses they could find in place of their own and be prepared for a quick departure. Allen Palmer wasn't impressed with the horseflesh around town, but there were some magnificent mounts in the stable that the garrisoned federals had been riding.

Palmer mounted a fine mare and came riding out of the stable, which prompted Lieutenant Frank Cunningham of the 13th Kentucky to come running. It was Cunningham's horse. Cunningham declared that if that horse left the stable it would be over his dead body. "That is a damned easy job," Palmer declared and shot Cunningham dead.[2]

After quite a commotion, but not involving further bloodshed, Quantrill and his men quickly rode out of Hustonville in the direction of Danville. The irregulars in blue arrived in Danville about 9 A.M.

"They took quiet possession of the place and swapped a few horses," the *Western Citizen* reported of the event. The local newspaper added, "Some of them helped themselves to boots at one of the shoe stores and left money in part pay for what they took."

While in Danville, a woman who had been in Hustonville earlier called Quantrill by name. Quantrill replied: "Why, madam, you were never more mistaken in your life. I am Captain Clark of the federal army." The woman was not convinced and told a federal officer she was certain the man was Quantrill. While his men had their horses shod and lounged around town, Quantrill went into a saloon to have a drink. As Quantrill reached for the glass, a Union officer walked up behind him with a carbine at his shoulder. He accused Quantrill of deception, saying he was the guerrilla chieftain from Missouri.

Quantrill said he had papers from the Secretary of War to prove his name was Clark and to identify his unit. He yelled for Orderly Sgt. John Barker to come to the saloon. Barker stepped in with several other guerrillas hot on his heels. Quantrill told the others all was well and asked Barker to show the lieutenant his papers. Barker felt inside his coat, then stepped forward, ripped the rifle away from the soldier with his left hand while dragging him to the floor.

With the muzzle of his dragoon pressed into the soldier's face, Barker said, "These are the papers, I reckon, you was expectin'." Quantrill was amused and called for drinks all around, sparing the life of the lieutenant, praising him for his coolness and insisting that nothing more be said of the affair. The lieutenant agreed.[3]

After dinner, Quantrill led the command toward Harrodsburg and they were within five miles of the city at sunset. They were: Quantrill, 2nd Lieutenant Chatham Renick, Orderly Sgt. John Barker, and privates Ves Akers, John Barnhill, Jack Graham, David Hylton, Clark Hockensmith, Frank James, Allen Palmer, Ran Venable, James Lilly, Andy McGuire, Donnie Pence, Richard Burns, Tom Evans, William Gaugh, Isaac Hall, William Hulse, Foster Key, Bud Pence, George Wigginton, John McCorkle, Henry Noland, Samuel Robertson, James Younger, William Basham, Richard Glasscock, Thomas Harris, Robert Hall, Payne Jones, William Noland, John Ross, Peyton Long, Lee McMurtry, Henry Porter and James Williams.[4] It was all of Quantrill's men who arrived in Kentucky Jan. 1, 1865, except Jim Little, who was killed near Hopkinsville by a bullet fired by a federal from a house the guerrillas had surrounded.[5]

With snow still on the ground since the 23rd and the mercury slipping toward zero, part of Quantrill's men went to 40-year-old widow Sallie (Riker) Vanarsdall's house within sight of the Oakland Church, and the rest, along with Quantrill, went to John Adams' place on a hill near the valley farm of the Vanarsdall family.

The guerrillas barely had time to eat when Bridgewater and his 40 or more Hall's Gap Tigers surrounded the Vanarsdall house and opened fire. The guerrillas fought back as they fled to a nearby log barn, but the fire was too intense for them to do much damage. John Barker, William and Henry Noland were fatally wounded. Bridgewater shot Quantrill's Lieutenant Chatham Renick with a rifle when the bearded guerrilla rode his white horse from the Adams place to the top of a hill overlooking the Vanarsdall house. Quantrill wanted Renick to find out the nature of the gunfire in the valley. The rifle shot killed Renick outright.

Glasscock, Williams, McGuire and Burns were wounded and had to surrender, while Robertson, Evans and Gaugh escaped injury, but also were forced to surrender. Frank James raced back to report to Quantrill on the state of affairs and those at the Adams house were able to flee through the snow and cold.[6]

A report by Hobson to Headquarters, First Division, Military District of Kentucky said in part, referring to the Jan. 29, 1865 fight:

> This morning at 2 o'clock the detachment from Stanford, under Captain Bridgewater, of State force, attacked the guerrillas on Little South Fork, west of Hustonville; killed 4, captured 35 horses and equipments; ran 30 or 35 of their men into the woods, most of whom were barefooted; only 7 got away mounted.
>
> Captain Clarke [Quantrill] escaped barefooted, but our men in three detachments are hunting for them and with good prospect of finding them as the snow is fresh on the ground.
>
> Very respectfully, your obedient servant.

In a dispatch from Danville, dated Feb. 10, 1865, Union Captain W.L. Gross reported to Assistant Adjutant General J.S. Butler that Colonel Weatherford had brought in William W. Maraman, James McCoy and James Hardin Younger of "Clark's (Quantrill's) men" who had been hiding in the woods since the Little South Fork fight.[7] Bill Maraman was the Bullitt County native who usually rode with Jerome, Magruder and Berry. Jim Younger was one of the Younger brothers who rode with Frank and Jesse James after the war as part of the most notorious outlaw gang in American history.

Maraman, born in 1847, was the son of Francis M. Maraman, Jr. of Bullitt County and Eliza Ann Troutman of Nelson County. Billy's grandfather, Francis M. Maraman, was from St. Mary's County, Md., and his paternal grandmother, Mary Lee, was born in Bullitt County, Ky.

In 1904, some of the people in Harrodsburg took issue with the local newspaper concerning the names of the men killed at the Vanarsdall place.

Somehow, Frank James got word of the controversy and wrote to the newspaper May 30, 1904, from Kearney, Mo. He believed John Barker died as he was being taken to Harrodsburg for treatment of severe wounds. He confirmed the others who died as Chat Renick and the Noland brothers, Henry and William. The four were initially buried at the Oakland Church Yard, then on June 3, 1904, were reinterred in the Confederate Lot at Harrodsburg.

Evans, 19, was accused of killing Lieutenant Cunningham in Hustonville and was kept chained on his back at the military prison in Frankfort. He was allowed to send a telegram to President Johnson, June 22, 1865, which stated:

President Johnson.

I did not kill Cunningham. Allen Palmer of Independence of Missouri is the man. Give me time and I will prove it by twenty (20) witnesses. If I fail then execute me. Please be merciful to me for [a] short time until I prove my innocence.

T.W. Evans.

Evans was released from confinement, but died Jan. 23, 1866.

Chatham Ewing Renick had been a sergeant in the Third Battalion, Company C, Missouri Infantry, CSA, before joining the guerrillas. He was a Confederate recruiter in the Trans-Mississippi Department. After serving under guerrilla Captain George Todd, Renick joined Quantrill in 1864 and held the rank of First Lieutenant. Renick was born in 1827 in Jackson County, Mo., the son of Robert Archer Renick and Mary Baker Ewing (courtesy Miles-Peck Collection).

CHAPTER 27

Missourians' "True Grit" Tested

Marion was not convinced the Missourians were true Rebs and he told other irregulars to keep an eye on them. After a great deal of discussion, it was decided that Quantrill would remain at the Alexander Thomas place in Spencer County while his men rode with Marion and other Kentucky guerrillas and if they displayed "true grit," there would be no more doubt. Quantrill reluctantly agreed.

Quantrill said he had learned Colonel James W. Weatherford of the 13th Kentucky Cavalry Regiment and Major Benjamin Bristow were in the Danville area and he wanted to capture them to exchange for his captured men or hang them in retaliation. His impatience with Marion was obvious, but he needed the cooperation of the Kentuckians. The test ride left Spencer County, Tuesday, Jan. 31, 1865, over soggy trails, since the cold was moderating and the snow melting.[1] The guerrillas trekked to the northeast and in the afternoon reached Simpsonville. They camped between Simpsonville in Shelby County and Smithfield, a Henry County community, and on Feb. 1, 1865, still in Henry County, the column moved through New Castle.

It was along the guerrillas' line of travel that three Union soldiers lost their lives and while those responsible for the deaths were never positively identified, local tradition blamed Sue Mundy.[2] A Feb. 2, 1865, story in the *Louisville Daily Journal* said Sue Mundy and Quantrill's guerrillas entered Simpsonville two days earlier and robbed the citizens and the stage. It also said that while moving toward Smithfield, on the Frankfort Railroad, the guerrillas encountered four federal pickets, took them into the woods and shot them, killing one and leaving three "mortally wounded."

140

The Feb. 3, 1865, *Louisville Journal* reported the Union soldiers who were shot were unarmed and in advance of some 300 men of the 15th Army Corps who had been icebound on the Ohio River and were moving overland to the railroad.

The story said the killings were two and a half miles from New Castle on the Carrollton Pike. Two days later, the *Journal* reported federal soldiers had left Carrollton searching for guerrillas and had, around noon on Wednesday, Feb. 1, 1865, split up into small groups, going to various houses for food.

Deputy Provost Marshall Americus Vespucious Carlisle, 21, of Carroll County, 2nd Lieutenant Lawson Burnfin, also 21, of Company E, 55th Kentucky Volunteer Infantry, and 34-year-old Private George Washington Lucas, also of Company E, 55th Kentucky Volunteer Infantry were killed by guerrillas, the newspaper said, but the name "Sue Mundy" did not appear in the story.

Oscar Kipping of Carrollton was 90 in 1969 when he told the story of his father going to get the bodies of the three soldiers. He said a Union soldier who lived on Goose Creek near Carrollton was home on leave and sent word to Carlisle that he was sick and needed an extension of his leave. Carlisle, accompanied by Burnfin and Lucas, started out to verify the soldier's excuse but never got there.

They stopped to get a bite to eat at a large log house where there were some women at home, but no men. Jerome Clarke and others reportedly arrived outside and ordered the three to come out and they would be treated as prisoners of war. Otherwise, everyone in the house would be killed.

Carlisle, Burnfin and Lucas walked into the road and were gunned down.[3] The bodies were taken to Lulie Wilkins' Carroll County residence by fellow soldiers before an undertaker came for them. The guerrillas had stripped Burnfin of his Union overcoat, a large gold ring and a watch. Carlisle's large gold ring was also taken. Only a small black ring was left on Burnfin's hand.[4]

From Lexington on Feb. 1, 1865, Assistant Adjutant General J.S. Butler sent this telegram to Colonel P.T. Swaine in Covington: "Quantrill is passing from Louisville and Frankfort Railroad and will probably go into Owen County, also Sue Munday (*sic*). How many of the Fifty-fifth Kentucky can be sent mounted through Grant to Owen?"

From Eminence, Feb. 2, 1865, Captain E.W. Easley telegraphed Hobson:

> Sue Munday's [*sic*] command, about thirty men, well mounted, passed through Smithfield this morning at 2 o'clock in direction of New Castle; left that place to the right; about two miles near that place attacked a detachment of the seventeenth Army Corps, en route to this place [Eminence] from Carrollton; wounded four or five of them; heard nothing of them since.

Three privates from Company E, the 55th Kentucky Volunteer Infantry were fatally wounded Feb. 1, 1865, in Owen County by guerrillas. The three, all 18, were Jesse Jones of Boyle County, John Burris of Taylor County and James T. Waid of Marion County.

The blue-clad column of guerrillas under Marion moved through Worthville in Carroll County, then made camp for the night. Jerome Clarke, meantime, was with Henry Magruder and others, as he had been since Monday, Jan. 30, 1865, when they were on a ride that began at Bloomfield and continued to Fairfield, where the three "met the rest of the boys," Magruder would say later. Then the group proceeded to High Grove, Mount Washington, Waterford, southern Shelby County, back through Spencer County to Nelson County and returned to Bloomfield. The trek covered 54.2 miles in about two days. None of these guerrillas were with Marion on his test ride with Quantrill's men, and as mentioned earlier, neither was Quantrill.[5]

CHAPTER 28

"He is not armed. He cannot hurt you much."

The Marion-led column moved into Scott County, Thursday, Feb. 2, 1865, with the federals in confusion about the identity of the leader. Communications referred to Quantrill, Clarke and Sue Mundy. With Quantrill using the alias "Captain Clark" shortly after entering the state, there was more than enough reason for the federals and the press to be confused.

No one suspected Marion as the leader, and for that matter, few knew him. Prentice was as confused as everyone else, reporting in the Feb. 2, 1865, *Louisville Journal* that Quantrill and Sue Mundy were on their way to Smithfield and a band of guerrillas under "Captain Clark" made a raid on Danville. Whether "Captain Clark" referred to Jerome or to Quantrill, Prentice had the person in two places at the same time.

It was the confusing telegraphed federal dispatches that had led Prentice into his reporting quandary. Maj. Thomas Mahoney, 30th Kentucky (federal) Infantry reported, in part, to Captain J.S. Butler from Lebanon on Feb. 1, 1865:

> Captain Searcy had a running fight with Clarke's guerrillas, three miles east of Chaplintown last Monday [Jan. 30, 1865], wounded one of them, had better horses, got away. Captain came to Bloomfield on Tuesday, Fifty-fourth [*sic*] run in on him, had a fight, wounding one man, killed a horse before learning who they were.

The column of guerrillas led by Marion came within 100 yards of the Scott County Courthouse at Georgetown on Feb. 2, 1865. Some 30 federal soldiers, members of Company G, 53rd Kentucky Volunteer Mounted Infantry, were stationed there. The Union blue, worn by the guerrillas, allowed them to take the federals and citizens by surprise.

The Union troops began figuring out what was happening and made ready to do battle, prompting Marion to turn the force toward Lexington, but he did not want to abandon Georgetown. A short distance from town the guerrillas "arrested" two citizens and sent them back into Georgetown as messengers, delivering a surrender demand from Marion. The officer in charge, 2nd Lieutenant Edwin N. Vallandingham, sent word back that he would think about surrender after firing his last cartridge.

The guerrillas, not eager to fight federals entrenched for an ambush, paused just a moment at Medley Powell's, about six miles above Stamping Ground, and killed his son, Fielding Powell, 22, then moved on toward Midway. He was killed because he and his father had resisted guerrillas on a previous visit and had driven them away. Back in Georgetown, the citizens planned a dinner of celebration for the men of Company G, who had, as they supposed, avoided a gun battle with a show of force.

As Marion's marauders continued into Woodford County, they reached the Midway Depot and set it afire.[1] While it burned, the guerrillas stayed busy, robbing the stores and cutting down telegraph poles. They took $700 from the depot agent and robbed two other men of several hundred each and their gold watches. The federals were still confused about whom they were chasing, as evidenced by E.H. Hobson's report out of Lexington, Feb. 2, 1865:

Commanding Officer, Crab Orchard:

Send part of your mounted force to Danville. Sue Munday [sic] burned the depot at Midway this evening. Moved in direction of Versailles. If your men hear of them they must follow them.

E.H. Hobson,
Brigadier-General.

The next stop for the Marion-led force was Robert Atchison Alexander's Woodburn Farm, where some of the best horseflesh in the country was bred for racing. Warren Viley, 73, was owner of the stock farm Stonewall, a neighbor of Alexander and the friend who had helped recover the valuable thoroughbred Asteroid after the first Woodburn raid Oct. 27,

1864. Viley's friendship was to be tested again as the column stopped at his place and took him along as a hostage.

As dusk began to spread over the bluegrass region of Kentucky on that Feb. 2, 1865, there was a flurry of excitement at Woodburn.

A farm hand hurried to the mansion and reported to Alexander that a large number of soldiers were coming down the lane. Alexander ordered the house to be closed and the front part barred. He got out a supply of guns and sent word for all the men on the farm to "be in readiness."

"By this time they came in two files into the kitchen yard," Alexander recounted later.[2] "I went to see who they were and, finding them clad in federal overcoats, presumed that they were federal soldiers. With my gun in my hand and a pistol in my belt, I stepped into the door and cried 'Halt!' just as the column had gone half by me. They halted and turned about at once, upon which I said, 'What will you have, gentlemen?' One of them answered, 'We want provender for two hundred horses.' I replied, 'That is a pretty large order. I have provender in various places, but I have no place to feed so many horses.'"

It was at this stage of the conversation that it was obvious the educated and conversant Quantrill was not present. A second voice told Alexander, "We are out pressing horses." Alexander asked to see an order for his horses and each guerrilla drew a revolver as the same voice said, "This is our order." Alexander's response was firm.

"Well, I suppose if you are bound to have horses, there is no necessity for a fight about it, but if you are disposed to have a fight, I have some men here, and we will give you the best fight we can."

With the sun sinking in the west, it was difficult to see the faces of the riders, but Alexander had no trouble in identifying a voice from the ranks of horsemen. "Alexander, for God's sake, let him have the horses," Viley said. "The Captain says he will be satisfied if you will let him have two horses without a fight or any trouble."

Alexander knew the trump card had been played, so he assured Marion he was a man of his word and walked out to shake hands with him. Marion then told Alexander to surrender his arms, but the horseman refused.

Marion seemed satisfied when Alexander said he would take all his guns in the house and there would be no firing. "Do so then," said Marion. "But if a gun is fired, I will burn up your whole place." Alexander got the last word as he warned Marion that if a gun should be fired, it would be his fault.

As some of the guerrillas rode to a stable near the house under Alexander's direction, the horseman found ankle-deep mud difficult to negotiate. Alexander was offered a ride and when a guerrilla took his foot from a stirrup, he got up behind, but the ride was short-lived. The horse began kicking and the guerrilla suggested Alexander continue walking. After reaching the stable, Alexander learned there was no deal with the guerrillas. They intended to take whatever they wanted and Marion started asking about the "bald horse."

The guerrillas took four thoroughbreds, but missed Asteroid, taken in the earlier raid, because a trainer was able to hide him and pass an inferior horse off as the famed stallion.[3] Alexander returned to the house and found two guerrillas gathering up all the weapons and threatening Daniel Swigert's family, who had been staying at Woodburn.

One nearly drunk guerrilla was waving a pistol around, trying to get Mrs. Swigert to tell if there were more guns in the house as a smaller irregular was trying to carry a load of guns outside. A nurse and the Swigert children looked on in horror.

"The Captain says if I will give him two horses without a fight or any trouble, I can keep my arms, and I am going to keep them," Alexander said. The guerrilla held the pistol to within 18 inches of Alexander's breast and blurted, "Damn you! You deliver up the rest of those arms or I will shoot you!" Alexander pushed the pistol aside so it was no longer pointed at him and put a bear hug on the guerrilla, who still held onto the weapon. In his letter to Henry Charles Deedes, his brother-in-law, Alexander described the encounter:

> We stood close to the door which opened into the passage and I made an effort to throw him out of the room, fearing the pistol might go off and shoot someone in the room. I was unable to throw him out at the first effort, but I had seized him in such a way that I had my left shoulder against his right shoulder and was somewhat behind him, [sic] in making the effort, I felt his right knee come in contact with my left knee and it instantly occurred to me that I should trip him. So, lifting him, I advanced my left leg, and throwing my whole weight against him at the same moment, giving him a twist to the left, we fell together out the door and into the passage [which was] about 8 or 9 inches lower than the floor of the dining room.
>
> I had a little the best of the fall, as he was undermost, and, in attempting

to rise, he called to the other man to shoot me, that I was killing him. I took a hasty glance at the man who stood with his arms still full of guns who seemed taken quite by surprise by my action. He, in answer to the other fellow, said, "He is not armed. He cannot hurt you much." Just then we rose together, I still holding onto the fellow with the same grip, my arm encircling him just at the elbow joint so as to pinion him. The fellow made a violent effort to get away and again called out to the other to shoot me. As I saw that he might get loose from me and would certainly shoot me if he did, I made my mind up to give him another fall just as the other called out to me, "Let him go, Mr. Alexander." I said, "I will not let him go. He will shoot me as I have no arms."

Again the fellow made an effort to get loose, and, giving him the benefit of my knee a second time, down we came together, I still retaining my grasp on him. This time we fell against an iron safe placed opposite the dining room door and against the wall in the passage, my elbow rubbing against the door of the safe and his arm, in the hand of which he held the pistol, must have struck the edge or corner of the safe, for the fellow said I had broken his arm (which, however, was not the case).

Again we rose up together, for I could not hold him down, though I could retain my hold on him, which I had first taken; and just as we were rising, the man with the guns said again, "let him go," adding that he would protect me.

As we rose, I said, "Do you promise me on the word and honor of a gentleman that you will protect me?" He answered, "I will," or "I do," and thinking that this was as good a bargain as I was likely to be able to make, I let him go. He made a strong effort to get away just as I released him and I, at the same time, gave him a shove so that he went through the door towards the kitchen. The other fellow stepped in between us and kept him moving till they moved into the kitchen. I watched them till they disappeared from the passage and, following them quickly, bolted the middle door between the passage and also the door through which I shoved the fellow and returning to the dining room where I found Mrs. Swigert, the nurse, and children. I told her not to open the door on any account, and, if the fellows should return and inquire for me, to say I had gone out.[4]

Alexander made his way to a spot where he could observe and saw a bonfire of straw burning in front of his trotting stable, which illuminated the guerrillas taking horses.

I then hastened to Lexington's stable and told my man there to take out such animals as were most valuable and they were likely to steal. I also sent a boy to the training stable to tell the trainer to remove most of the valuable horses, but before the boy got there, a portion of the rascals had got there and taken out 4 horses. They asked for "Asteroid," but in the dark of the evening, the trainer gave them an inferior horse and so saved the best horse in my stables.

They got "Norwich," brother to "Norfolk," however, a 4 year old mare that was a good one, and a three year old filly by "Lexington" which we think well of, besides the colt they mistook for "Asteroid," making four from my racing stable. They also got four from my trotting stable, and 4 from my riding stable and three more from various places making 15 in all.

Alexander said in his letter that "Bay Chief," the horse Marion seemed so anxious to get, was worth fully as much as any horse he owned, except "Lexington."

"I doubt I would have touched fifteen thousand dollars in green backs for him ('Bay Chief')," Alexander added. And in recalling the raid, he continued: "The second most valuable was my trotting stallion 'Abdallah.' Both these are dead. The first from a wound in the back; the second, being captured by Federals, was ridden to death by a Federal soldier. The third, 'Norwich,' was still in the hands of the guerriillas (*sic*) when I last heard from home. Six horses and mares are still missing, including the two which are dead and their value is not less than $32,000. We can console ourselves with the idea that it might have been far worse...."

The guerrillas left Viley at the nearby residence of Frank Kinkead and took Kinkead as a guide. One report said Viley was so exhausted he fell from his saddle and could not continue. A federal guard of some 25 men out of Versailles gave chase as the guerrillas and their stolen horses headed for Clifton on the Kentucky River.[5]

With men of Company H, 12th Ohio Cavalry out of Lexington hot on their trail, the guerrillas crossed the river at Clifton Ferry about 12:30 A.M., which gave them a two-hour lead on the pursuing federals. The guerillas stopped at Bacon Bush's, about two miles from the river, to have breakfast. Soon Second Lieutenant Levin A. Harvey caught up and ordered his men to open fire. A brisk skirmish lasted about ten minutes before developing into a running gun battle.[6]

That's when "Bay Chief," ridden by Marion, was hit in the muzzle and the quarters. As the great horse lay dying, Marion found another mount and escaped. Since Marion was unknown to those who saw him on the raid, sources said the guerrillas were led by Quantrill, or Sue Mundy or Ben Foreman, but *Giants of the Turf* was on the right track in 1960, when it reported: "... a party of men led by a Captain Merrian, believed to be a fictitious, name, rode up to the trotting stable at Woodburn." Bill Marion's name was, in fact, fictitious as mentioned earlier. His real name was Stanley Young.

It was also in the fight at Bush's that Tom Henry was gravely wounded in the right breast. After falling from his saddle, he was shot twice in the face by a federal cavalryman. Despite wounds that appeared to be fatal, Henry crawled to the home of a Confederate sympathizer and was nursed back to health.[7]

"Abdallah's" rider, in making his escape from Bush's, abused the horse terribly and three days later, "Abdallah" was found in Lawrenceburg. He died there Feb. 6, 1865.[8]

Quantrill resumed his role of commander as his men returned to Spencer County from Marion's test ride. Marion praised the Missourians, saying: "Braver men I never saw in battle, truer men never fired a gun since the war began."[9] John Newman Edwards, in his *Noted Guerrillas or the Warfare of the Border*, said Quantrill prevailed upon Marion to restore the remaining blooded horses to Alexander and Marion agreed.

"Alexander presented Quantrill with a magnificent thoroughbred, and Frank James with another, known everywhere by his name of 'Edwin Forrest,' and noted everywhere for his speed and for the prowess of his rider," Edwards wrote in his 1877 book.

Alexander made no mention of the return of any of the stolen horses in his March 4, 1865, letter to Deedes, but did mention that several were still missing.

CHAPTER 29

Battling the Hall's Gap Tigers

Quantrill had anxiously awaited the return of his men from their adventure under the command of Marion so he could mount a rescue mission for those captured just ten days earlier near Hustonville.

Magruder, Jerome Clarke and others who had not made the second Woodburn Farm raid became acquainted with Quantrill and agreed to go along. Quantrill had learned that Colonel James W. Weatherford of the 13th Kentucky Cavalry and Colonel Benjamin Helm Bristow of the Eighth Kentucky Cavalry were in the Danville area. He sought to capture them to trade for his men or, if that should fail, hang them in retaliation.

It is likely Quantrill unveiled his plan to the Kentucky guerrillas at the home of Dr. Isaac McClaskey a short distance northeast of Bloomfield. There was a party at the doctor's house, about Feb. 6, 1865. The doctor had arranged a feast and provided musical entertainment. Area girls had come to mingle and dance with the guerrillas, who included Jerome Clarke, Magruder and Quantrill.[1]

There was other news to discuss at the gathering. Federal soldiers had moved quickly into the town of Fairfield on Feb. 5, 1865, and surprised two of Zay Coulter's men, the Truax brothers. The boys were visiting their sister when the federals arrived and began questioning them. A gunfight ensued and one of the brothers was killed and the other wounded. The federals then went to the residence of Dr. Wootton, where they discovered Confederate George Blandford and gunned him down. It was to his advantage that Blandford was shot at the doctor's house because he survived.[2]

On Feb. 7, 1865, the guerrillas gathered at John Hinkle's just south of Bloomfield off the Springfield Road and made ready to ride.

They rode all day through a steady, accumulating snowfall and the temperature remaining in the lower 20's.[3] Their first action came as the guerrillas spotted a train of nine Union supply wagons at New Market in Marion County and opened fire. Captain George G. Lott in Lebanon reported to Captain J.S. Butler, assistant adjutant-general on Feb. 8, 1865:

> I sent out train of five post teams and four of the Thirtieth's wagons [30th Kentucky Volunteer Infantry] this morning. They have been captured by a band of about forty guerrillas, but one man of the guards has escaped and brought us word. Major [Thomas] Mahoney is mounting men of the Invalid Corps and starts in pursuit. He has sent for Captain Searcy's company at Springfield.

Magruder later recounted the attack:

> At sunset we took the road to New Market, which place we reached in the night, and learned that there were two Government wagons there, guarded by some Yankees. We at once charged them, captured and killed three soldiers, burned the wagons and killed the mules. We stayed there long enough to rob the stores....[4]

The guerrilla gunfire on the wagon train fatally wounded Quartermaster Sgt. Archibald Kite Miller, 23, and Private Martin V. Finnell, 25, both of Boone County, along with Private John Peebles, 20, of Ballard County.[5] Privates Shedrick Thomas Butler, James M. Defries, William C. Russell and Calvin Carmack Smith were taken prisoner by the guerrillas and executed in Bradfordsville. Mahoney and his 35-man invalid corps gave it all they had when they caught up with the guerrillas at the Bradfordsville toll gate, but Mahoney reported his men "could not master horses and lead their long guns."[6]

Mahoney's men dismounted in Bradfordsville and the guerrillas charged, creating excitement in the ranks. Some of the invalid corps horses got away and ran to the guerrillas.[7]

Several Bradfordsville buildings were torched as the guerrilla band quickly scattered the invalid corps and took command of the town. Among the structures put to the torch was John Yowell's Bradfordsville Hotel and livery and a house once occupied by the town's first doctor, Joseph Rose. They found Dr. John Fleece's horse outside a house and took it along. The doctor was visiting a patient and unaware his horse would not be there when he prepared to go home. They moved eastward through northern Casey County and, southwest of Hustonville, stopped at the residence of Pryor

When a combined guerrilla force led by Quantrill passed through the counties south of Lexington, Ky., there was a consistent need for fresh horses. They stopped at Prior Prewitt's house southwest of Hustonville, Ky., but Prewitt refused to cooperate with the guerrillas and was shot to death. Perry Brantley and local historian Allan Leach found Prewitt's grave marker in a cow-decimated family cemetery and confirmed the date of the farmer's death and thus the date of the incident. *Above:* The Prior Prewitt house. *Below:* Perry Brantley (left) and Allen Leach, righting Prewitt's grave stone (photographs by Thomas Shelby Watson).

H. Prewitt.[8] A knock at the door may have been unheeded by Prewitt, 54, or he may have conversed through the door without opening it. A single bullet fired through the door killed Prewitt Feb. 8, 1865. Prior and Nancy (Cunningham) Prewitt had seven children.

It was ten o'clock on that bitterly cold Wednesday night and the ground was covered with snow as Quantrill, Frank James, Jerome Clarke, Henry Magruder and the others of the combined band of guerrillas surrounded Colonel Frank Wolford's house along the Little South Fork, only to find he wasn't home.

The next target was Colonel George D. Weatherford's, but first the men sought a break from the numbing cold. They took over the two-story log home of William and Susan Mills and all lay down on the floors, many kicking off their boots.[9] After less than three hours of rest, the sleeping men were awakened by Bridgewater and his Hall's Gap Battalion, under sanction of the Union Army as a home guard unit to hunt down and kill the Confederate guerrillas.

Bridgewater described the attack in an Oct. 25, 1865, report to D.W. Lindsey, adjutant general of Kentucky:

Bullitt County, Ky., native Henry Clay Magruder had no regard for the lives of federal soldiers. He killed them on the battlefield, after they were discharged or when they were home on emergency leave. Magruder, Jerome Clarke and Samual Oscar "One-Arm" Berry were often together during the closing months of the Civil War. Quantrill relinquished command of a joint guerrilla operation to Magruder after heavy losses in a skirmish with Captain Jim Bridgewater's "Hall's Gap Tigers" near Harrodsburg, Ky. It was proof of the confidence other Confederate guerrilla leaders had in Magruder (courtesy McClaskey Family Collection).

We charged the position upon two sides but owing to the strong fencing and the frozen hillsides all of them escaped except five who were instantly killed.

The guerrillas made a stand behind a post and rail fence but could not stand the assault of the Hall's Gap Tigers. Five were killed dead and how many wounded I can't say. We captured between thirty five and forty Horses and Equipment [*sic*].

Most of the Horses were proven [verified stolen] and taken by the citizens of Marion, Casey and other adjoining counties. Among the captured Horses were about five Race Horses belonging to Mr. Alexander of Woodford County. One of them "Anna Butler" was a Beautiful animal. All of them were restored, pursuant to order from Frankfort.

Magruder claimed later that Quantrill turned command of the men over to him because he knew the country. Since Jerome Clarke was not among the dead, it is believed he was with some 20 men led by Magruder between Harrodsburg and Lebanon and around Springfield to the Bloomfield Pike.[10]

They camped on a hill overlooking the road leading westward to Bloomfield from Chaplin and watched a force of a hundred federals in pursuit of them. As the last of the bluecoats moved out of sight, the guerrillas broke camp and headed for the Chaplin River area, where there were friends and hiding places.[11]

CHAPTER 30

Not Enough Friendly Rebels

The winter was unrelenting and so was Bridgewater. The guerrillas knew it was time to take a break, get warm and contemplate their next move. They rode east of Chaplin to the residence of Butler Remey Thomas, where Mollie Thomas was undoubtedly delighted that Jerome had returned safely from his most recent raid. Magruder, after scouting the Bloomfield area on his own and finding the federals gone, rode back to the Thomas farm to share his findings with Quantrill.

They bunked out for the night, but true to their normal routine, they were already planning to return to the saddle at the rooster's first crow. Home cooking and warm fires were just what the doctor ordered for the haggard horsemen. The Dawsons of "Dawson Hungry Lodge" southeast of Bloomfield were cousins of John Jarrett, who visited them along with his commander, Quantrill. Jarrett was the son of Joshua Jarrett and Martha Ann Dawson. One of Martha Ann's brothers, Charles, married Milly Duncan and to them were born ten children. One of those children was Nancy, born Dec. 31, 1845. She was 19 when Quantrill, 27, took a shine to her.

Quantrill composed poems for "Nannie," as he called her, and clearly expressed affection, or perhaps intended seduction, in the wording.[1] A poem by Lord Byron, written for his fellow poet Tom Moore, was an instrument of Quantrill's effort to gain the attention of Nancy Dawson. He rewrote "An Ode to Tom Moore" on a piece of paper and dated it Feb. 26, 1865. It was folded and left in a wooden jewelry box for Nancy to find. The date is important because the federal army blamed Quantrill for a raid on Hickman the next morning. The distance from Bloomfield to Hickman is 233 miles. The first line of the real poem was:

"My boat is on the shore." The Quantrill version was:

My horse is at the door,
And the enemy I soon may see;
But before I go Miss Nannie,
Here's a double health to thee!
Here's a sigh to those who love me,
And a smile to those who hate;
And, whatever sky's above me,
It hath springs which may be won.
In this verse as with the wine,
The libation I would pour
Should be peace with thine and mine
And a health to thee and all in door
Very respectfully your friend

Feb. 26, 1865   W.C.Q.[2]

Nancy Dawson was the object of William Clarke Quantrill's attentions and the recipient of his love poems. The youngest of ten children, Nancy was referred to as "Nannie" in the poems. Family members verify that the log home of Charles and Milly Dawson, a short distance south of Bloomfield, was a frequent stopping place for the Confederate captain. When he visited the Dawson residence in 1865, Quantrill was 27 and Nancy was 19 (Dawson Family collection).

(Courtesy the Dawson Family Collection and Kenneth Spencer Research Library, Lawrence, Kan.)

Among Quantrill's other poems is an undated one that clearly shows he had strong feelings for Nancy Dawson. "The Hot Burning Tear" contains the repetitive line, "Who will care for thee Nannie, when I am gone?" That changes at the end to: "I will love thee, My Nannie, when ever I am gone."[2] The Byron influence was apparent in Quantrill's poetry and there's a hint of an unhappy childhood. His use of the comma instead of the apostrophe to mark contractions is noticeable, but the words are readable.

This was an undated, original love poem by Quantrill to Nancy Dawson:

The hot burning tear, will come to my eye,
When I think I depart at the grey breaking dawn;
And deep from my bosom will come the sad sigh,

Who will care for thee Nannie, when I am gone?
Soon far, far away, o'er the deep rolling sea,
The boat of my fortune will swift bear me on;
From the home of my childhood, dear one I flee;
Oh!, who will love Nannie, now that I am gone?
Tho, many the Richmonds that crowd on the field,
And brave in the battle of love they are drawn;
Tho, pointed and bright are th, [sic] darts that thy deal,
Yet who will *love*, Nannie, now that I am gone?
Who will smile at her laughter happy and clear?
Who will sigh deeper when her sad sighs are drawn?
Who will share sorrow or shed tear for tear?
Oh! who will *love* Nannie, now that I am gone?
Here's a heart that will love yet fondly and true,
Tho fate in its fancy does drive me far on;
Tho my home be a rock' mid the ocean bright blue,
Yet I'll care for thee Nannie tho, far I am gone.
Yes, I'll think of the smile that once me did cheer,
And sigh for the sigh that I know not are drawn;
And weep but the deeper for the distant tear
Yet, I'll love thee, my Nannie, tho far I am gone.
Tho, the wings of the morning doth bear me away,
Or the shades of dark night doth spirit me on;
Or an Angel doth grasp me far brighter than day,
I will love thee, my Nannie, when e'er I am gone.

(Courtesy the Dawson Family Collection, first publication)

Quantrill also penned poems entitled "The Misty Shades of Evening," "Disappointment," and "Love: Dedicated to Miss Mollie on Her Wedding Day." They are also from the Dawson Family Collection.

Quantrill supposedly entered Kentucky a married man, having taken the hand of teenager Kate King in Missouri.[3] The daughter of Robert and Malinda King of Blue Springs, Mo., was just 13 when in 1861 she became infatuated with Quantrill. At 23, Quantrill saw a lot of Kate, going horseback riding with her to the chagrin of her parents, and when her father made it clear she was not to see him again, they went to a preacher's house and were married. They spent their honeymoon in an abandoned house.[4] While Kate remained with Quantrill in Missouri, there is evidence she used the names Nancy Slaughter and Kate Clarke.

Quantrill left Kate in St. Louis when his force was headed toward Kentucky, and so the story goes, he provided her with a modest amount of money.

Frank James stopped at the Alexander and Finetta Sayers residence at Deatsville in northeast Nelson County and, finding that they were another true Southern family, became very close to them. He also became very fond of the Samuels family in an adjacent community by the same name and at one point was courting Mary Rachel Samuels, but she broke off what was labeled "an engagement" by some in favor of Thomas Edward "Bud" Pence.[5] Frank was 22, Mary 17 and Bud 23 in 1865. McCorkle was related to the Wiggintons of Spencer County and visited them, as well as the Aaron Decker Foreman family of the same county. Tom Harris, George Wigginton and John Barnhill of Quantrill's guerrillas were close to McCorkle and spent many nights at Foreman's as well.

McCorkle became quite fond of 18-year-old Jennie Foreman, yet once the war was over, he never saw her again.[6] Jerome Clarke visited with Mollie Thomas and her family frequently and Henry Magruder reportedly had a female friend with whom he spent time, but her identity was not generally known, and only rare local tradition told of her existence.

On Feb. 18, 1865, the former Morgan followers and associates attacked Fort Jones near Colesburg, where men of the 12th U.S. Colored Heavy Artillery were stationed. A dispatch described what happened.

General Ewing
Louisville, Ky.

Colesburg, Ky. February 18, 1865.

I took sixty men and went to Fort Jones, from thence to Lebanon Junction. Magruder's guerrilla band, numbering thirty one men, came within three quarters of a mile from here, killed three of my men who were on their way from Jones to draw rations. Sue Munday's [*sic*] came within 200 yards of the fort, numbering some sixteen men. Another force is reported on the west of Lebanon Junction. They robbed a number of citizens etc.

Have returned to Colesburg.

Do not anticipate further danger.

C.B. LEAVITT
Major, Commanding
Station.[7]

The three men killed in Hardin County Feb. 22, 1865, were Sgt. Alfred Jones, Company B, 12th U.S. Colored Heavy Artillery; Private John S. Ward, Company 2, Ohio Heavy Artillery; and Private Samuel Young, Company B, 12th U.S. Colored Heavy Artillery. On Feb. 21, 1865, Marion stopped at the farmhouse of Dr. John Lilly near Little Union in southern Spencer County.

"Marion and his men, guerrillas, impressed two horses from me and left two tired horses in their place," Lilly wrote in his journal. "Later in the day, 4 of Captain (Robert Hunter) Young's men, federals, came to my house and took away my bird gun worth $50 or $75 and two coats and gloves worth $40."

Henry Magruder and Jerome Clarke knew that they were constantly being hunted and that if they were ever caught, their fates were pre-determined. They also knew that if they could return to the regular army before the war ended, they stood a better chance of being paroled. And so, with guerrillas Henry Metcalf, Jim Jones, Henry Porter and others, they headed southwestward.

"I then started for Lyon's command," Magruder said after the war. "(We) started through Petersburg and went on to Beach Fork, where we swam our horses by a canoe." They continued to gradually work their way down the Ohio River Valley, passing through Garnettsville, Big Spring, Webster, and Clifton Mills and skirting Hardinsburg.

In Hancock County, they robbed James Snider's store at Pellville of $315, plus what goods they wanted. They obtained three good horses at Peter Purcell's farm.[8] They crossed into Daviess County, went to Knottsville and had their horses shod, paying for everything to avoid suspicion. Nevertheless, someone went to nearby Owensboro and reported their whereabouts and home guardsmen began searching for them.

It was Sunday, Feb. 19, 1865, when the gang stopped at Benjamin Muffett Taul's in Breckinridge County.[9] Taul responded to a knock at the door and the guerrillas rushed in and began eating what food had been left out.

They forced Taul to get dressed and ride with them on a horse they had stolen from a neighbor some time earlier. The guerrillas continued taking fresh horses during their visit to the river valley and even took a pony on which Taul was forced to ride. It proved to be entertaining for the guerrillas and they laughed as Taul kept fighting to stay astride the animal.[10]

The irregulars grabbed a meal at Jones' father's and spent the night at Jones' brother's house. As they continued toward Cloverport near the Ohio River, the assemblage was joined by guerrilla Bill Davison. He led them to a safe place, five miles from Cloverport, where they stayed two days.[11] It was Feb. 24, 1865 when Jerome Clarke, Magruder, Davison and the others with them stopped at Minor E. Pate's house, some ten miles southeast of Hawesville on the Hardinsburg-Shawneetown Road in Hancock County. It was near the Hancock-Breckinridge County line. Squads of federal soldiers were scouring the countryside looking for the guerrillas, and on March 3, 1865, the Rebs returned to the saddle for what would prove a short and fateful ride. They were about a mile from the Pate farm when they spotted three home guardsmen, Silas Taylor, Charles Hale and William Stinnett, all from the Pellville area, near the intersection of the Hardinsburg and Cloverport Roads. The three, who were scouting for Union Captain John A. Clark's company, immediately opened fire on the guerrillas with rifles. Stinnett spurred his horse and left his two companions to the fight. Taylor and Hale dismounted and had a tree-to-tree running gunfight with the guerrillas. Davison began chasing Hale and firing at close range, but Hale was on target with his reply, firing a bullet that shattered the Hawesville guerrilla's right arm and lodged in his lower chest or abdomen. Hale and Taylor reached a cabin where they were able to hold off the guerrillas for 45 minutes. That was long enough for Captain John Clark to arrive with seven additional home guardsmen.[12] The guerrillas left the two men to defend their cabin and rode away.

"We then went on half a mile further and ran into the balance of them, some forty in number," Magruder recalled. "The first we knew of them was their fire, delivered at a distance of about twenty feet. Davison was hit twice — once in the side and once in the bowels."[13] A federal's bullet smashed into Magruder's left breast and Jones was killed as 16 bullets ripped into his body. Jerome Clarke and the rest of the guerrillas returned the fire as they fled, searching to find a safe hiding place. Magruder gave them directions to a cousin's house, but after two days, he was moved to another location.[14]

The wounded Magruder was taken to the woods on Joseph Claycomb's farm, where he suffered for a week in the cold with inadequate medical care, yet he had food and water. Joe Claycomb's young son, Green Claycomb, was recruited at gunpoint by Jerome Clarke and put to work, helping to carry food and supplies to the camp.[15]

Magruder told Porter to take the men back to Nelson County and he did, except for Jerome Clarke and Henry Metcalf. They moved Magruder to a tobacco barn on the John and Elizabeth Cox farm in Meade County near the Meade-Breckinridge County line. John, 28, and Elizabeth, 24, summoned an area physician, Dr. Jesse Pittman Lewis, to treat Magruder on a daily basis.

Davison, with blood spilling from his wounds, rode three miles north of the ambush to the Silkman Bottom on the Ohio River east of Hawesville, trying to reach the home of his cousin, Thomas Newman. Struggling from his horse, Davison lay down in the woods, where he remained two days. Eliza and Sarah Newman, his teenage cousins, heard the neighing of his horse, found Davison and took him home. Soon, with word circulating that Davison was being sought in the area, the Newmans moved the guerrilla deep into the woods and hid him in an old cabin.

Davison's mother, Jane Dupuy Davison, was awakened in the middle of the night not long after her son was moved to the cabin. A man she didn't know told her to bring bedding for her son and to follow him. They rode to the Hancock County cabin where Davison's mother, the Newman sisters and Dr. William Stapp nursed the wounded guerrilla until Davison's death March 7, 1865. He was buried, at his own wish, in a secluded place near the cabin.[16]

On the day of Davison's death, a Prentice column headlined "All About Sue Mundy" appeared in the *Louisville Daily Journal*. Prentice claimed that he had received two letters — one signed by Sue Mundy and three of "her" chief officers, together with a note in Sue's name alone. Prentice said "Sue" had offered to pay for publication of the letters "in whatever currency we prefer." "Well, let us think what we will take pay in," Prentice wrote.

We don't want it in Confederate notes, for our pockets wouldn't hold enough to pay for "a nip" apiece for Sue and ourselves. We don't desire it in lead for we have mettel [*sic*] enough in us already. We don't want it in steel, for we have quite as much point now as we need. We prefer not to take it in hemp, for we are a temperance man [*sic*] and have decided objections to getting high.

We won't accept it in kisses, for we would rather be kissed by the Devil's daughter with her brimstone breath than by a tomboy. We'll not submit to have it in hugs, for those who have seen Sue in her guerrilla costume say that she is a little bare. She has done a great deal of stealing, but she can't steal our heart, and we don't care to have her steal her own against us. She has committed great waste, but she can't commit her own little one to our arms.

We fear that we can't make a bargain with you, pretty and gentle Sue. Still if you will name time and place, and promise not to have any improper aims at us and not to look through other sights in getting a sight of us, in short, not to be at all snappish toward us, and not to frighten us as ghosts are said to be frightened by a cock, we may meet you and talk matters over confidentially. Abstemious as we are, we would rather accept the contents of one of your pilfered whisky-barrels than those of your pistol barrel.

We would rather feel the wadding of your bosom than your pistol wad. We would prefer to see all the stock you have ever "lifted" rushing furiously toward us rather than behold your Colt's stock lifted at us. We should be almost as willing to see the nipples of your bosom as the nipples of your firearms. You may drill your troops as thoroughly as you please, but please don't go to drilling a big hole through us.

'Twould be better that you pull hemp from a cross beam than a trigger at us. We have had many openings before us, but none so perilous as the muzzles of your Deringers. You can spit fire enough at us yourself without calling in the aid of your side or pocket arms. Many think that it makes no difference on what day of the week a man dies, but we confess that we shouldn't like to die of a Mundy.

We don't want to be in front of you if the breech of your weapon is going to commit a breach of the peace. We desire to be away if you mean to use the ugly prime of death against our handsome prime of life. If you come, don't bring Quantrell [sic] along with you on any account, for every limb in our forests would of its own accord twist itself into a withe at his appearance. Though somewhat of a woman killer in our youth, we have got entirely over that in our fall manhood. Let the interview be soon, for we apprehend that before long you will be like many hen's eggs we have seen — laid in the straw.

Folks call you Mundy, but we suspect that you are all the week round. Tell us whether you are as unprincipled as some say, or whether you have "a living principle within." The very times, like or unlike yourself, are pregnant of great things. Undoubtedly you are now in a perilous situation, but you may in due season be triumphantly delivered. But pray don't send aught to be left in a basket within our gate, for the thing will not be a sin to be laid at our door.

You have been an awful girl, Sue, we must say. You have killed so many persons, of all colors, that no doubt, white, yellow and black ghosts haunt you continually, the black ones coming by day because black doesn't show at night. Our Journal may bring you and your fellows to justice and thus be to you and them not only a newspaper, but a noose paper. The authorities civil and military command us to cut down you and your gang wherever we can find you, but, if we wake up some morning and see you all hanging about here, we'll be hanged ourselves if we cut down one of you. And now for the present goodby.[17]

The disjointed, somewhat humorous column makes the reader wonder if Prentice would not be sorry to see his Sue Mundy character captured, although his attitude appeared to be that of an unconcerned journalist. No matter what his true feelings might have been, they were to become inconsequential.

On Sunday, March 12, 1865, the privacy of the barn on the Cox farm in Meade County near the Breckinridge County community of Webster was invaded. Captain Lewis O. Marshall and 50 federal troops of Company B, the 30th Wisconsin Volunteer Infantry, under command of Major Cyrus J. Wilson, a recent retiree of the 26st Kentucky Volunteer Infantry, arrived at Brandenburg aboard the steamer *Grey Eagle* and marched ten miles to the Cox farm.[15] When the troops arrived around daylight, Lewis pointed out the hiding place of Magruder, Clarke and Metcalf.

Private John Weirick of Company F 30th Wisconsin Volunteer Infantry, and seven others ran up to the barn door where Weirick knocked with the butt of his pistol, but there was no answer. Then a large rock was used to smash in the door and there was an instant answer from Jerome Clarke in the form of blazing guns, as he fired from a revolver in each hand.

Some 40 rounds were fired into the barn by the federals before their captain ordered them to "fall back," but Private John G. White didn't follow orders.

Perry Brantley holds a revolver once carried by Jerome Clarke. It was given to him by a family whose relatives lived on the farm 40 miles southwest of Louisville where Jerome Clarke, Henry Magruder and Henry Metcalf were captured. Stamped on the barrel of the Colt 1851 Navy is "Sue Mundy" (photograph by Thomas Shelby Watson).

White sat down with his gun to his shoulder looking at the door. Weirick told him to get away or he might get shot. "I had not more than spoke the words until a ball struck him," Weirick was to recall. White was shot in the chest. Privates John Robbins and W.A. Wadsworth suffered less serious wounds and one other private also was hit.[18]

Marshall wanted to torch the barn, but Wilson sent in a flag of truce by Dr. Lewis and gained an audience with Jerome Clarke. Wilson approached the barn door and Jerome stood facing him inside, with a pistol in his hand. Wilson asked Clarke for his surrender.

"If I surrender to you, you will kill me," Jerome replied. Wilson told Jerome he would not kill him if he surrendered. "Your men will do it," Clarke replied. Wilson said his men would not kill him there either. Wilson told Clarke he had no doubt that he would be killed once he was taken to Louisville, but that his surrender would give him a few more days to live.

Jerome invited Wilson inside the barn and they sat and smoked together. Magruder insisted that Clarke surrender and Jerome said he might wait a while first. But Wilson said he could give him just five minutes to decide, then he would have to order a resumption of fire because he had the lives of his men to consider.

Wilson told Jerome there might be a chance in a thousand or ten thousand of his escape if he surrendered. Jerome asked to be treated as a prisoner of war and Wilson agreed.[19] "There is enough published against me to kill me," Wilson later recalled Jerome as saying. "I know I will be killed at Louisville," Jerome lamented. Wilson replied that he had no doubt at all that Clarke had but a few more days to live. Clarke, Magruder and Metcalf surrendered.

CHAPTER 31

The Truth Is Revealed

The heavily-shackled prisoners were taken to the steamboat *Morning Star* and transported up the Ohio River to Louisville. When the boat docked at the Louisville wharf, Jerome Clarke and Henry Metcalf were placed aboard horses in irons and a horse-drawn ambulance was summoned in which Magruder was loaded. A "square" of soldiers, designed to prevent an escape, accompanied the captives.

As the parade slowly proceeded up the sharp Fourth Street incline toward Main Street, word began to spread that Sue Mundy had been captured. Crowds gathered to get a glimpse of the "she devil" they had read about in the *Louisville Daily Journal*. The prisoners were escorted to the U.S. Military Prison at Tenth and Broadway streets and physicians were summoned to check on Magruder. Otis Hoyt, a surgeon with the 30th Wisconsin Volunteer Infantry, observed that Magruder's wound was on the left side of the sternum, halfway between the nipple and sternum, between the fifth and sixth ribs.

He said the ball did not go through Magruder's body, but admitted he never examined him on the other side to see if it did. Magruder's general appearance was used to determine whether the wound would prove fatal.

He said nearly two thirds of Magruder's left lung was below the wound and that no large blood vessels were ruptured. Hoyt said Magruder's pulse was between 90 and 100 when he was brought in.[1]

On Tuesday, March 14, 1865, Jerome Clarke was taken under heavy guard to the headquarters of Lieutenant Colonel William H. Coyl, 9th Iowa Infantry, the post commander, whose headquarters was a large house on the south side of Chestnut Street (216 West Chestnut), four doors west of Second Street.

It was there, sitting in heavy irons on his wrists and ankles, that Jerome Clarke knew he would have no defense against the charges that were outlined. He said he was a regular Confederate soldier and that Quantrill and Captain Marion had committed the crimes.

He was told the court-martial he would face would not hear evidence on those points. There are those who say there was no trial, although the Old Military Records Division of the National Archives possesses a court-martial document entitled "The United States vs. Jerome Clark Alias Sue Mundy."

It is 32 pages long, with an additional three-page statement by Jerome Clarke, which is basically a plea to call witnesses so he could prove he was a legitimate Confederate soldier. No witnesses for the defense were allowed. On the back of Jerome's statement is the endorsement of the court-martial findings by Major General John McCauley Palmer.

"The proceedings and findings are approved and the sentence confirmed, Jerome Clarke, alias Sue Mundy, will be hanged by the neck until he is dead on Wednesday, the 15th day of March, 1865 at 4 o'clock P.M. at Louisville, Ky. The commanding officer of the Post of Louisville, Ky. is charged with the execution of the sentence." The endorsement was dated March 13, 1865, the day before Jerome Clarke's trial began.[2]

There was one charge against Jerome Clarke—"being a guerrilla." The specification under the first charge alleged that Jerome did "unlawfully and of his own wrong, take up arms as a guerrilla, and did join, belong to and act and cooperate with guerrillas, he the said Jerome Clarke, alias 'Sue Mundy,' not then acting with or belonging to any lawfully authorized military force at war with the United States, and not being commanded thereto by any lawful civil or military authority."

The specification accused Jerome of acting as a guerrilla in Nelson, Marion, Henry and Woodford Counties, September through December, 1864. Under previous courts-martial proceedings, the only thing needed for conviction under the "being a guerrilla" charge was to state the time and place and they did not have to be exact.

In the second, and only other specification, Jerome was accused of wounding John G. White, John Robbins and W.A. Wadsworth, three of the 30th Regiment Wisconsin Volunteer Infantry who had fired into the barn where he was hiding with Magruder and Metcalf. Jerome was represented by Judge Advocate Lt. Col. William H. Coyl, but it would not have mattered who was appointed to defend him because it was the Union Army who was really on trial for being outwitted so many times by the long-haired Kentucky guerrilla. Jerome was going to lose.

Major Cyrus J. Wilson of the 26th Kentucky Volunteer Infantry took the stand first as a government witness and described the capture of Jerome, Magruder and Metcalf. Wilson testified that he found Dr. Lewis and "compelled him to tell of the whereabouts of Magruder." Wilson said the doctor "acted as a guide" and showed them the barn where the guerrillas were hiding. Wilson said he sent in a flag of truce by the doctor, then arranged the meeting with Jerome to discuss terms of surrender.

Wilson also discredited a tale that Jerome once dressed in female attire to fool Morgan, perhaps the first time Prentice had been publicly discredited. "He (Jerome) spoke of the publication concerning him fooling Morgan ... said that was 'all damn stuff' and there was nothing to it about him having an introduction to Morgan as Sue Mundy and asking and receiving from him a lieutenancy."

Captain Lewis O. Marshall, Company B, 30th Wisconsin Volunteer Infantry, testified that four of his men were wounded at the barn. He said that during the lull after the gunfire, he went to the Cox house and found John Cox and his brother sitting at a table. He says two rusty pistols were confiscated and the two men were taken back to the area of the barn.

Marshall said he saw the flag of truce, a hankerchief on a stick, and asked who sent it in. He was told Wilson did and that he was wanted in the barn. Marshall asked Jerome, "Is this Sue Mundy?" Jerome's reply was, "I am the man they call Sue Mundy." He testified that Jerome and Magruder turned over four guns each and denied that he had assured Jerome that he would be treated as a prisoner of war. Asked if Jerome told him how he came by the name of Sue Mundy, Marshall said Jerome's explanation was: "There was a girl by the name of Sue Mundy who had stolen a horse and who started the report that it was him."

Asked if it was not Prentice who gave him the name, Marshall replied: "I do not think he did." Marshall was also asked if Jerome did not tell him there were three people known as Sue Mundy. He denied hearing Jerome say that, but added that maybe one of his lieutenants did. There had been a report, Marshall said, that three guerrilla bands were in the neighborhood and might try to rescue Jerome. The source told Marshall, "It would go like wildfire and there were plenty who would carry it through." But it didn't happen.

One day before Jerome's court-martial began, Prentice received a letter from guerrilla Bill Marion. The *Louisville Daily Journal* story said:

A Curiosity.— We have received the following communication for publication, which we print verbatim, as a literary curiosity. We have no doubt that it is genuine. It is evident that the education of Captain Marion, as he styles himself, was sadly neglected in his younger days. He is as bad a soldier as he is a poor scholar:

March 13th, 65, Mead Co. Ky.

to General Palmer or the Commadant of the post of louisvill, Ky. sir you have Captured two of my men Clark or Sue Mondy you style him an Megruder an also lieut Medcalf Gentlemen J. W.W. Marion Capt Commanding Confederate forces in Kentucky do Solemnly declare if you do treat them as guirillas that I will Shoot or hang fifty of your men you may think get them first but you will find that I will get them. I am a Confederate soldier an my men are all Regular soldiers but you drive us to desperation [*sic*] let it be if you Murder those Brave men I haunt the city of louisville until I have revenge them look how you treated one of my men when wounded an captured in Anderson County at Bacon Bush, you Brutally shot him while lying on the ground But you failed to kill him or keep keep [*sic*] him. So far as I am Concerned I ask no quarters of you an if you don't treat those Boys as prisoners of ware I will Show none to you So if you thint there is no hell for you you [*sic*] pitch out.

W.W. MARION
Capt-CS.A

Prentice published Marion's letter March 25, 1865, well after Jerome's court-martial.

As testimony continued at the court-martial, William M. Bradley, Company A, 14th Illinois Infantry, placed Jerome two and a half miles northwest of New Castle on Feb. 1, 1865. He said Jerome, riding a dark bay, was part of a group of 15 who forced him and some others into a field and shot them. He was wounded in the chest, but said a man with whiskers shot him. Jerome was clean-shaven and Bradley said he wore "something over his shoulders all fringed off."

Private Hiram H. Meadows, Company C, 1st Wisconsin Infantry Regiment, testified that Sue Mundy and ten of his men captured him, his brother and some other soldiers Christmas Day, 1864. He says that on a forced march, his brother gave out and was ordered shot by Mundy. He said his brother died instantly. Asked where it happened, Meadows said he didn't know because his regiment was marching through a part of the state where it had never been before. He said they were kept for three days, then escaped in a storm, crossed the Cumberland River, and went to Nashville, then Louisville.

Private Alfred Hill of Company B, 23rd V.R.C. testified that he caught a train at St. Mary's and someone said that a man who fired into the train from 100 to 250 yards away was Sue Mundy. Hill said he saw "Sue" again at New Haven where citizens were being robbed. He said "Sue" and four others fired at him and his compatriots from 250 yards away. Brakeman John Briant of the Bardstown Branch Railroad said he had not seen Jerome for eight or ten months but "always knew him." He remembered that Jerome Clarke and

It wasn't his real name, but he wanted to be known as Bill Marion. Stanley Young, of Nelson County, Ky., sought to protect his family's reputation by changing his name as he operated as a Confederate guerrilla. To his guerrilla brethren he became known as "Captain Marion," yet he did not serve in the military (courtesy Miles-Peck Collection).

Maraman (spelled Merryman by the clerk) were just lying around Brunnersfield (Bloomfield?). Then he recognized Jerome during the capture of the Bardstown train, although he didn't see Jerome rob anybody. He said the train was burned and the mail rifled through.

Briant said he also saw Jerome in the fight at Bardstown against the 54th Kentucky. He said he was looking out the garret of his house.

That ended the trial, except for Jerome's prepared statement:

I will state to the court the time I entered the Army. I first entered it on the 4th of July, 1861 joining Captain Morris Company from Henderson. The company was sent to Camp Burnett and was put into the 4th Kentucky Infantry.

General Buckner sent me — detailed me, to go with a detachment to Bowling Green, Kentucky. The detachment was from our regiment. We stayed there some two months and then our company was converted into an artillery company under command of Captain Graves.

We stayed there two months longer until the fight was about to come off at [Fort] Donelson when we were moved down there. The fight lasted four days and our force surrendered. I was sent with General Buckner to Louisville and was a prisoner here 6 months. After being exchanged I was sent to Vicksburg to join the regular army in the infantry branch.

I swapped places with a man, got into Kirkpatrick's Second Kentucky Battalion. I was under General Morgan also. I was in the fight at Chattanooga and Ringold. Stayed there all winter and then went to Decatur, recruited a company and General Lyons took command of us. We moved around through Georgia, North Carolina and Virginia and made a raid on the salt works and had a fight there.

After that, General Morgan got orders to go into Kentucky. We had [our] first fight at Mount Sterling, next at Lexington. Went on through, reached Cynthiana had a fight and captured Hobson. General Burbridge came next morning about daylight and attacked us and by a charge of cavalry scattered and whipped us.

I was wounded there in the hand. I joined Captain Alexander's company of 20 or 30 men to go south. We were camped near the Lebanon Railroad and Big Springs, some 5 or 6 miles distant from the road and met a scout from Elizabethtown, had a fight and Alexander was shot through the head and we were scattered.

This rare picture of Jerome Clarke was in the possession of his great-nephew, the late Marcellus Jerome "Jerry" Clarke, of Anchorage, Ky., a Louisville suburb. Jerry Clarke refused to believe, in an interview with author Thomas Shelby Watson, that his kinsman and namesake committed the unlawful acts attributed to him in the *Louisville Daily Journal* and other newspapers. This photograph was the basis for an oil painting of Jerome Clarke that "Jerry" Clarke willed to the University of Kentucky (courtesy Sally Ridley).

We were looking for a camp. One fellow said Nelson County would be a good place so we went there and threw off our Confederate uniforms and put on citizens clothes. I stayed at a house there two or three weeks and one day I went to [a] meeting and heard some ladies say there was one of Morgan's men, a Rebel solder. The man of the house where I stayed told me that everybody charged me with being a Rebel soldier. I asked him what I had better do.

He said he did not know, that Magruder with a scout of 8 or 10 men was near there passing through and I better go with them. I went with them and the first place I was ever at was on the Lebanon Railroad. Captured the train and paroled the soldiers and I think burnt the train.

I met Sam Beard at Pound Gap and went with him; got into a fight [and] Beard was killed. I came back to Nelson County again and knocked around there for several months. I got orders through Captain Jones from Colonel Breckinridge to report to Paris, Tennessee. Saw Captain Jones and he told us to go on to Paris. Brandenburg is where Medkiff got with us. When we got down below we were bushwhacked and Magruder was wounded. He asked me to bring him back to Meade County and stay until he got well. I did so and there is where I was captured.

Jerome asked to call witnesses from Camp Chase and other points to prove he was a Confederate soldier. The court was cleared and the tribunal huddled.

They replied a short time later "after mature deliberation" that such evidence would not be material because the accused was charged with certain crimes that would cause even a detached federal soldier to be punished. They said that only evidence to prove he did not act as a guerrilla while being detached would save him, but the case was closed.

Crowds had gathered outside Coyl's headquarters to get a glimpse of Sue Mundy when he was returned to prison.

CHAPTER 32

"I Do Truly, Fondly and Forever Love You"

The Rev. Talbott of St. John's visited Jerome March 15, 1865, and found that he was unaware the execution was to be that afternoon and that he was to be hanged rather than shot.

Jerome prayed with Talbott, seeking forgiveness for his sins, and was baptized. Four letters were dictated by Jerome. One went to his great-aunt and foster mother Mary Ann Brents Tibbs at Crow's Pond in McLean County. A second was sent to a sister, either Mary Susan Elizabeth Barker in Logan County or Emily Catherine Clarke Ricks in Simpson County.

A third letter was sent to a cousin, probably Charles Benjamin Bradshaw, son of William Bradshaw and Nancy Clarke Bradshaw. The fourth letter went to Jerome's sweetheart, Mary Porter "Mollie" Thomas of Chaplin, who married William H. Russell Feb. 18, 1874. With each letter, Jerome included a lock of his hair.

The letter to Mollie Thomas said:

> My Dear Mollie: I have to inform you of the sad fate which awaits your true friend. I am to suffer death this afternoon at four o'clock. I send you from my chains a message of true love, and as I stand on the brink of the grave I tell you I do truly, fondly and forever love you.
>
> I am ever truly yours.
>
> M. Jerome Clarke.

The execution of Jerome Clarke was witnessed by *Courier-Journal* writer Young E. Allison when he was a lad of 12. He recounted it Feb. 6,

1887, in the Louisville newspaper that was the result of George Prentice's *The Louisville Journal* merging with the *Louisville Courier.*

At a quarter after three that fateful Wednesday afternoon, Allison wrote in the *Courier-Journal,* four companies of troops marched into the street and forming a square, stood resting on their guns. "In the street to the west of the soldiers, the Post band then marched and waited with their horns in their hands."

Allison's account continued:

Soon an open carriage drove into the square, up to the sidewalk, and then, the doors of the prison opening, Sue Mundy came out, preceded by several soldiers. Dr. Talbott accompanied the prisoner and held his arm. About his ankles were irons that impeded his movements somewhat, but his arms were at liberty.

He was assisted into the carriage, and took his seat facing the horses. In his hand he carried a fine white cambric hankerchief [*sic*], and, putting this to his eyes, he leaned his head against the side of the carriage.

At this moment an express wagon passed rapidly by, going in the direction of the scaffold. In the wagon was a rough pine coffin. It was the home into which Sue Mundy was preparing to move. Doctor Talbott sat beside him in the carriage; the driver mounted in his seat; there was a hush upon the crowd (estimated at 10,000 to 12,000). Suddenly the snap of a military order was heard, the muffled roll of the drum rang out, and twenty brass instruments united in the crashing dissonance of the first chords of the Dead March.

Simultaniously [*sic*], the military body moved, the horses in the carriage pranced gayly [*sic*] for a moment, and then the march to the scaffold began. Passing out of the streets into the common, the great crowd spread out on either side of the military nucleus like the huge, lazy wings attached to a floating bird. (The scaffold was on a block bounded by Broadway, Magazine, 17th and 18th· a fairground referred to as "the common.") From far across the plain the patient crowd about the scaffold saw the black mass moving, heard the scream of the brass in the Dead March, and began to seethe and boil in agony of impatience and expectation. Under the platform the rough pine coffin had been deposited, waiting for a tenant.

The condemned man in the carriage did not raise his head. His face was buried in his handkerchief, and Doctor Talbott talked to him earnestly. When the carriage reached the foot of the scaffold, it was halted, while the officer commanding disposed his troops about the instrument and drove back the crowd to a respectful distance. Not even then did the prisoner look up, and those in that immense throng speculated upon the event. But there was no sign of weeping.

At last all things were in readiness, and then Sue Mundy, putting up his handkerchief, raised his face, upon which there was no sign of tears or of fear, but one of serious contemplation. His lips were constantly moving as if in prayer. He rose, walked up the steps, and took his place on the trap door, while the guards tied his limbs and arms.

What he said nobody could hear, but one of those who stood near the platform said his lips continually formed the words; "Lord, have mercy upon my poor soul." His physical beauty was apparent to all the crowd. He was dressed in a dark-blue cavalry jacket, down the front of which was a single row of brass buttons, bearing the Kentucky coat of arms; dark cassimere [sic] trousers, and a pair of boots cut down to fit like shoes. His hands and feet were beautifully small, and the symmetry and grace of his person were unusual. Upon the long curls sat the black velvet cap, which was then removed and flung under the platform.

The post commander read the charges and the order of death, and asked if the condemned had anything to say. Sue Mundy said a few words in low tones to Dr. Talbott, who repeated them aloud. It was the same plea he had made in person, that he was a regular soldier and not guilty of the murders charged to him. He added that he hated no one, but loved everybody, and hoped to go to heaven. Then Talbott repeated Jerome's last words: "I believe in and die for the Confederate cause."[1]

A white cap was pulled over Jerome's head and at the count of three the supporting post of the trap door was knocked away. The fall did not appear to break his neck and he fought the noose furiously, some said so hard they thought he would break his bonds and escape. But such was not to be. Marcellus Jerome Clarke was dead at the age of 20 and Sue Mundy died with him.[2]

There was a fight involving two men who sought to retrieve the cap from beneath the platform and both were arrested. They were fined in City Court the next day and the cap became the property of the provost marshal. Jerome's jacket was ripped open by some in the crowd as rumors flew that there was money sewn in the lining. The would-be thieves found no money. Meanwhile, in the middle of Broadway, a large bull appeared and was pawing the Earth. Whether an escapee from the stockyards or nay, those in the dispersing crowd were only interested in avoiding injury. As was the case in those days, several citizens were armed; they opened fire, killing the bull.

Others in the crowd feared Sue Mundy's gang had arrived to exact revenge and a near riot ensued. Soldiers came running with fixed bayonets from the Tenth and Broadway prison. With no more shots fired, the crowd calmed and order was restored.

CHAPTER 33

The Eagle's Claws Tighten

It was March 22, 1865, and Rebecca Wootton was visiting her sister, Lis Stallard. The Pitts and Lis Stallard residence was just north of Powell Run off the Fairfield-High Grove Road in Spencer County.

She wrote in her diary that Bill Marion, Sam Berry and Tom Henry stopped by and since she and her sister had already eaten dinner, they prepared a meal for the guerrillas. "They behaved very politely," she added, and well they should have. Rebecca's husband treated Berry when he was severely wounded in the left shoulder Jan. 16, 1865, in Bardstown.[1]

The next day, back home in the north Nelson County village of Fairfield, she noted that the bridges over the Rolling Fork River were burned, and on March 26, 1865, Rebecca wrote:

"Three squads of home guards come through town at eleven o'clock and after they pass, two guerrillas come below town and fire on them and return with about 40 pursuing them and they press horses, everything nearly, as they go."

It rained hard in Fairfield March 30, 1865, as Rebecca entered in her diary:

The guerrillas hang a Lieutenant Hackett of [a] home guard company in retaliation for Isaac Ludwick who was shot by them on the 28th of January. The young man was hung in J.C. Duncan's woods near the town of Bloomfield. They followed on and made a charge on 40 and killed three of their number. One guerrilla was wounded in the hand.

Warren Hackett was a member of Captain Edwin Terrell's decoy guerrillas. Hackett wrote a letter to Joshua Hansbrough in Clay Village, Shelby

County, dated March 29, 1865, which explained exactly what was happening:

> I am now in the hands of the guerrillas. I am to be hung in a few minutes. I am at the farm of James Duncan, a few miles east of Bloomfield. Dear Joshua, I want you to pay the bearer of this note and my body for taking care of it. He will bring it to you. I want you to take it to Uncle Jack Gales, have it put away. He will make a bill of expenses. Give my love to all and to yourself.[2]

Hackett had also been accused of gunning down Wesley Cook of Shelby County as Cook stood at his front door. Wesley Cook's son, Martin, had been associating with guerrillas and someone had snitched on what he thought was a secret plan by Martin to stop and visit his home.[3]

In her diary, Rebecca Wootton wrote: "The country is completely submerged in trouble on account of the present state of affairs. We have no assurance of anything that we own or have. It seems as if we were in the eagles' claws."

On March 31, 1865, Rebecca observed that the guerrillas came riding through Fairfield and one was on her sister's riding mare "Rosa." Sometimes Rebecca wrote about mundane subjects, perhaps to keep her mind off the constant threat of violence. April 1, 1865, found the doctor's wife making soap and complaining about getting smoke in her eyes during the process and that it made her throat so sore she couldn't sleep.

The next day was bright and beautiful in the north Nelson County town. "We'd hoped to have a still and quiet day, but not so," Rebecca wrote. "At 10 o'clock we have (Union) Colonel (Harvey M.) Buckley's and Major Russell's men in. They do no harm, only horse flesh they will have. They are soon gone and in the evening, Terrell's men come in throwing rocks, bursting doors, demanding watches and eatables. They are called State Troops. They said they had killed a man by the name of Paris, a Confederate soldier." Joseph T. Paris was home on furlough from the Rebel army and was riding with his sweetheart to Waterford Baptist Church in Spencer County when they approached Terrell and his men. The young woman said they must turn around and return to her home. But they continued on and Paris glanced back and saw that one of them was signaling him to approach. He attempted to reassure her, saying: "They will not molest me." With tears in his eyes, Paris then admitted to his sweetheart, "I am lost." One of the federal guerrillas rode up and knocked Paris off his horse. As his companion watched in horror, Paris was taken to a site near the road and hanged.[4]

Perhaps Rebecca's most memorable diary entry was much earlier in the year. It was May 21, 1865. Terrell and his men arrived in Fairfield and stayed in the neighborhood that night. Rebecca wrote: "The next morning they took my husband (Dr. Wootton) and put a rope around his neck and dragged him around by the neck awhile and then they took my good horse and rode him off so he was not any account to them nor me." She didn't say how the doctor was doing, but he survived the incident.

A black woman identified as "Laura" of Nelson County was allegedly a rape victim of Berry on April 8, 1865. In testimony given after the war, Laura said she lived with Ben Adams the year before and Leck Adams the year before that. She said she had seen Berry six months earlier at Ben Adams' place. "He forced me to unlock a trunk and get money out of it. He made me go upstairs and after he got upstairs he told me what he wanted to do to me. He was going to ravish me. I cried and begged him not, but he (said he) would do it. He had his pistol drawn on me all the time," she testified.

"He was a tall man, very saw-boned and had his right arm off," she said. She didn't know three other men who accompanied him, but only Berry was accused of the rape. Her husband was in the army and she was free, the witness said. Berry held his pistol in his left hand, she testified later. Her child was upstairs and she was afraid to come down when the guerrillas arrived. She was called down by them, then forced to go back up. The defense questioned how Berry could raise her clothes and ravash her while holding a pistol in his only hand.

"Well, he did it," she said. Berry gave her a quarter for her trouble and she kept it, she added.[5]

CHAPTER 34

Lee Surrenders, Guerrillas Face Quandary

It was a date to remember — April 9, 1865. The American Civil War, for all practical purposes, ended as Brigadier General Robert E. Lee surrendered his Army of Northern Virginia to Grant at Appomattox Court House, Virginia.

Those who had chosen not to return to their ranks were left without a true cause for which to fight and the U.S. Army could apply more resources in the effort to wipe them out. That was evident in Fairfield April 12, 1865. Rebecca Wootton wrote in her diary she saw "a good many soldiers come out towards my house. They were called Quantrill's and Marion's men. They came to Fairfield and then went out the Springfield road. The 59th Ky. federal came in a few minutes in pursuit of them."

The two forces clashed near Bloomfield the evening of April 13, 1865. Major Cyrus J. Wilson, the man who captured Jerome Clarke, reported he had one man killed and three wounded. He also reported killing two guerrillas and wounding three.[1]

On April 14, 1865, President Abraham Lincoln was assassinated and the telegraph lines swiftly carried the news to all parts of the country. By the next day, Quantrill, his men and other guerrillas were celebrating. On March 27, 1898, Jim Davis, 33, the son of the 1865 Spencer County Judge Jonathan Davis (not Jim Davis the guerrilla), recalled many facts about Quantrill in the *Lexington Morning Herald*. He said that Quantrill and Berry prevented Marion from shooting Judge Davis one day in early 1865. Marion had ordered Davis to burn the Spencer County Courthouse within three days or be killed. Marion met Davis on the road and was told by the judge that he had taken an oath to protect the records and property of the citizens and could not burn the courthouse.

Quantrill and Berry would not allow Marion to shoot the judge and from that time, the judge's house, in the area that would later become known as "Wakefield," was always open to those two guerrillas. Jim Davis said in the *Lexington Morning Herald*:

> The last time he [Quantrill] came was on the 15th day of April, 1865. His band had dwindled down to about 25 or 30 men, as he had numerous fights with the federal cavalry, who were after him from time to time.
>
> He and his men were all under the influence of liquor and behaved in a most boisterous manner than I ever saw them. My wife (Mary Jane) and several other ladies were on the porch and Quantrill, taking off his hat, bowed to them and said: "Excuse us ladies, we are a little in our cups today. The grand-daddy of all the greenbacks, Abraham Lincoln, was shot in a theatre at Washington last night."
>
> In a short while they called for glasses and drank toddies. One-Arm Sam Berry, raising his glass of toddy high above his head, pronounced the following toast: "Here's to the death of Abraham Lincoln, hoping that his bones may serve in hell as a gridiron to fry Yankee soldiers on."
>
> The gruesome toast unnerved the ladies and my wife exclaimed, "Oh Captain Berry, how can you utter such remarks?" He smiled sardonically and told her that he meant every word of it.[2]

Despite being in a good humor after Lincoln's death, the guerrillas dared not put their guard down for long. Reports from the *Official Records* show after Lee's surrender, guerrilla catching became a major priority for the federal army.

The man with the scraggly beard who wanted to kill Judge Davis became a quarry of the hunt, as this dispatch explains:

> Hdqrs. First Division, Department of Kentucky,
> Lexington, Ky., April 17, 1865

> I have the honor to report that my scouts and detachments of mounted men in every section of my division are doing good work in breaking up guerrilla bands. Troops beyond Mount Sterling captured six guerrillas on yesterday. On Friday last when at Lebanon, I directed Captain [George W.] Penn to move with his company of mounted State Guards, and if possible intercept Marion, the noted guerrilla. One company, Fifty-third Kentucky, has been ordered to move from Camp Nelson through Bloomfield and Mackville, for the purpose of driving Marion toward New Haven. This plan worked as I

expected, and this morning I have the gratifying intelligence that Captain Penn's men killed Marion on yesterday. [Marion was killed at the still-house in Manton, a Marion County community].

My mounted force is so arranged at this time that it will result in the killing and capturing of every guerrilla in the division or compel them to surrender.

Mose Webster's men will, I think, come in and give themselves up in compliance with an arrangement entered into between my adjutant, Captain J.S. Butler, and Mose Webster. I will endeavor in a few days to have mounted force in the counties of Monroe, Metcalf, and Barren.

> Very respectfully,
> E.H. HOBSON,
> Brigadier-General, Commanding.

Ed Terrell tried to prove to the military that he and his men were earning their pay. A report of Lieutenant Colonel John G. Rogers, 54th Kentucky Infantry, offered a clear example of Ed's egocentricity:

> Lebanon, Ky., April 17, 1865.

Marion, the guerrilla, was killed yesterday by Captain Penn's company of Kentucky State troops. Captain Terrill [sic] is on his way to Louisville with the body and may claim the honor. He took the body while [Captain George W.] Penn and his men were pursuing the balance of the guerrillas.

He [Terrell] had only two men in the fight and they had pistols only. Marion was killed by a carbine cartridge. I send this in justice to Captain Penn. Particulars by mail.

> Jno. G. Rogers,
> Lieutenant-Colonel, Commanding Post.

Major-General Palmer,
Headquarters, Louisville.

Hobson was right, because Grant County–born Moses Webster and his men called it quits. Bantering followed over whether Webster, a 30-year-old lawyer and Confederate captain, was bad enough to be tried in Louisville as a guerrilla. Captain J.S. Butler said, "the case does not require it." Judge Advocate Coyle differed, saying Webster was a guerrilla and murderer. Webster had good lawyers and was freed on bond. He died in the Kentucky Confederate Home at Pewee Valley at the age of 93.

CHAPTER 35

"Here They Come!
Here They Come!"

On April 18, 1865, Rebecca Wootton observed 16 of Quantrill's men passing through Fairfield, "getting out of reach of Negro troops and Yankees in Bloomfield." She saw federal troops passing through April 19, 1865, headed for Bardstown, and on the 22nd, wrote in her diary that home guardsmen were en route to Bloomfield.

April 29, 1865, Rebel soldiers begin to arrive in the Bloomfield area from the war, to surrender to federal authorities and return to their homes. There were 72 men who fought for the South from Bloomfield and several gave their lives.[1]

On the morning of May 10, 1865, storm clouds began to spread over Kentucky. Quantrill had been at John Bedford Russell's house on Ashes Creek in Spencer County at the Spencer-Nelson County line. While there, Russell's daughter, Betty, 18, presented Quantrill with a beautiful saddlebred horse for his use.[2]

McClaskey family tradition says Quantrill and his men rode out that Wednesday morning and stopped at the home of Newell McClaskey, then proceeded northward in the direction of Taylorsville. The horsemen turned in at the gate of farmer James Heady Wakefield where a Negro blacksmith, Almstead Jacobs, operated a shop. Jacobs said in later months that he had counted 21 riders in Quantrill's band as they passed by. Wakefield reported Quantrill had 15 men with him that day, and that was nearly the same total heard most often in local recollections by old-timers.[3]

In his *Noted Guerrillas, or the Warfare of the Border*, John Newman

Edwards had a partial list of the men with Quantrill. He listed: John Ross, Allen Palmer,[4] William Hulse, Lee McMurtry, brothers Bud and Donnie Pence, Dick Glasscock, Clark Hockensmith, Isaac Hall and David Hylton (sometimes seen as Helton).[5] A Bloomfield-area guerrilla, Eliphilet "Babe" Hunter, was there, according to his son, Phil Hunter.

Also there were Payne Jones and Robert Hall, but Donnie Pence, recently wounded, may not have been present. There also may have been a few other Kentucky guerrillas who went with Quantrill to the Wakefield farm, but evidence is lacking. Counting Quantrill, the total was most likely 13.

It had been raining and as Quantrill and his men approached Wakefield's barn, the rain became a deluge.[6] The horsemen, dripping wet, dismounted and took cover under the barn's sheds that projected out 15 feet on three sides of the structure. Hunter, 25, spoke with Quantrill just before the guerrilla chief climbed into the mow with the intention of taking a nap. Quantrill had recently told his followers he knew the South was losing the war and wanted to get the men to Virginia so they could surrender with Brig. Gen. Robert E. Lee and be paroled.

The son of Kentucky-born parents, Lee B. McMurtry took part in the Lawrence, Kansas, massacre as a member of Quantrill's guerrillas and was in the bloody Fayette and Centralia, Missouri, battles. McMurtry, wounded at Fayette, was rescued by Jesse James and Dick Kenney. After the Civil War, McMurtry became a successful cattleman in Wichita Falls, Texas. He died at the age of 68 (courtesy Miles-Peck Collection).

That goal having been lost, he was now going to ask them to follow him to Mexico where he would start a revolution. Quantrill told Hunter he had worked out a plan in which his men would enter the country two at a time, then get together again once across the border. He said efforts would then be made to raise a large force from the people.[7]

Others also talked in the barn, sampling whisky supplied by Wakefield, and a few were involved in a sham battle, using corncobs as weapons. Terrell and his decoy guerrillas arrived at the blacksmith shop where Terrell spotted horse tracks in the mud, leading up the steep farm road to Wakefield's place. It may have taken only a quizzical glance from Terrell to get a response from the blacksmith, who later told John Langford of Terrell's force he counted 21 in Quantrill's band. It was believed Terrell had 30 men with him,[8] although one of his decoys said in 1936 that there were 19 and that Quantrill had the same number of guerrillas. The claim had not been heard before.[9]

Langford said 32 years after the war in a letter to Editor William W. Scott of the *Iron Valley Reporter* in Canal Dover, Ohio, that Terrell had 28 men in the fight. If Jacobs sought to help the Union by pointing the way for the decoy guerrillas to find Quantrill and his followers, the act was fraught with symbolism because Jacobs was a black man.

Terrell directed his men up a slope where they followed a farm road toward the west that led them straight to the barn lot. They were drawing their revolvers and unslinging their carbines when Dick Glasscock, who had been standing under the protruding barn shed talking to farmer Wakefield, spotted them coming.

"Here they come!" he shouted once and then again.

Palmer was to say later he could hear the voice of Terrell over all the noise, letting go with a Rebel yell he'd learned when he was on the Confederate side. Spencer County resident Elmer Stevens said his uncle Ben Stevens was with Terrell's scouts and heard someone, apparently in the barn, blowing a whistle. At the first indication of trouble, one of Quantrill's men grabbed a feed basket, raced from the barn into an adjacent field and posed as an innocent farmer calling the hogs. When the attackers ignored him, he fled.[10]

There was a scurry for horses as bullets began crashing into the barn. The gift horse became wild and Quantrill could not get mounted. Several guerrillas jumped their horses over a gate in the southwest corner of the barn lot. Three ran a hundred yards southeast to a pond, leaped in and allowed only their noses above water to grab breaths of air until they found an opportune time to run again.[11]

Dick Glasscock and Clark Hockensmith were the last two on horseback and headed toward a grove of sugar maples, Quantrill following on foot. He yelled to them and waited, firing to check the pursuit. Quantrill ran alongside Glasscock, trying to mount, but Glasscock's mare was shot in the hip. Quantrill then tried unsuccessfully to mount behind Hockensmith. Quantrill, running toward a horse trail that could have been an escape route, was shot in the back. John Langford's bullet glanced off the right shoulder blade and ranged down, lodging in the right groin and leaving Quantrill paralyzed below the hips.[12]

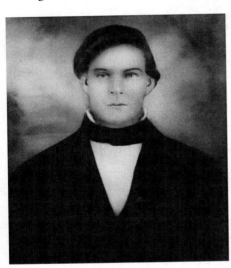

A member of Captain Edwin Terrell's federal decoy guerrillas, Horace W. Allen enrolled in the Union army August 5, 1861, and was mustered on September 9 into Company A, Second Kentucky Volunteer Cavalry. The son of Samuel and Melissa (Larue) Allen of Larue County, Ky., was born November 9, 1834. The 5-foot-11, light-haired, blue-eyed Allen was wounded in the Battle of Perryville. He was discharged in 1864 at the end of his three-year term, but soon joined Terrell's guerrilla-hunting unit (photograph courtesy Roxanne Pleva and Rex Allen).

Terrell rode up and fired as Quantrill lay on his left side, the bullet ripping off the trigger finger of the guerrilla chief's right hand. Both Hockensmith and Glasscock were killed as they continued trying to flee the hail of lead.

In a published quote years after the incident, Sylvester Cheatham of Terrell's command said it was he who shot Quantrill. Max Allen, the grandson of Horace Allen, another of Terrell's decoys, insisted that Connelley and other authors were wrong. He said Horace Allen inflicted Quantrill's mortal wound.[13]

Quantrill was taken to the Wakefield house, where he claimed to be Captain Clarke of the Fourth Missouri Cavalry, but Terrell doubted that to be the case. Terrell's men began ransacking Wakefield's house until the farmer gave Terrell $20 and Terrell's Shelby County colleague Joe Taylor $10 to stop. The deal was sweetened with a quantity of whisky for each.[14]

Quantrill gave Terrell his gold

watch and $500 with a promise of another $500 his men would raise if he would grant a parole and let him die at Wakefield's. Terrell took the money and watch and wrote a worthless parole.[15] Frank James, John Ross, William Hulse and Allen Palmer sneaked into the Wakefield house that night, but could not persuade Quantrill to allow himself to be rescued. James had been visiting the Sayers family at Deatsville and other members of the band were also absent when Terrell attacked. Quantrill told his would-be rescuers he was going to die and sent word to Henry Porter of his band to seek paroles for the men.

Two days after he was shot, Quantrill found himself being readied for a trip to Louisville as Terrell arrived with a Conestoga wagon, pulled by two mules. A blanket that James had obtained from the Wakefields was spread over the guerrilla captain. Quantrill was suffering greatly from the wound after 21 miles of travel, and the caravan spent the night in Jeffersontown, where, at Quantrill's request, Dr. Samuel N. Marshall came to examine him and found

John Ross was one of Quantrill's more dedicated men and was one of those who escaped uninjured from the skirmish at James Wakefield's farm. He was also among a small group who sneaked into Wakefield's house and sought to rescue the wounded Quantrill. Harriett Ross, the guerrilla's mother, cared for Quantrill until his death (courtesy of the Miles-Peck Collection).

his back was broken. Dr. William Wallace Senteny also took a look at Quantrill's wound. Quantrill told Marshall he remembered seeing him another time and Marshall recalled the visit as well. Marshall said he had treated Quantrill in Shelby County, but had recently moved to Jeffersontown. "So have I," Quantrill was quoted by the doctor's wife as telling him.[16] The next morning, the nine-mile trip to the military prison was completed.

Quantrill died at the U.S. Military Prison Hospital in Louisville, 27 days after he was shot. The Sisters of Charity had cared for Quantrill after military doctors stopped treating him. Harriet Ross, the mother of guerrilla John Ross, stayed with Quantrill until his death, June 6, 1865, at 4 P.M.[17]

The sisters obtained a wooden coffin and Quantrill was buried in St. John's Cemetery on Louisville's northwest side. His mother, Caroline Quantrill, had his grave opened 22 years later, and in doing so, opened a Pandora's box. Through various twists of fate, Quantrill traveled in death nearly as much as he did in life. A boyhood friend of Quantrill, *Iron Valley Reporter* Editor William Scott, accompanied Caroline Quantrill to Louisville in order to help her recover her son's body. After hiring a man to help dig, Scott removed Quantrill's skull, a lock of hair and several bones, placing them in a zinc-lined box. The skull and bones found in the Louisville grave made their way to Scott's newspaper office, then to author William Elsey Connelley, then to the Kansas State Historical Society, which found some of them belonged to a 17-year-old boy and had fallen into Quantrill's Louisville grave from an adjacent burial.[18] Quantrill's bones, the left and right tibia (shin), right humerus (upper arm), a right radius and left ulna, both lower arm bones, plus the lock of hair, made it to a grave in Higginsville, Missouri, in 1992. A few years later, an effort was made at Kent State University to reconstruct a Quantrill face, based on his skull, but the outcome bore little resemblance to him.[19] Quantrill's skull was supposed to be reburied in a Dover, Ohio, family plot along with the recovered bones, but parts of Quantrill's ribs and backbone had crumbled and with other unrecoverable parts, would remain in Louisville forever, with only his skull finding the long way home.

Scott's son and other young men decided to use the skull in connection with a high school fraternity initiation in Dover. The boys would place their right hands on it and swear allegiance. There were light bulbs mounted in the eye sockets to make the skull look more foreboding. The Dover Historical Society tracked down the skull and displayed it for several years at the J.E. Reeves Historical Home and Museum in Dover. Historian Sam Ream let the skull sit on his mantle when a debate arose over what should be done with it. Finally, Oct. 30, 1992, the skull was placed in a baby coffin and buried in the Quantrill family plot in Dover.

Kate (King) and Quantrill never saw each other again after she was left in St. Louis, except perhaps when Quantrill was on his deathbed. There are conflicting reports over whether she may have been there. Kate was married two more times after Quantrill's death, to men with the surnames Woods and Head. She died Jan. 9, 1930, and was buried in the Maple Hill Cemetery in Kansas City, Kansas. Quantrill's remains are in Kentucky, Kansas, and his native Ohio.

CHAPTER 36

Terrell Kills the Blacksmith

Terrell continued his unceasing hunt for guerrillas, for to do otherwise would cut off his federal Army check and lessen his chances of getting to pillage the homes of Rebel sympathizers. Terrell was paid $50 a month as "chief of scouts," while his second in command, John Thompson, was paid $35 and Horace Allen got $30. His other 28 men in May 1865 received $20 each, according to a copy of the decoy guerrillas' payroll.

On May 25, 1865, Terrell and his decoys captured Union County native Tom Henry in Bloomfield and they were headed to Louisville with him when they stopped in Taylorsville. Some of Terrell's men needed to get their horses shod.

John Weathers of Terrell's band rode up to blacksmith Innis Wootton's shop on the west end of Main Street near Brashears Creek. "Hand me a drink of water," he demanded of the blacksmith. "There is the well, John, as near to you as it is to me. Help yourself to it," Wootton replied. "God damn you, if you don't get me some water, I will shoot the piss out of you," Weathers retorted, drawing a pistol.

Wootton also refused to shoe Weathers' horse, but said there was a Negro in the shop who could shoe him if he wanted to. Terrell came riding down the street and Wootton's married daughter, Louisa, begged him to make Weathers put up his pistol, and Weathers holstered the firearm. Wootton walked out in the street to talk to Terrell and Weathers followed with his version of what happened. Wootton called Weathers a "damned liar" and Weathers struck the 59-year-old muscled blacksmith. They clutched and began scuffling. Another of Terrell's men came forward to part them but Terrell said, "Let them fight it out."

Wootton then pushed Weathers into a mud hole, grabbed a rock and began beating him. Terrell drew a revolver and Wootton's daughter held up her hands in a supplicating manner screaming, "Don't! Don't, Captain Terrell! Don't shoot my father!" She grabbed Terrell's pistol, but Terrell jerked away and fired.[1] The ball entered under and near Wootton's left shoulder blade and came out the right breast. Wootton fell face down, tried to raise himself, but collapsed. He was carried to the porch of his house but died soon after.[2] Terrell and his prisoner, Tom Henry, continued their journey to Louisville.

On the evening of the fifth of June, 1865, Rebecca Wootton of Fairfield, the sister-in-law of Innis Wootton, had guests for dinner. Confederate veteran John Purdy of Bloomfield arrived with Sam Berry and Dick Mitchell. It was the last time she would cook for guerrillas. Berry and Mitchell were looking for a way to preserve their lives without having to flee the state. Berry sent word to Major Cyrus Wilson through a Taylorsville man, Tom Kirk, that he and Mitchell wanted a meeting with him. Meanwhile, Henry Porter traveled to Louisville and met with Palmer, asking that he and the rest of Quantrill's men be allowed to return to Missouri unmolested.

Palmer told Porter the guerrillas must surrender for trial and that if his terms were not satisfactory, he would not detain them, but give them 24 hours of grace to return to the place "from whence they came." Palmer added that if that should be the case, he would keep up the war on them.

An incident that occurred On April 25, 1865, appeared to make it impossible for the guerrillas to ever receive paroles. Mary A. (Hibbs) Clark, a 31-year-old resident of the New Haven community in Nelson County, was riding an unfrequented road to a neighboring town in quest of medicine for an ailing neighbor. She was overtaken by guerrillas John Brothers and William A. "Texas" Hoskins and apparently taken back to her house before she was raped.[3] Mary Clark did not know Brothers or "Texas." The federals rounded up two suspects, Privates Elijah Ford and George A. Martin of Company G, 8th Kentucky Cavalry, but she said they were not the ones responsible for the attack.[4] Brothers and Texas immediately started a tale that Quantrill's men were responsible for the crime against Mary Clark. When the tale reached Palmer, he was incensed and issued Special Order No. 64 in which he said no guerrilla or Rebel soldier in Nelson County or who had been within the county in the past ten days would be allowed to surrender himself, other than for trial, until the perpetrators of the rape were arrested. "They are guerrillas and are known to the people of that county," Palmer said in the special order, and offered a reward of $500 for either of the men, dead or alive.

The special order would make it impossible for Quantrill's men to receive paroles unless they were able to capture the guilty men and turn them in to Palmer. Brothers and Texas had ridden with Berry, but were not Quantrill's men. Frank James and William Hulse, hearing that Missourians were being blamed, were in the saddle and searching for the guilty parties before Palmer heard of the crime.[5]

Edwards offered the following description and Palmer trusted its authenticity enough to print it word-for-word in his own book. James and Hulse tracked Brothers to a house, looked inside and saw three men at a table having dinner. They burst in and James announced: "'Keep your seats, all of you; keep your hands up; keep your eyes to the front.' Two of the three sat stone still, scarcely breathing, hardly lifting or letting fall an eyelid," Edwards wrote. "Brothers, desperate even in extremity such as this, snatched swiftly for his pistol. Frank James blew his brains out across the table."

Edwards also, but erroneously, said Quantrill's men killed Texas. Berry, upon hearing of James killing Brothers, went to the Sayers house at Deatsville with others and shouted at the front gate for James to come out. Finetta Sayers told Berry that James was not there and Berry left, which probably saved Berry's life. James was upstairs, fully armed and watching from a window, according to Sayers family tradition.

An initial Berry-Mitchell-Wilson meeting was held at the two-story log residence of Thomas E. Green across the Taylorsville-Bloomfield Turnpike from the Wakefield farm where Quantrill had been shot and captured.[6] Later, and a short distance away at Squire Heady's, another meeting was held, and finally, at Henry Russell's, Berry and Mitchell showed up with Texas in tow and handed him over to Major Cyrus J. Wilson.[7] Berry obtained a parole from Wilson June 2, 1865, but Mitchell didn't trust the federals and left the state, eventually becoming a lawman in Yazoo, Miss., where he was mortally wounded during a disturbance in the street.

The parole was worthless and Berry was tried by a court-martial in Louisville Sept. 13, 1865, which was just what he had sought to avoid, saying he'd rather have "gone to hell." At Berry's trial, Wilson was asked if he signed the parole under direct authority of General Palmer. "Well, I didn't know whether I did or not," Wilson said. "It was the first parole I had given, the first of the kind."[8] Wilson said he could not have caught Texas otherwise. Wilson also paroled guerrilla Sol Thompson and nine of his men, saying he was afraid they would scatter if he waited for a courier to ask Palmer's permission to set them free.

Epilogue

Dressing Up

Despite stories in publications over the years that Jerome Clarke dressed as a woman for purposes of spying, there was always something questionable or lacking about their credibility. That something was reliable attribution.

One story is very interesting, but apparently untrue as were others. Dr. C.H. Buck, a Dayton, Ohio, dentist and Clarke family descendant, wrote a letter to a relative in Kansas City, Mo., in 1955 about Jerome Clarke.

The letter said:

> Back about 1919 I met Hamilton Busby [*sic*], former editor of the Louisville Courier Journal in Louisville, Ky. At that time Mr. Busby related a very interesting story about "Sue Mundy."
>
> He recalled that, one Sunday morning during the Civil War he looked up from his desk into the muzzle of a Navy six pistol [*sic*] pointed at him. Louisville was occupied by Union forces at that time but in some manner Sue Mundy had slipped thru the lines and into Mr. Busby's office. He was disguised as a woman and informed Mr. Busby that unless he stopped writing derogatory things about him and his men and their exploits Mr. Busby would be very likely "...to come up missing."

Buck said that having delivered his ultimatum, "he departed and was captured a few days later by Union forces."

Jerome Clarke had been heading southwest with a group including Magruder, Henry Metcalf, Jim Jones and Henry Porter since Feb. 24, 1865, following along the south side of the Ohio River until the March 3,

1865 skirmish. Then he hid out with Henry Metcalf and the wounded Henry Magruder until they were captured Sunday, March 12, 1865. It isn't known why the story, as allegedly related by Busby, was not published decades earlier. The *Courier-Journal* was formed in 1868, three years after Jerome's death and the end of the Civil War.

Nettie Oliver of the Filson Historical Society in Louisville said, after checking the society's biographical index that covers hundreds of volumes of biographical materials relating to Louisvillians and Kentuckians, "No Hamilton Busby was listed." Also, from 1919 through the 1920s, the Louisville city directories show no Hamilton Busby, she said.

A story in a national magazine in 1965 was titled "The Soldier With Two Sexes," and except for excerpts from the glowing descriptions of the fictitious "Sue Mundy" as painted by John Newman Edwards and some quotes from the Rebellion Records, nothing is attributed. The writer mistakenly identifies Bloomfield as "Bloomsburg," and confuses Jerome with Quantrill when the latter had to flee from a skirmish near Harrodsburg through an accumulation of snow.

A March 1997 article in a monthly publication said, "When Mundy joined Magruder, he donned the guise of a woman for the first time, but he continued to dress in this way until his death." When Jerome Clarke began riding with Magruder, Sue Mundy had not yet been created and there were no stories, published or otherwise, that Clarke had dressed in women's clothing.

There is no lack of Sue Mundy Historical Highway markers in Kentucky, including one at 18th and Broadway in Louisville that would certainly confuse the uninformed. It states, in part, that Clarke saw action at Chickamauga and then became one of "Morgan's men." The plaque also says that after Morgan's death, "this Confederate raider became notorious as woman (*sic*) marauder." Jerome Clarke never became notorious as a woman marauder, but the fictitious Sue Mundy did. Thomas Shelby Watson wrote part of the marker content, but disagreed with the part just mentioned.

Another Clarke descendant, Wand B. Duncan of Bowling Green, wrote to the late Kentucky historian J. Winston Coleman, seeking information on Jerome Clarke. Duncan referred to another member of the Clarke family in the letter, stating:

"Judge Bradshaw also told me they had a picture of him (Jerome

Clarke) in his feminine getup, but it had been put away so thoroughly some years previous they had been unable to find it."[1]

The most repeated story about Jerome Clarke dressing as a woman is the fictitious account of him trying to "fool" Morgan, mentioned earlier. The story by Prentice claims that Jerome was introduced to Morgan as "Miss Sue Mundy," dressed in women's clothing, and Morgan was not able to tell that Jerome was actually male. That is likely because of the fact that Morgan was dead, having been shot in the back Sept. 4, 1864. Prentice did not create the character Sue Mundy until Oct. 11, 1864.

Magruder Tried

Henry Magruder steadily improved from his chest wound, and was able to lie on a stretcher through his court-martial, which began in Louisville Sept. 13, 1865.

A long parade of witnesses were summoned, including E.H. McKay of Bloomfield, deputy United States collector, who testified that Magruder and Dick Mitchell visited him, trying to figure out the names of the richest men in town. He said Magruder was fleshier, ruttier and his hair darker than when he had previously seen him. McKay said he was also familiar with Jim Davis, Tom and Jim Henry. McKay testified that the guerrilla bands ranged from two or three to 30 or 40. Mitchell was still at large at the time of Magruder's trial.

During the visit to McKay's house, Mitchell and Magruder sat in front of the fireplace and asked McKay about his collections as they looked at his papers the 13th or 14th of January, 1865, McKay recalled several weeks later. Their clothing was covered with different colored cord and various figures, McKay testified. Some was of velvet, some silk. The red jackets were made of a red cloth, like that used for saddle cloth.

McKay said Magruder and Mitchell generally were armed with pistols, Magruder carrying five or six, and they had some shotguns and carbines strapped to their horses. Although farmer Joe Miller of New Haven was related to Magruder, it didn't prevent the young guerrilla from robbing him. In July 1864, Magruder arrived at his house with others, Miller testified, but he also misspoke under oath. He said Magruder was with "Sue Mundy, Colter (sic) and some others." It was some three months before Prentice invented the character "Sue Mundy." Miller said the guerrillas who came to his house were wearing dusters.

Two burst in and at pistol point demanded his buggy mare, gold watch, guns, especially pistols, and money. He said Magruder was the son of his niece, Amy Magruder. After robbing him, Miller said the guerrillas, numbering five to seven, then went into Nelson County and attacked the train, about a mile and a quarter from his house. His gold pen that was taken in the robbery was found by a woman after they attacked the train.

Magruder entered pleas of guilty to murder, with Jerome Clarke, in the deaths of Jacob Winstead, James Engle, Charles Barnett and Joseph Barnett on Jan. 8, 1865, at Lebanon Junction. He also admitted taking the lives, with Jerome Clarke, of Surgeon John L. Shirk and Captain Robert M. McCormick on Dec. 29, 1864, in Nelson County. He entered pleas of guilty, with Sol Thompson, in the killing of Edward Caldwell and Frank Crady. He denied killing Thornton Lee and John Wetherton in Springfield and three men — Foster, Wintham and Masters — in Jackson County, Tennessee. He said he did not kill William Fox and David Snodgrass in Edmonson County and denied killing, with Jim Davis, Charles E. Spalding in Washington County. Magruder also said he did not wound Amanda Hastings in Monroe County and said he did not rape Catherine Raymer. The court-martial agreed with Magruder's pleadings, in which he also admitted being a guerrilla and carrying out the crime of murder, either of which was a capital offense. Magruder was able to stand at the gallows Oct. 20, 1865. He was one of the last people to die as a result of Civil War crimes. He took a few puffs from a cigar, asked that the butt be given to his mother, and was hanged.[2]

On Aug. 12, 2000, a small gathering of historians, reenactors and dyed-in-the-wool Rebels gathered on a Bullitt County hill to do homage to Henry Magruder. There, in the Ezekiel Magruder Cemetery near Lebanon Junction, Henry's field stone grave marker was joined by an official Veterans Administration marker. There was a 21-gun salute and the singing of "Amazing Grace," "My Old Kentucky Home, Good Night" and "Dixie Land."

Solon Thompson

"Sol" Thompson, after being paroled, rode with Major Wilson into Louisville, where he hoped to receive amnesty, but was arrested and tried by a court-martial. It was explained by the military that any guerrilla charged with murder could not be paroled. Thompson was tried and convicted of being a guerrilla and killing Union soldier Frank Crady Nov. 14, 1864. He was sentenced to hang July 12, 1865, but the execution was delayed for 20 days until Aug. 1, 1865. A large number of Union soldiers and several officers were on hand to witness the hanging of Thompson, along with the guerrilla's mother, Elizabeth.

General Louis Watkins, just moments before the scheduled execution, "respited the prisoner until further notice" because Palmer had not been heard from. The mother's tears of sorrow turned to tears of joy as Thompson was returned in chains to a cell. Thompson was resentenced to ten years in prison, but after a short stay was released because of the helpless conditions of his parents and the recommendations of many citizens. Thompson died Feb. 22, 1922.

Henry Metcalf

The third man in the Meade County tobacco barn where Jerome Clarke and Henry Magruder were captured, Henry Metcalf, was charged with being a guerrilla and with participating in the Edward Caldwell murder. There were also three counts of murder participation with Henry Magruder involving three people in Nelson County who were not named in the charges.

Metcalf was sentenced to hang, but the punishment was reduced to five years in prison and he was taken to the Kentucky Penitentiary, June 3, 1865. There was a concerted letter-writing campaign on his behalf and since the war was over and Metcalf was 34, he was discharged by order of the War Department Oct. 13, 1865.

Sam Berry

Sam Berry's parole was taken from him soon after he surrendered, but it was worthless anyway. He was tried and convicted by a federal court-martial and sentenced to be hanged March 2, 1866, in Louisville. Five days later, Palmer commuted the sentence to ten years at hard labor in the military penitentiary at Albany, N.Y.

Berry, because of having only one arm, was kept confined and avoided the hard labor. Repeated letters and petitions from friends, acquaintances and officials, including the governor, could not get him a parole. In one letter to President Andrew Johnson, it was pointed out that Berry frequently saved the lives of people threatened by "desperate men" and a supportive statement carried many signatures. The letter asked that Berry be pardoned and restored to his family. It said Berry's wife, Amanda (Rose) was in "very delicate health" and the couple had one small child. One of the signatures on the letter was that of George D. Prentice, the *Louisville Daily Journal* editor who had invented the name "Sue Mundy" and who had blasted Sam Berry numerous times in his newspaper in connection with guerrilla activity.

The defense counsel at Berry's court-martial, W.B. Hoke, wrote to Brigadier General Lovell Harrison Rousseau on March 21, 1866, painting Berry as a victim of circumstance who was ordered to Kentucky to bring those who had turned guerrilla back to their Confederate ranks.

"When the party that he had collected left on the 13th of Oct., '64, he was then confined to a sick bed and was left. He tried soon after his recovery to follow but was badly wounded by Home Guards and kept hid for some time not able to travel. He then fell in with the guerrilla bands for protection waiting for them to leave the state. All this we have proven," Hoke wrote.

After failing a second time to get out of the state, Hoke wrote, Berry "returned to Spencer County (and) had his friends to make up a school." Hoke said Berry offered to prove, and could have proven, he saved the lives of more than 30 Union soldiers who were threatened by guerrilla bands.

Hoke pointed out that General Palmer agreed to meet Berry and parole him but sent Major Cyrus Wilson, who paroled him, administered the amnesty oath and told Berry if the parole was not satisfactory to Palmer, he would return Berry's horse and pistols and give him 24 hours' notice (head start). "They never returned the horse or pistols or gave any notice," Hoke said. He added in the letter, "He (Berry) is not a bad man." Hoke's plea fell on deaf ears.

In a letter to the president as part of the last of ten appeals on his behalf, Berry wrote:

My hair has whitened and form emaciated and my health broken. At 30 years of age, I find myself an old man. I have not seen for nearly eight years my wife, nor shall never more, she having died of a broken heart several years since, leaving an only child, a son, whom I have never seen, to the care of such friends as he may find. Do you not think my offense atoned for?

Sam Berry died in prison July 4, 1873, at the age of 36.

Jim Davis

James Warren "Jim" Davis, who also used the names Harvey Wells and William Henry, was the guerrilla who suffered from epilepsy. He was tried June 21 through July 13, 1865 by a military courts martial in Louisville, found guilty of being a guerrilla and was sentenced to be hanged.

Davis' mind had been declared impaired by fits and several who knew him said he had been subject to the epilepsy since he was 14. He usually became "very wild and disorderly" when out of control because of one of the seizures. A board of surgeons was asked Aug. 5, 1865 to examine the mental and physical condition of Davis and reported that Davis was not insane and could determine right from wrong. Davis suffered several attacks of epilepsy while in prison at Louisville during July, 1865. He was described as becoming very quarrelsome and would want to fight before an attack.

His execution, scheduled for Sept. 21, 1865, was suspended pending further orders by President Andrew Johnson. The suspension was confirmed by the War Department Sept. 28, 1865. John M. Palmer wrote to the president July 24, 1865, urging that the sentence be carried out. Burbridge sent a collection of affidavits from the Lexington area from people who knew of Davis' affliction, but C.W. Alexander quoted former neighbors of Davis as saying they knew nothing of his epilepsy. He said R.A. Alexander had known him for many years and knew nothing of it.

President Johnson commuted the Davis sentence on Feb. 19, 1866, from hanging to 10 years in prison, and Davis was sent to prison in Albany, N.Y., Feb. 26, 1866. Johnson commuted the sentence April 12, 1867, because of Davis' health and set him free.

Jim Bridgewater

Bridgewater's reputation had not been good during the war and included many instances of horse theft, including his men taking a farmer's plow horse while the granger was at work in the field.[3]

When Bridgewater became a candidate for the Kentucky legislature, running against Judge Thomas W. Varnon, he at once made political enemies. On July 8, 1867, Bridgewater was sitting in the Commercial Hotel office at Stanford, playing checkers, when several of his political enemies from Crab Orchard stormed in and opened fire. Walter Saunders was given credit for the neck wound that took Bridgewater down, although the body was riddled with bullets.[4] Saunders, Jim Henry Tucker, Dan Collier, Mack Adams and Tom Hays were exeonerated in the killing on the basis of self-defense, because local authorities believed the contention that Bridgewater had threatened the six men previously.

Hays had determined Bridgewater's location in the hotel, and after he reported to the others at the Myers House stable, the six rushed with their firearms in hand across Main Street and straight to the checkers game. Saunders is credited with firing first and the shot broke Bridgewater's neck, sending "Jim Bridge" to the floor as his hand swept blindly for his sidearm. By the time Bridgewater sank to the floor, he had bullets in his head and body and would never fight again.[5]

It was said that if Bridgewater had ever looked up from his checkers, Saunders or some of the others would have met the devil. Many citizens gave Saunders hero status and elected him sheriff, mainly for ridding the community of Bridgewater.[6]

The trouble between Saunders and Bridgewater began when Saunders was plowing near the road at his Cedar Creek residence near Crab Orchard and found a pistol. He tied the pistol on just before Bridgewater came by on horseback. Spotting the pistol, Bridgewater demanded Saunders give it to him. When Saunders handed it up, Bridgewater also spotted a nice ring on Saunders' finger. Bridgewater demanded the ring as well, but Saunders asked that he not take it because it had belonged to his since-deceased mother. Bridgewater shot Saunders in the shoulder and ripped the ring off his finger.

A witness to the incident got Saunders to a doctor who saved his life. Saunders is quoted as telling the physician: "Doc. Save that bullet from my shoulder. I'm going to remold it and kill him (Bridgewater) with it." And he did.[7]

Ed Terrell

Ed Terrell's ruthlessness did not stop and he was blamed for robbery and murder after the war. The *Louisville Daily Journal* of April 26, 1866, carried a reward notice from Governor Thomas Bramlette, promising $500 each for Terrell and John Weathers, a Terrell sidekick. They were wanted for the Jefferson County murder of Hercules Walker and the Spencer County killing of blacksmith Innis Wootton. Walker was a notorious character who had been accused, along with two others, of killing several members of a Hill family near Louisville on Jan. 1, 1861. Hercules Walker, James Walker and Jefferson Rogers were acquitted after a change of venue sent their cases from Jefferson County to Shelby County. No witnesses for the prosecution showed up at their trial. The fourth man, Benjamin Lount, Jr., was set free on bond and also was never punished. Hercules Walker's name appeared occasionally in the Louisville newspapers in connection with various troubles attributed to him. Military authorities tossed him into a prison cell at Louisville in February 1864 for an unstated offense. It seemed ironic that two of the more ruthless outlaws of the time, Herc Walker and Ed Terrell, would cross paths. It was 6:30 P.M., April 27, 1865, when Terrell rode out to the Walker farm on Preston Street Plank Road, nine and a half miles south of Louisville, uninvited, but not unarmed and not alone. It was estimated as many as 20 of Terrell's men rode with him.[8]

Terrell called Walker outside, told him he (Terrell) was the leader of a guerrilla band and understood Walker had been supplying and feeding Rebel guerrillas. Walker acknowledged that he had been doing just what Terrell said. Terrell then asked Walker if he would supply his men some ammunition and Walker agreed.

While Walker was getting the ammunition, Terrell ordered one of his men to summon Walker over by the desperado's barn and kill him. The man refused, knowing Walker's reputation as a dangerous gunman. A second of Terrell's men also turned down the invitation, but young Horace Allen of Larue County jumped at the chance and killed Herc Walker.

An inquest by Coroner J.C. Gill on April 28, 1865, determined that Walker died the result of a single pistol wound to the head. Allen was pardoned for Walker's murder Nov. 8, 1866. Why was Terrell gunning for Walker? It has been speculated, but not confirmed, that military or civilian authorities, or both, wanted the troublesome Walker dead, and if Terrell lost his life in the battle, so much the better. Terrell had become an enigma to the Union Army and although he and James Bridgewater led the only home guard or decoy guerrilla units who had proven effective in hunting down the Confederate irregulars, their reputations for lawlessness had grown to immense proportions.

Terrell and Harry Thompson teamed up for a crime spree that included robbery and murder. Finding that stock trader William R. Johnson from Illinois was carrying a large sum of money with him in Shelbyville on Aug. 25, 1865, Terrell and Thompson took him for a walk to the town's Clear Creek Bridge. Johnson's body, minus the cash, was found in the creek a short time later.[9]

Terrell and Thompson were arrested, and although Thompson played the banjo to conceal the noise as Terrell did the digging, the effort to tunnel to freedom was discovered Sept. 21, 1865, and they were unable to escape from the Shelby County Jail. On Jan. 8, 1866, Terrell was charged with the murder of Hercules Walker, who was, as noted, actually killed by Horace Allen, one of Terrell's men. A hung jury saved Terrell and Thompson from the hangman's noose March 24, 1866, and within 48 hours the two desperadoes had successfully broken out of the Shelby County Jail. Terrell and John L. Weathers were captured soon after the Shelby County Jail escape and sent to Taylorsville to stand trial for the murder of blacksmith Innis Wootton. Within four days, on April 13, 1866, members of Terrell's gang arrived in town and at gunpoint persuaded the jailer to free the two. A bit longer and it would not have been necessary to bother the jailer because Terrell had nearly completed a hole through the ceiling and roof.

In the May 1, 1866, *Frankfort Commonwealth*, there appeared the offer of a $1,000 reward posted by Governor Thomas E. Bramlette on April 24, 1866, for the apprehension of Terrell and Weathers. The wanted poster read:

WHEREAS, IT HAS BEEN MADE KNOWN to me that EDWARD [*sic*] TERRELL stands indicted in the Jefferson Circuit Court for the murder of Hercules Walker, and in the Spencer Circuit Court for the murder of Innis Wootton, and in Shelby Circuit Court for the murder of William R. Johnson, a citizen of Sangamon County, State of Illinois, and that one JOHN WEATHERS stands indicted jointly with said Terrell in the Spencer County Circuit Court for the murder of said Wootton, said Terrell and Weathers having made their escape from the Spencer county jail, are now fugitives from justice and going at large:

Now, therefore, I, THOS. E. BRAMLETTE, Governor of the Commonwealth aforesaid, do hereby offer a reward of FIVE HUNDRED DOLLARS

($500) cash for the apprehension of the said murderers and their delivery to the jailer of Jefferson county.

The notice included descriptions of the desperadoes:

Edward [*sic*] Terrell is 21 years old, long chestnut hair, blue eyes, fair complexion, weighs about 130 pounds, 5 feet 9 inches high. John Weathers, about 6 feet high, sallow complexion, long dark hair, weighs about 160 pounds, dark eyes.

Others said Terrell was shorter than 5-foot-9, and of course his name was Edwin, not Edward. Even with a price on his head, Ed Terrell continued to bask in bursts of glory. The people of Shelbyville cheered loudly when Terrell and some of his men rode into town May 18, 1865. Some black federal soldiers had been breaking up patent farm machinery and using the wood for kindling to build fires for warmth during a cool snap. When shop owner Thomas C. McGrath attempted to stop them, one of the black soldiers shot and killed him. The soldier's superior officers quickly arrested him and the entire group of black soldiers hurried to the courthouse. Citizens began arming themselves and roaming the streets as Terrell and his followers roared into town. Ed and his companions stormed the courthouse, put a rope around the neck of the soldier accused of killing McGrath, and were about to toss him from the third-floor balcony when a troop of Union soldiers rode in and stopped them. Terrell and his "scouts" were paid off and disbanded May 24, and from that day on, Edwin Terrell was known as "Bad Ed." Hearing that Palmer wanted to hang him, Terrell fled to Mexico for a short time, but was back in Kentucky by late August.

Terrell's fate was sealed on the evening of May 26, 1866. He'd been boozing it up at the Armstrong Hotel in Shelbyville with his uncle John R. Baker. A posse was quickly organized and men with guns occupied the windows of buildings, awaiting his return through town. Terrell and Baker saddled up and appeared to be leaving Shelbyville, but paused outside Redding's Hotel to speak to owner Merritt Redding. Someone yelled "Halt!" and Terrell fired in the direction of the voice. Then, multiple shots rang out and Terrell was wounded. Baker suffered multiple wounds, but stayed on his horse, riding several yards before falling into the street dead.[10]

The paralyzing wound, much like that suffered by Quantrill, claimed Terrell's life Dec. 13, 1868, at Louisville City Hospital. Terrell had asked

Dr. Thomas Marshall of Mount Eden to remove the bullet still in his spine in hopes he would walk again, but the hero-turned-outlaw died in surgery. Tailor J.H. Masonheimer is generally credited with firing from an upstairs window the shot that led to Terrell's death.[11]

Before Terrell died, he was cared for at his grandfather Baker's home in the Harrisonville area of Shelby County. A family story told to Thomas Shelby Watson by the late Ottis Goodwin of Louisville was that Terrell, although paralyzed and unable to rise from his bed, was able to gain access to a loaded pistol, probably provided by one of his men who came to visit, and took a shot at his brother-in-law, Abe Gray. The shot missed its mark. It isn't known why Terrell was gunning for the man who married his sister, Alice.[12]

Henry Turner

William Henry Turner, the son of Harvey and Catherine Donohoo Turner of Bardstown, surrendered to Captain R.H. Young, 54th Kentucky Infantry, at Samuels' Depot in Nelson County, May 9, 1865, as a prisoner of war. His surrender was with the agreement that he was to undergo an investigation and if he was not guilty of murder or robbery, which he contended, he was to be released "unconditionally." He was tried by court martial in Louisville.

Defense counsel R.H. Cochrell pointed out testimony that a fleshier man was the third one with Sam Berry and Bill Marion when the Spencer County Courthouse was burned, despite Alphonso Kirk's testimony it was Turner. The commission found Turner guilty on all counts, including robbery and aiding and abetting in the murders of Thornton Lee and John Wetherton during the Springfield raid.

A sentence of death was approved July 17, 1865, by Palmer. The execution was scheduled for July 21, 1865, but the sentence was commuted to ten years. A petition for pardon pointed out that Turner was 17 years of age during Morgan's first raid into Kentucky and was persuaded to join up. He was separated from the command on Morgan's second raid into Kentucky. Major C.B. Throckmorton testified that on several occasions, Turner saved his (Throckmorton's) life by telling him when the guerrillas were coming. A pardon petition acknowledged Turner was in Taylorsville at the courthouse burning, but Throckmorton wrote to Union officers on Turner's behalf. Jonathan D. Wickliffe wrote to Brigadier General

Rousseau, Dec. 13, 1865, requesting clemency for Turner, then Rousseau wrote to President Andrew Johnson, April 29, 1866, asking that Turner be freed. On April 30, 1866, after Turner had spent 14 months in prison at Camp Chase, Ohio, President Johnson ordered Turner released.

Turner returned to Bardstown and went to work for his brother, Edward, who was clerk of the Nelson County Court, then held office as a clerk himself. In 1881 Turner married Mary F. Smith and they had two daughters, Lois and Eula.

Francis Payne Stone

Payne Stone of Smithfield faced a federal court-martial in Louisville on June 28, 1865, although he had taken the oath of allegiance May 11 the same year in New Castle. Stone, a 2nd Lieutenant in Co. A, 6th Kentucky Cavalry, was described by witnesses as having been seen with guerrilla Henry Metcalf and other irregulars. Farmer Hanson Harding of Shelby County said Stone introduced him to Metcalf and he cooked for five men who took two of his horses when they left.

Despite John Milton's testimony that Stone shot him in the arm and side Dec. 20, 1864, Stone was acquitted July 10, 1865. The military appeared to be tired of searching for witnesses to testify at the courts-martials and no longer had a guerrilla of high notoriety to hang.[13]

Nathaniel Marks

A Rebel convicted of being a guerrilla who operated in Morgan and neighboring counties during 1862 and 1863 became a victim of the Union army hangman in Louisville Jan. 20, 1865. Nathaniel Marks, a native of Glenville, Virginia, had developed consumption after two years of confinement in the military prison and told those gathered for his execution they would shorten his life by only a matter of weeks. Marks, who claimed he was a Confederate soldier and not a guerrilla, was survived by his mother, wife and one child, living in Grayson County.

J.H. Vincell

An Owensboro area irregular, J.H. Vincell was taken before a court martial April 1, 1865, and was accused of "taking up arms as a guerrilla."

Witness Jesse More said he saw Vincell on the street Jan. 2, 1865, the day the Daviess County Courthouse was burned. J.G. Bailey testified that Vincell said he had helped set fire to the courthouse. The proceedings were adjourned until June 14, 1865, and on that date, Vincell was acquitted.[14]

Robert Britton

Another Confederate accused of being a guerrilla was Robert Britton, who served under Payne Stone. When the court-martial got under way Aug. 16, 1865, in Louisville, Stone was called to testify. He said that Britton, a native of Shelby County, did only what he was told and Stone, in turn, said he answered to his commander, Colonel George Jessee. Britton remained in Shelby County in the months near the end of the war and just afterward, specifically the Simpsonville community. Providing more evidence that the military was tiring of the courts-martial proceedings, especially the low-profile, unspectacular ones, Britton was released from custody.

Henry Spaulding

A Larue County indictment named brothers Henry and William Spaulding, William Hughes and Charles Roberts as the guerrillas who burned down the county courthouse in Hodgenville Feb. 21, 1865. Hammonville merchant W.B. Ousley testified in another case that Henry Spaulding, 21, was one of a band of guerrillas led by Sol Thompson who robbed him of money, goods and horses on March 4, 1865. Witness A.K. Flory, a Larue County farmer, said Charles Roberts of the gang shot at him. He also said Spaulding's brother, William, rode with the group of 16, as did John Linton. Henry Spaulding was sentenced to five years in prison, the term expiring Aug. 9, 1870.[15]

Jake Bennett

Another guerrilla who escaped the hangman in Louisville was Jake Bennett. After his surrender, May 21, 1865, at Carthage, Tennessee, Jake made his home in Clay County, Tennessee, where he became a prominent citizen and served three terms as sheriff. He married a local girl, Martha Dulcena Dale, and to them nine children were born.

Martha died Feb. 22, 1882, and Jake moved across the state line into Cumberland, Ky., where on Nov. 29, 1887, he married Fannie P. Beazley. It was while on his honeymoon that Jake and Fannie visited his father, Washington Bennett, 86, in McLean County, and a sister, Mrs. W.J. Everely, in Ohio County. At the age of 47, Bennett was described as a "stout and able bodied man" despite 26 bullet holes in his skin. In 1899, Jake served as a prison guard at the Tennessee State Prison in Nashville and it was after one of the shifts as guard that he became ill. He died two days later, Dec. 6, 1904. Jake and Fannie had one daughter, Mary Lee.[16]

Joseph R. Jonigan

Pardoned by President Johnson after being sentenced to hang by a court-martial in Louisville, Joseph R. Jonigan of Union County had operated as a guerrilla with Jerome Clarke and Henry Magruder. Jonigan was a Confederate soldier in Butler's First Cavalry, Co. G. He was granted a furlough in August 1863, at which time he returned to Kentucky and became a guerrilla.[17]

Eliab Garrett

Eliab Garrett was found guilty by a court-martial in Louisville in September,1865 of being a guerrilla, and was sentenced to four years in the penitentiary. The *Louisville Daily Journal* reported Feb. 7, 1866, that the findings of the military commission were approved, "but in consideration of certain facts which came to the knowledge of Gen. Palmer after the trial, tending to mitigate the conduct of Garrett, and rendering his punishment as an example unnecessary, the sentence has been remitted, and the prisoner released from custody."[18]

"Black" Dave Martin

Captain David S. Martin, Co. E, 6th Battallion, First Brigade, CSA, was taken before a court-martial in Louisville on July 5, 1865. As so many had done before him, Martin said he was a regular Confederate soldier. He claimed the force under him was not strong enough to defeat federals who were obstacles to their return to regular units. Martin was convicted

July 13, 1865, and sentenced to two years at hard labor.

Palmer used the power of his pen to declare that Martin was no worse than others who had been granted paroles and declared: "This man is not worse than they and as he has a helpless dependant family he will be discharged." Martin, called "Black Dave" because of his dark, Caucasian complexion, was set free.[19]

Thomas L. Henry

After his surrender to Ed Terrell, Tom Henry, 24, thought he would get a parole once he was taken to Louisville, but that was not the case. The Morganfield native found himself facing a court-martial. The son of William Henry and Elizabeth Russell had been mustered into the Confederate army Aug. 30, 1862, and became a member of Co. H, 10th Kentucky Cavalry. Henry was arrested in his home county April 10, 1863, sent to the military prison at Camp Chase, Ohio, but then released May 9 the same year after agreeing to the oath of loyalty to the Union. Henry, unable to sign his name, made his mark on the release document.

After seven days of testimony by witnesses, Henry was found guilty Nov. 20, 1865, of being a guerrilla and sentenced to five years at hard labor, but charges that he murdered Pickney (also seen as Pinkney) Hill and Jacob Winstead were not proven. In the most unusual conclusion of a guerrilla court-martial in Louisville, Henry was set free Feb. 20, 1866, on a technicality.

Gen. Palmer wrote:

The proceedings of the trial of Tom Henry, having been returned to these headquarters for correction, it is discovered that a more serious error exists therein than the one pointed out, and in this case it is deemed that the error cannot be remedied; to wit: It does not appear that the Judge Advocate of the court, on the consideration of this case, was sworn. He having been appointed to that duty subsequently to the former findings and sentence. The proceedings are disapproved. The accused will be released from custody.

Henry's survival in the woods after being severely wounded is one of the more remarkable stories attached to the Rebel guerrillas.[20]

Jerome's Final Resting Place

When Jerome Clarke's body was taken to Simpson County in southwest Kentucky at the Kentucky-Tennessee border, he was buried in a family cemetery. A decision was made by descendants of the Clarke family to move Jerome's remains to the Greenlawn Cemetery in Franklin, the Simpson County seat.

Left: Confederate guerrilla Tom Henry, shown here with his wife Lizzie, credits Frank James with saving his life after he was severely wounded by federal soldiers who left him to die. James is credited by Henry with crawling a mile through woods under the cover of darkness to deliver food and water to him as he lay wounded. The following night, Henry was helped to safety by James (courtesy Peyton Heady Family Collection). *Right:* Alexander Franklin James entered Kentucky with William Quantrill's guerrillas January 1, 1865. James was a few miles away at the Alexander and Finetta Sayers residence in Nelson County when Quantrill was mortally wounded. He was among the remaining members of Quantrill's band who surrendered and received paroles, allowing James and the other Missourians to return home. Within a short time, Frank, his little brother Jesse, and other Civil War veterans formed the infamous "James Gang" (Kentucky Historical Society).

On Aug. 1, 1914, a small group gathered at the rural gravesite. Wand Duncan, writing to historian J. Winston Coleman in 1953, said the casket was first taken to an undertaker, who wanted to make sure the remains were those of Jerome before taking them to Franklin for reburial. There, in the undertaker's shop, was a grandfather of Jerome, not identified in the letter, who was "quietly pledged to secrecy," Duncan wrote. The grandfather had attended a funeral for Jerome and his interment and was considered the best person who could identify the body that had been buried for 49 years.

"The casket was of metal, copper as I recall," Duncan wrote. "The weight of the covering earth through the years had caused corrugations both at the side and ends. With difficulty the top was removed, and the contents were once again visible to the eye of man. Inside was a skeleton in a mouldy uniform, but unmistakably the Confederate Gray. A mass of long black hair surrounded an empty skull and the neck was broken. As to the identity of the remains there was no room to doubt."[21]

Notes

Introduction

1. Kentucky Historical Society, *Journals of the Kentucky General Assembly*. May 16, 1861, Kentucky voted in favor of neutrality. Aug. 5, 1861, the lawmakers reiterated the vote as the Senate voted 27–11 and the House 76–24 in favor of remaining neutral.

2. Lewis Collins, *History of Kentucky*, 91–93; Dr. Thomas D. Clark, Kentucky historian laureate, interview by Thomas Shelby Watson, Oct. 1999.

3. *Journal of the Congress of the Confederate States of America* 1861–65, Vol. 1; Dr. Lowell H. Harrison, "Governor Magoffin and the Secession Crisis," *Kentucky Historical Society Register* 72; Harrison, interview by Thomas Shelby Watson, Oct. 1999; Dr. Thomas D. Clark, interview by Thomas Shelby Watson, Oct. 1999; Russell Harris, Kentucky Historical Society, interview by Thomas Shelby Watson, Oct. 1999.

4. Dr. Lowell H. Harrison, *The Civil War in Kentucky* (University Press of Kentucky; reprint edition, January 1987).

5. Harrison, interview.

6. Ibid.

7. Benjamin Dunlavy Journal (Shakertown Collection, Pleasant Hill, Ky.); William Thomas "Salt River Tom" Love, Spencer County, Ky., diary; others.

8. Charles Kerr, *History of Kentucky* (Chicago: American Historical Society, 1922), 846.

9. Young E. Allison, *Select Works of Young E. Allison* (Louisville: John P. Morton & Co.), p. 446.

10. Duke, Basil W. and R.W. Knott, eds. *Southern Bivouac. New Series: A Monthly Literary and Historical Magazine*, vol. 2. Louisville: B.F. Avery, 1885–87.

11. Ibid.

12. Henry C. Magruder. *Three Years in the Saddle: The Life and Confession of Henry C. Magruder, the original "Sue Munday," the Scourge of Kentucky. Written by Himself,* 1865. The alleged confession of Henry C. Magruder, based on interviews with Magruder by the Rev. Jeremiah Jeptha Talbott, rector of Saint John's Episcopal Church in Louisville. It was published by Cyrus J. Wilson, the federal officer who captured Jerome Clarke, Henry Magruder and Henry Metcalf. Republished by McDowell Publications, Utica, Ky.

13. *Louisville Daily Journal*, Jan. 25, 1865, p. 2, c. 2.

14. Ibid.

15. Charles Messmer, "Louisville During the Civil War," *The Filson Club History Quarterly* 52, no. 2 (April 1978): 243.

16. Hambleton Tapp and James C. Klotter, *Kentucky's Decades of Discord, 1865–1900* (Kentucky Historical Society, 1977), 1–3.

17. General Order 59. National Archives and *The Filson Club Quarterly* 35, no. 3 (July 1961): p. 299, Sept. 14, 1864.

18. *U.S. vs. Samuel O. Berry.* Union soldier John Robinson was fatally wounded in the streets of Harrodsburg, Oct. 7, 1864. Berry was charged with murder in the death, but a witness at Berry's court-martial testified that a long-haired man fired the first shot into Robinson's side. Berry's hair was short.

19. *U.S. vs. Jerome Clarke, alias Sue Mundy.* Testimony of Major Cyrus J. Wilson of the 26th Ky. Vol. Infantry: "...he spoke of the publication made concerning him fooling Morgan. He said that was all 'damn stuff' and there was nothing of it about his having an introduction to Morgan as Sue Mundy and asking and receiving from him a lieutenancy."

20. Allison, p. 446.

21. Frederick L.A. Eichelberger, chief author of *Military History of Kentucky*, in a letter to Jerry Clarke of Anchorage, Ky., Jan. 3, 1940. Jerry Clarke was a great-nephew of Jerome Clarke. From collection of the late J. Winston Coleman, Lexington.

22. Allison, p. 446.

23. Richard S. Brownlee, *Gray Ghosts of the Confederacy* (Baton Rouge: Louisiana State University Press, 1958), 118.

24. *U.S. vs. Jerome Clarke, alias Sue Mundy,* Louisville, March 15, 1865.

25. *Louisville Daily Journal,* Dec. 31, 1862, p. 1, c. 3.

26. *Kentucky Standard,* Bardstown, Ky., Feb. 24, 1910, Vol. 10.

27. Interview. Marcellus Jerome "Jerry" Clarke, great-nephew of the man who became known as "Sue Mundy," interviewed at his Anchorage, Ky., residence May 23, 1972. Tape in possession of author. Jerry Clarke died March 31, 1976, at the age of 82.

28. National Archives. Old Military Records.

29. Church Record. Handwritten by William Thomas Love, Van Buren, Ky.

30. *Louisville Daily Journal,* Dec. 31, 1862, p. 1, c. 3.

Chapter 1

1. Ibid. Harrison.

2. Basil Wilson Duke, *Morgan's Cavalry* (Cincinnati: Miami Printing and Publishing Co., 1867).

3. Duke, ibid.; Bayless Hardin, *Brigadier General John Hunt Morgan of Kentucky* (Kentucky Historical Society, undated). Morgan was born in Huntsville, Ala., June 1, 1825. He was reared in Kentucky and lived in Lexington from his 18th year until enrolling in the Confederate Army in 1861.

4. Ibid.

5. The Orphan Brigade Kinfolk Association wrote in an information packet that one explanation for the name "Orphan Brigade" is that Kentuckians of the 4th Kentucky never returned home from February 1862 until the war ended. Another possibility: General John Breckinridge is quoted as saying after an attack at Murfreesboro, Tenn.: "My poor Orphan Brigade! They have cut it to pieces!"

6. *U.S. vs. Jerome Clarke, alias Sue Mundy.*

7. *War of the Rebellion: A Compilation of the Official Records of the Union and Confederate Armies.* Usually called the *Official Records,* or simply O.R. Dated Feb. 18, 1862, from Columbia, Tennessee

8. Report of the Adjutant General of the State of Kentucky.

9. *U.S. vs. Jerome Clarke, alias Sue Mundy.*

10. Averell was the correct spelling, although Duke had it Averill.

11. Bruce S. Allardice, *More Generals in Gray* (Baton Rouge: Louisiana State University Press, 1995), notes that Giltner, a former Carroll County, Ky., sheriff, was a colonel of the 4th Kentucky Cavalry and was commissioned a general late in the war, although the commission never reached him; George D. Mosgrove, *Kentucky Cavaliers in Dixie* (Louisville, 1895), 47; George L. Willis, *Kentucky Democracy,* 3 vols. (Louisville, 1935), 1,201.

12. Duke, *Morgan's Cavalry,* 516.

13. Duke, ibid., 516.

14. Duke, ibid., 517.

15. Duke, ibid., 519.

16. Duke, ibid., 519–520.

17. *U.S. vs. Jerome Clarke, alias Sue Mundy.*

18. Duke, *Morgan's Cavalry*, 522.

19. *Lexington Observer and Reporter*, June 15, 1864.

20. Kentucky Historical Society.

21. Lewis Collins, *History of Kentucky*, 134.

22. Duke, *Morgan's Cavalry*, 524.

23. O.R., Series 1, Volume XXXIX/1 (S#77).

24. *U.S. vs. Jerome Clarke, alias Sue Mundy*; Collins, *History of Kentucky*, 134.

25. Duke, *Morgan's Cavalry*, 526.

26. Ibid., 525.

27. James L. Balance Journal, Shaker Village near Harrodsburg.

28. Duke, *Morgan's Cavalry*, 526.

29. *U.S. vs. Jerome Clarke, alias Sue Mundy.*

Chapter 2

1. U.S. Census and cemetery records show the granddaughter was the daughter of Innis G. Jones, a son of John R. Jones and Jones' first wife, Elizabeth Lewis. When her father died, young Elizabeth moved in with her grandfather. Elizabeth Lewis was born May 28, 1795, and died Christmas Eve, 1862, at the age of 67.

2. The house, in the fall of 2006, was still standing along Ky. Highway 55 at the Bloomfield exit of the Martha Layne Collins Blue Grass Parkway and was known as Springhill Winery & Plantation Bed and Breakfast. An outdoor drama based on the John R. Jones shooting was being presented on the front porch and lawn.

3. James Horan, *Confederate Agent* (New York: Crown Publishers, 1954), 260–261.

4. *Louisville Daily Journal*, June 23, 1864, p. 3, c. 1; also: Dr. Alexander Hamilton Merrifield, *Wartime in the Bloomfield Country*, 1903. Report of historian Fincastle Chapter, D.A.R., 1940–41, Louisville. Merrifield said Jones had a horse and saddle the Rebels wanted; Sarah B. Smith, *Historic Nelson County* (Louisville: Gateway Press, Inc., 1971). "They demanded a certain saddle that he [Jones] treasured very much." Interview with Smith, 1971, Bardstown, said local lore indicated the saddle was silver-studded.

5. *Louisville Journal*, June 23, 1864, p. 3, c. 1. The description of Jones firing "through the flags" is thought to mean Iris plants. Small glass panes beside doors are also called "flags," but the door in question did not appear to have the panes.

6. Letter, Josephine Thomas of Bloomfield to Gillie Bodine, visiting in McLean County, June 21, 1864. Thomas-Stiles letters, courtesy John B. Thomas, Jr. All rights reserved.

7. Ibid.

8. Ibid.

9. James M. Prichard, "General Orders No. 59: Kentucky's Reign of Terror," *Civil War Quarterly* 10, p. 32.

10. Merrifield.

11. James M. Prichard, *Tree Shaker*, Civil War pamphlet, Louisville, undated.

12. O.R. Headquarters, 1st Div., District of Kentucky, Lexington, Aug. 12, 1864, to Brig. Gen. E.H. Hobson, commanding 1st Brig., 1st Div., District of Kentucky, "General, I have the honor to enclose herewith order from Headquarters Dist. of Kentucky with endorsements authorizing the execution of Richmond Berry and May Hamilton. The endorsement by Captain Butler directs the prisoners to be left at Bardstown, but since in consideration of the unsafeness, they are by direction of the Gen'l Comdg. to be sent to you. I am General very Respectfully yours [sic] Obt. Sevt. Geo. Hamilton Captain & P.M.G."

13. Interview. Emma Wilson Brown of Bloomfield, at 103, said in April, 2002, local tradition was that the executions were "opposite where Clyde Allen used to live," on the old Bardstown Road, within the limits of Bloomfield.

14. Smith.

15. Daughters of the Confederacy, *Minutes of the Eighth Annual Convention of the Kentucky Division* (held in Paducah, Oct. 12–13, 1904; Louisville: Press of George G.

Fetter Co., 1905), p. 111; *Kentucky Standard*, Bardstown, May 27, 1909.

16. Spaulding Hall Museum, Bardstown.

17. *Kentucky Standard*, Bardstown, May 27, 1909. "Tragic Recollections" by Mrs. Clay Duncan, read before Joshua Gore Chapter, United Daughters of the Confederacy.

18. *Glasgow Times*, Glasgow, Nov. 20, 1900.

19. Ibid. The same article, quoting the *Bloomfield Sentinel*, notes that a graphic account of the executions overseen by Bristow was circulated in Cincinnati prior to the 1876 presidential convention and may have been a factor in Bristow's defeat for the presidential nomination. The shots in the face of Berry: truth or politics?

20. Merrifield.

Chapter 3

1. *Three Years in the Saddle*.
2. Ibid., p. 10.
3. Ibid., p. 13.
4. Ibid., p. 69.
5. Ibid., p. 69.
6. Ibid., p. 108.
7. *U.S. vs. Henry C. Magruder*.
8. *Three Years in the Saddle*, p. 70.
9. O.R., Series I, Volume XXXIX/2.
10. *Three Years in the Saddle*, p. 70.
11. *U.S. vs. Jerome Clarke, alias Sue Mundy*.
12. Ibid.
13. *Three Years in the Saddle*, p. 73.
14. *Louisville Daily Democrat*, Tuesday, June 21, 1864, p.3, Col. 5.
15. Ibid., Monday, June 20, 1864, p. 2, c. 2.
16. Letter to Governor Bramlette from G.W. Caplinger, dated June 25, 1864.
17. *Louisville Daily Journal*, July 12, 1864, p. 3, c. 1.
18. *Louisville Daily Journal*, Aug. 2, 1864.
19. *Louisville Daily Democrat*, Aug. 8, 1864, p. 2, Col. 2.
20. Ibid.

21. *Louisville Daily Democrat*, Aug. 11, 1864, p. 2, Col. 2.
22. *Louisville Daily Democrat*, Aug. 17, 1864, p. 2. c 2.
23. *Louisville Journal*, Aug. 19, 1864, p. 3, c. 1.
24. *Louisville Daily Democrat*, Aug. 30, 1864, p.2, c 3.

Chapter 4

1. Joseph Millard, "The Spy Who Saved the Union," in *True Civil War Stories* (Fawcett Publications, 1961).
2. Dr. Alexander Hamilton Merrifield, *Wartime in the Bloomfield Country*, paper read before the Filson Club, Louisville, 1903.
3. Ibid.
4. Merrifield, "Wartime in Nelson County," in *The Kentucky Standard*, Nov. 19, 1903, University of Kentucky.
5. John Boling, *Guerilla Times in Meade County* (Utica, Ky.: McDowell Publications).
6. *U.S. vs. James W. Davis*, National Archives.
7. *Nashville Daily Times & True Union*, Sept. 2, 1864, p.2, Col. 3.
8. *Louisville Daily Journal*, Sept. 13, 1864, p. 3, Col. 3.

Chapter 5

1. *U.S. vs. Henry C. Magruder*.
2. *Louisville Journal*, Sept. 13, 1864, p.3.
3. Ibid.

Chapter 6

1. Basil W. Duke, *Reminiscences of General Basil W. Duke, C.S.A.* (New York: Doubleday, 1911). Stories and anecdotes collected by Duke.
2. Thurman Sensing, *Champ Ferguson* (Vanderbilt University Press, 1942).
3. *Louisville Daily Democrat*, Sept. 14, 1864, p. 3, Col. 5.

Chapter 7

1. *U.S. vs. Samuel O. Berry*, prosecution witness William Wilkinson, stage driver.
2. Ibid.
3. Ibid.
4. Ibid., testimony by Thomas Stagg.
5. Ibid., testimony by Dr. J.L. Smedley.
6. Ibid., testimony by Stagg.
7. Ibid.
8. *U.S. vs. Samuel O. Berry*. Prosecution witness Thomas Stagg indicated Berry was the first to shoot Robinson, but prosecution witness Milton Young said he was "under the impression" that "Sue Munday" fired first. He said a long-haired man was first to shoot Robinson. Berry had short hair.
9. *U.S. vs. Henry C. Magruder*, testimony of prosecution witness Ludwell McKay, Wednesday, Sept. 21, 1865.

Chapter 8

1. Mary Charles Stout, great-granddaughter of Massie. Interview by Thomas Shelby Watson, 1972.
2. Dr. John E. Lilly, Spencer County Journal (diary).
3. Letter. The account of Israel Shepherd Massie, son of Edward Massie in Mary Charles Stout collection, Louisville. Family tradition is that the two youngest children held onto their father. There was a 4-year-old, but the family does not believe she stood with her father.
4. *Louisville Daily Journal*, April 18, 1865, stated that: "He [Foreman] is the infamous scoundrel, who by his own hand, murdered E.D. Massie." The name is also seen as Froman and Frohman, but Foreman is correct.
5. From Anderson County Circuit Court murder indictment. The names of all who took part were not listed.
6. William Gunn, Commander of Allotments of Kentucky Volunteers, letter to Burbridge, Nov. 7, 1864.

Chapter 9

1. *Louisville Journal*, Oct. 17, 1864, p. 3, c. 2. The use of the term "Negro boy" by Prentice could have meant a young boy or perhaps it was racist slang for an adult. He was further identified as a slave, "belonging to Mr. Vernon."
2. Ibid.
3. Ibid.
4. Ibid.
5. *Louisville Courier-Journal*, Louisville, June 11, 1904.

Chapter 10

1. Letter, Josie Thomas from her Nelson County residence to relatives, June 21, 1864. Courtesy John B. Thomas Jr.
2. *Kentucky Standard*, Bardstown, Thurs., Nov. 3, 1938, p.2, c. 5–6.
3. *U.S. vs. Samuel O. Berry*, prosecution witness Henry Tinsley.
4. Ibid.
5. Ibid.
6. Ibid.
7. Ibid.
8. *Three Years in the Saddle*, p. 76.
9. Ibid.

Chapter 11

1. The month of Alfred Porter Thomas' birth was not ascertained, so his age is an approximation based on family records that list it "circa 1842."
2. Letter, Feb. 13, 1865, to military command in Louisville. Author uncertain. Source: Kentucky Archives.
3. Ibid.
4. Letter, from Lawrenceburg, Ky., Feb. 16, 1865, T.H. Hickman to Brig. Gen. Edward Hobson.
5. *Louisville Daily Journal*, Oct. 27, 1864, p. 3, c. 2

Chapter 12

1. *Louisville National Union Press*, Tues., Nov. 1, 1864. p. 2, c. 5.

2. *U.S. vs. Jim Davis*, court-martial, Louisville, June 21, 1865-July 13, 1865. Alexander's testimony described the raid but could not identify Davis as being one of the guerrillas.

3. Ibid. Witness Henry Granison, a slave at Alexander's, testified that the five men who stole the horses took him along. He said the men were dressed in gray clothing and the man who rode "Asteroid" was a "low, chunky man."

4. *Louisville Courier-Journal*, March 3, 1901, "The Harpers and the Departed Glories of Nantura." Sec. 3, p. 3.

5. Ibid.

6. Ibid.

7. Daughters of the Confederacy, *Minutes*, p. 52; *Louisville Courier-Journal*, Jan. 6, 1882, p. 6, c. 1-2.

8. *Louisville Courier-Journal*, Jan. 6, 1882, p. 6, Col. 1-2.

9. Daughters of the Confederacy, *Minutes*, p. 52.

10. Ibid.

Palmer at Louisville, March 24, 1865. Author said widow of William Fox saw Magruder kill her husband and she knew Magruder from having seen him twice before; said Catherine Raymer and her sister were raped when a gang stopped at the Philip Raymer house and said six young ladies were raped by guerrillas while at school. No records have been found to indicate Catherine Raymer's sister was raped and the school rapes story also lacked support.

12. Ibid., testimony by Catherine Raymer.

13. Nov. 17, 1864, attachment to report by Captain Joseph J. Borrell, Co. K, 37th Kentucky Mounted Infantry, by Nelson County Sheriff James Wood and John A. Terrell, state deputy provost marshal for Nelson County.

14. Dispatch to R.A. Alexander, Louisville, Military Headquarters, from Captain J.J. Borrell, 37th Kentucky, L.B. No. 8_1864, p. 53.

Chapter 13

1. *U.S. vs. Samuel O. Berry*, testimony by Butler Remey Thomas.

2. Ibid., testimony by Henry Tinsley.

3. Ibid., testimony by James Moore.

4. Ibid., testimony by Mitchell Russell.

5. Ibid., testimony by John Green.

6. *U.S. vs. Henry Magruder*, court-martial, Louisville, testimony by Elijah Jones, Sept. 13, 1865.

7. Ibid.; findings of court-martial, Sept. 27, 1865, were that Magruder was "not guilty" of the murders of Lewis and William Fox.

8. Louisville & Nashville Railroad records, University of Louisville Archives.

9. *U.S. vs. Henry Magruder*, court-martial, Louisville, testimony by Elijah Jones, Sept. 13, 1865.

10. *U.S. vs. Henry Magruder*, court-martial, Louisville, testimony by Philip Raymer.

11. Letter, anonymous author from Brownsville, to Major General John M.

Chapter 14

1. *Three Years in the Saddle*, ibid.

2. Ibid; also local tradition, including a paper, *Wartime in the Bloomfield Country*, Dr. A.H. Merrifield.

3. *Louisville Daily Journal*, Nov. 16, 1864, p. 3, c. 2.

4. O.R., Series I, Volume XLV/1 [S# 93].

5. Ibid.

Chapter 15

1. *U.S. vs. Henry C. Magruder*, testimony by J.H. Sherard.

2. Ibid., testimony by J.H. Sherard.

3. *U.S. vs. Solomon Thompson*, testimony by William Allen.

Chapter 16

1. *Louisville Journal*, Nov. 29, 1864, p. 2, c. 2.

2. *U.S. vs. Samuel O. Berry*, testimony of Jacob Perkins, Jan. 22, 1866.

3. Ibid. The word "resent" in this context could have meant to resent another's superiority.

4. *U.S. vs. Samuel O. Berry*, testimony of Jacob Perkins, Jan. 22, 1866.

5. Ibid., testimony of William E. Riley.

6. Ibid., testimony by James Devine.

7. Ibid., testimony by neighbors William Yeager and William Yates.

8. Ibid., testimony by Martha Hall.

9. Ibid.

10. Ibid.

Chapter 17

1. *U.S. vs. Samuel O. Berry*, testimony by C.B. Butler.

2. Ibid., testimony by Grandison Robertson, Jan. 15, 1866. Also testimony of grocer G.J. Bosley in *U.S. vs. Henry C. Magruder*.

3. *U.S. vs. Henry Magruder*, testimony by Grandison Robertson. Also testimony by Robertson in *U.S vs. James A. Davis*.

4. Ibid.

5. *U.S. vs. Henry Turner*, testimony by John M. Bell.

6. Ibid., testimony by W.T. McElroy.

7. *Louisville Daily Journal*, Dec. 8, 1864, p. 1, c. 1.

8. O.R., Series 1, Volume XLV/2 (S# 94).

Chapter 18

1. O.R., Series 1, Volume XLV/2 (S #94).

2. Ibid.

3. Ibid. and local tradition.

4. Ibid.

5. *U.S. vs. Samuel O. Berry, Jr.*, testimony by Samuel Snider.

6. Ibid., testimony by John Russell.

7. Ibid., testimony by John Froman.

8. Ibid.

9. *U.S. vs. Samuel O. Berry, Jr.*, testimony by John Russell.

10. Ibid. Russell said Dick Mitchell was

in the gang that day, but there was no other supportive testimony to that effect.

11. *U.S. vs. James W. Davis*, testimony of Ann Blanton.

12. Ibid.

13. *U.S. vs. James W. Davis*, testimony by Joseph Watson.

Chapter 19

1. Statement of Captain A. Ballard of the *Morning Star*.

2. Benjamin Dunlavy, Shakertown, Ky., diary and Dr. John Lilly's Spencer County Journal.

3. *U.S. vs. Samuel O. Berry*.

4. *Louisville Daily Democrat*, Dec. 29, 1864, p. 1, c. 3.

5. *U.S. vs. James W. Davis*, testimony by George H. Corbitt.

6. *Louisville Daily Journal*, Jan. 11, 1865. The name is spelled Spaulding in a newspaper report on the shooting.

7. *U.S. vs. Henry Magruder*, testimony by the Rev. J.M.P. Kearny.

8. *U.S. vs. James W. Davis*, testimony of Dr. J.C. Pash.

9. *U.S. vs. Henry Magruder*, testimony of Fanny Spalding.

Chapter 20

1. East Family Journal, Shakertown Collection, Benjamin Dunlavy.

2. Confederate States of America paymaster voucher, Feb. 16, 1863, names Captain W.C. Quantrill, commander of cavalry scouts, recipient of $280 for two months of service. Also identified as a captain of Confederate scouts on a request for forage in 1862. Was granted 2,400 lbs. of corn to feed 211 animals.

3. William Elsey Connelley, *Quantrill and the Border Wars* (Cedar Rapids, Iowa: Torch Press, 1909).

4. *U.S. vs. Henry Metcalf*, prosecution witness Peter Caldwell.

5. *U.S. vs. Henry Magruder*, prosecution witness George Caldwell.

6. *U.S. vs. Tom Henry*, prosecution witness Margaret Caldwell.

7. *U.S. vs. Henry Magruder*, prosecution witness George Caldwell.

8. Ibid., prosecution witness Margaret Caldwell.

9. Ibid.

10. *U.S. vs. Henry Metcalf*, prosecution witness J.W. Caldwell.

11. Ibid., prosecution witness J.W. Caldwell.

12. Ibid., prosecution witness H.D. Cowherd.

Chapter 21

1. Diary of William Thomas Love, aka Salt River Tom, copy in possession of author, and comments of family relative Ottis Goodwin, interview by Thomas Shelby Watson, 1973.

2. Interviews with Ottis Goodwin, Juber Gray and other family members by Thomas Shelby Watson, 1973.

3. General Services Administration, Old Military Records, Washington D.C.

4. National Archives, paymaster files, U.S. Army.

5. Interviews with Joe Taylor and Terrell family descendants by Thomas Shelby Watson.

6. *U.S. vs. Henry Magruder*, prosecution witness Harvey K. Wells.

7. Ibid.

8. Louisville & Nashville Railroad records, University of Louisville Archives.

9. *U.S. vs. Henry Magruder*, prosecution witness William Hill.

10. Ibid., prosecution witness James D. Hill.

11. *Louisville Journal*, Jan. 10, 1865, p.3, c.1

12. Copy of the Hancock County marriage bond in possession of Brantley and Watson.

13. *Cannelton (Indiana) Reporter*, Feb. 23, 1865, p. 1, c. 4.

14. *Louisville Journal*, Jan. 30, 1865.

Chapter 22

1. *U.S. vs. Henry Turner*, prosecution witness Dr. G.W. Foreman.

2. Louisville & Nashville Railroad records, University of Louisville Archives.

3. *Three Years in the Saddle*, p. 92.

4. Ibid., p. 95.

5. Ibid., p. 97.

6. *Louisville Daily Democrat*, Jan. 19, 1865, p. 2, Col. 1.

7. *Three Years in The Saddle*, p. 98.

8. Ibid.

9. *Kentucky Standard*, Thursday, Dec. 15, 1938, p. 8, col. 1–3. The Walters residence was one mile north of Thomas Shelby Watson's residence.

Chapter 23

1. John N. Edwards, *Noted Guerrillas or Warfare of the Border* (St. Louis: Bryan and Brand & Co., 1877), pp. 416–417.

2. Old Military Records, National Archives.

3. Harry D. Tinsley, *History of No Creek* (Frankfort: Roberts Printing, 1953), pp. 181–185; *Owensboro Messenger-Inquirer*, Glenn Hodges, Nov. 30, 1992.

Chapter 24

1. Camp Nelson Restoration and Preservation Foundation.

2. Spencer County Journal, diary kept by Dr. John Lilly.

3. Benjamin Dunlavy Journal, Shakertown Collection, Pleasant Hill, Ky.

4. Edward Shinnick, ed., *Shelby Record* 14, no. 8 (Feb. 21, 1913): p. 9.

5. Ibid.

6. *U.S. vs. Henry Turner*, prosecution witness Alfonzo Kirk.

7. Ibid.

8. Ibid., prosecution witness Thomas J. Barker. Prosecution witness Alfonzo Kirk, 16, indicated in his testimony that it was Marion's idea that the opportunity be given to Barker to remove the Masonic

regalia, but Barker testified it was Berry who walked into church and made the offer.

9. Ibid., prosecution witness Alfonzo Kirk.

10. Edward Shinnick, ed., *Shelby Record* 14, no. 8 (Feb. 21, 1913): p. 9.

11. *Louisville Daily Journal*, Jan. 26, 1865, p.3, col. 1.

12. *Three Years in the Saddle*, p. 112. While Henry Magruder claimed that Jerome Clarke took part in the raid on the cattle drive, Clarke later told military authorities he was incapacitated with a wound and was not there. *U.S. vs. Jerome Clarke.*

13. *Three Years in the Saddle*, p. 111.

14. Ibid.

15. Edward Shinnick, ed., *Shelby Record* 14, no. 8 (Feb. 21, 1913): p. 9.

16. *Three Years in the Saddle.*

17. Ibid.

18. National Archives and interview with John Trowbridge, Kentucky Military History Museum.

19. *Louisville Daily Journal*, Feb. 3, 1865.

Chapter 25

1. *Three Years in the Saddle.*

2. Rebecca Wootton's Fairfield, Ky., diary. Rebecca enters the date of the killing of Ludwick as Jan. 28, 1865.

3. *Three Years in the Saddle.*

4. Ibid.

5. Champ Clark, *My Quarter Century of American Politics* (Harper & Brothers Publishers, 1920).

6. *Three Years in the Saddle.*

7. Ibid. Lucinda Harriet McKay Selecman was the widow of John Fisher Selecman. In a letter to the *Kentucky Standard*, Bardstown, Dec. 15, 1938, p. 8, col. 1–3, W.J. Nelson of Louisville said Berry was hidden at James Brewer's near Fairfield and at Thomas Walters' in Spencer County.

8. *Three Years in the Saddle.*

9. Dr. Alexander Hamilton Merrifield, *Wartime in the Bloomfield Country*, a paper written in 1903. Terrell shot at Merrifield's

gate, Walnut Grove, owned in 2006 by Jerry and Linda Bruckheimer.

Chapter 26

1. Benjamin Dunlavy Journal, Shakertown Collection, Pleasant Hill.

2. O.S. Barton, *Three Years with Quantrill: A True Story Told by His Scout John McCorkle* (1914; reprint, Norman: University of Oklahoma Press, 1998). McCorkle, a Quantrill guerrilla, claims he was there when Cunningham was shot.

3. Edwards, *Noted Guerrillas; Louisville Journal*, Feb. 10, 1865, p. 1, c. 4.

4. Ibid., 401.

5. Ibid., 392.

6. Ibid., 408–409.

7. O.R., Series I, Vol. XLIX/1, p. 694.

Chapter 27

1. Dr. John M. Lilly, diary, Spencer County Journal.

2. Letter to Paul Burnfin, Corbin, Ky., June 9, 1969, from Charles F. Hightower, with details of the incident. Also, letter from Lulie Wilkins of Carrollton to: "Parents and friends of the late Lieutenant Lawson Burnfin."

3. Ibid., Hightower letter.

4. Letter, Wilkins. Feb. 2, 1865.

5. *Three Years in the Saddle*, p. 118; *Louisville Courier-Journal*, April 29, 1874, p. 2, c. 2.

Chapter 28

1. Jerome Clarke was not present at Midway on Feb. 2, 1865, as previously mentioned. That means Kentucky Historical Highway Marker 537 on U.S. 62 at Midway is incorrect when it states that Jerome and Quantrill burned the Midway Depot and stole 15 horses.

2. Letter, March 4, 1865, from R.A. Alexander to his brother-in-law Henry Deeds in England. Copy provided by A.J. Alexander. Also in the letter, Alexander

spells the name of his prized horse "Astroid." Most other references use the spelling "Asteroid," which is correct for a celestial planetoid.

3. Ibid.
4. Merrifield.
5. *Louisville Journal*, Feb. 5, 1865, p. 2, col. 1.
6. *Louisville Journal*, Feb. 10, 1865, p. 1, col. 2.
7. *Noted Guerrillas*, p. 417.
8. Dan M. Bowmar III, *Giants of the Turf* (Lexington: The Blood-Horse, 1960); John Hervey, *Racing in America* (Jockey Club, New York). University of Kentucky Special Collection, p. 331.
9. *Noted Guerrillas,* p. 417.

Chapter 29

1. *Noted Guerrillas.*
2. Rebecca Wootton's diary.
3. Benjamin Dunlavy Journal, Shakertown Collection, Pleasant Hill.
4. *Three Years in the Saddle*, p. 116.
5. Letter from Robert Lockbaum to Perry A. Brantley, Jan. 7, 2001; M. Juliette Magee, *Ballard's Brave Boys*, and census records.
6. O.R., Series 1, Vol. XLIX/1(S #103)
7. Ibid.
8. Surname is spelled Prewett on tombstone found face-down in the Prewitt-Cunningham family cemetery that had been decimated by cows. Stone found and righted by Perry A. Brantley and Allan Leach in Sept., 1997. A hole in the door, that local tradition identified as having been made by the bullet that killed Prewitt, was clearly visible during that visit.
9. Local history compiled by Eula Ray Kirkland and Allan R. Leach; O.R., Series 1, Vol. XLIX/1 (S #103).
10. *Three Years in the Saddle*, p. 117.
11. Ibid.

Chapter 30

1. Dawson family tradition is that Quantrill was referred to by the seemingly endearing nickname, "The Captain," when he visited their large, two-story log house south of Bloomfield. The late Emily Dawson of Bloomfield said in an interview with Thomas Shelby Watson she believed her great-aunt Nancy had no romantic involvement with Quantrill. Nancy Dawson was never married.
2. Quantrill's poetry courtesy the Dawson family. All rights reserved. Unauthorized use prohibited. "My horse is at the door" poem was donated by the Dawson family to the Kenneth Spencer Research Library, University of Kansas, Lawrence, Kansas.
3. Barton, *Three Years with Quantrill*. When ghost writers or stenographers take information from the recollections of the story teller, there can be misunderstandings. The name "Thurman" was likely misunderstood and the actual name was "Foreman." This is proven through census and other records.
4. Ibid.
5. Sworn, notarized statement by Ida Alcorn, who was a neighbor and friend of Mary Rachel Samuels Pence and her daughters, Mattie and Mayme Pence, Jan. 28, 1974. In possession of author.
6. O.R., Series 1, Vol. XLIX/1.
7. *Cannelton (Indiana)Reporter*, March 2, 1865, correspondence from Hawesville, Feb. 23 and 25, 1865.
8. Ibid.; Hancock County Fearful Times.
9. *U.S. vs. Henry Metcalf,* testimony by M.L. Toll, Breckinridge County farmer.
10. Ibid.
11. *Three Years in the Saddle*, p. 122.
12. *Cannelton (Indiana) Reporter*, March 2, 1865, correspondence from Hawesville, Feb. 23 and 25, 1865.
13. *Three Years in the Saddle*, p. 122.
14. Ibid.
15. Ibid.
16. *Hancock Clarion*, July 12, 1935; July 19, 1935.
17. John M. Palmer, *Personal Recollections of John M. Palmer: The Story of an Earnest Life* (Cincinnati: Roberts Clarke

Co., 1901). Palmer said a "man from Elizabethtown" called upon him at the Louisville Hotel and reported the three guerrillas were in the barn on the Cox farm. Palmer did not identify the man in his book.

18. *U.S. vs. Jerome Clarke, alias Sue Mundy,* Specification 2 of Charge first, three soldiers wounded by Jerome Clarke.

19. *U.S. vs. Jerome Clarke alias Sue Mundy,* Wilson testimony.

Chapter 31

1. *U.S. vs. Henry C. Magruder,* witness Otis Hoyt, a surgeon with the 30th Wisconsin Volunteer Infantry. The defense asked Hoyt to examine Magruder in court to see if the ball passed through his body, but the military commission would not allow it.

2. Interview, C.A. Shauchnessy of the National Archives. "All I can say is the endorsement is on the back of the final page of Clarke's statement to the court."

Chapter 32

1. Young E. Allison, *Louisville Courier-Journal,* Feb. 6, 1887; Allison, *Select Works of Young E. Allison* (Louisville: John P. Morton & Co., 1935), p. 443.

2. Records of L.L. House Mortuary, Franklin, Ky. In July, 1914, Jerome Clarke's body was moved by the Simpson County Chapter of the United Veterans of the Confederacy from the Clarke family burial ground near Franklin to Greenlawn Cemetery in the same city with full Confederate military honors. L.L. House said the remains of a Confederate uniform were seen, along with long black hair, and the neck bones were broken.

Chapter 33

1. *Kentucky Standard,* Bardstown, Thursday, Dec.15, 1938, p. 8, col. 1–3.

2. Maude Johnston Drane, *History of Henry County, Ky.,* 1948, p. 127.

3. G.W. Demaree, "Some local history of the dark days of the Civil War," *Shelby News,* Shelbyville, Ky., July 23, 1903, p. 1, col. 3–4.

4. *Kentucky Standard,* Phillip H. Hunter, 1930s, exact date uncertain.

5. *U.S. vs. Samuel O. Berry.*

Chapter 34

1. O.R., Series 1, Vol. XL/1.

2. *The Morning Herald.* Lexington, Sunday, March 27, 1898.

3. Ibid. Quantrill, in bowing to the ladies, exhibited proper social training that was absent from other guerrillas. In U.S. vs Tom Henry, Quantrill's mannerly side was also displayed at the Spencer County residence of Alexander W. Thomas in late March or early April, 1865. After Thomas and his wife served dinner to as many as 16 men, including Quantrill, Tom Henry and Henry Magruder, Quantrill departed, telling his host, "Good evening, Mr. Thomas. I am much obliged to you for your kindness." Thomas said Quantrill was the first combatant since the war began to thank him for anything the Thomas family provided.

4. O.R., Series 1,Vol. XLIX/1 Pt. II, P. 511. (E.H. Hobson letter).

Chapter 35

1. Dr. Alexander H. Merrifield, *Wartime in the Bloomfield Country.* Report of Historian, Fincastle Chapter, D.A.R., Louisville, Margaret Calhoun Bryan, 1940–41.

2. Connelley, *Quantrill and the Border Wars,* p. 471.

3. Letters, Curtis Ochs to Joe Creason, *Louisville Courier-Journal,* 1955; to Creason, 1955, from J.H. Edelen, Raywick, Ky., quoting Ben Kirkpatrick of Terrell's force saying there were 12 or 14 guerrillas at Wakefield's farm.

4. Notarized statement, Texas State Archives, Aug. 2, 1926. Allen H. Palmer states that he is the same person as Allen Parmer who enlisted in Confederate service in 1861 at the age of 13 and that he

joined Quantrill in 1863. He signed his name "Allen H. Palmer." Palmer married Frank and Jesse James' sister, Susan Lavenia James, Nov. 24, 1870.

5. Congressman Ben Johnson, handwritten in an 1882 atlas later owned by Jack Muir of Bardstown, said Donnie Pence was seen riding through Bloomfield with Quantrill and others the day Quantrill was shot, leaving a presumption that the recently-wounded Pence could have been there. Photos of Johnson's notes in author's files.

6. Rebecca Wootton, four miles from the Wakefield farm, in her diary, described the intense rain.

7. Interview, Phil Hunter, son of "Babe" Hunter, Aug. 30, 1973, tape in possession of author. Phil did not know names of those with his father.

8. Connelley, *Quantrill and the Border Wars*, p. 471.

9. Paper, *The Career of William Clark [sic] Quantrill in Kentucky and his Ending*, by Benjamin Rufus Kirkpatrick, Kansas State Historical Society, Manuscripts Department, Oct. 10, 1935.

10. Interview, Elmer Stevens of Taylorsville. Bob Green, a Wakefield neighbor, told the feed basket story to Stevens.

11. Ibid., local tradition related by Elmer Stevens to author.

12. Letter, Clarinda, Iowa, Sept. 8, 1888, John Langford to William W. Scott, Canal Dover, Ohio, who was planning to write a book on Quantrill. Scott died before getting the book published and William E. Connelley obtained his research, then produced *Quantrill and the Border Wars*. Langford, a member of Terrell's decoy guerrillas who was there and claimed to have shot Quantrill, should have known exactly how many of Terrell's men were at Wakefield's that day. He said in a letter to Scott in 1897 there were 28. Sylvester Cheatham of Terrell's command said in 1871 there were 19 and that it was he who shot Quantrill. The actual number of men with Quantrill was more likely 13 as local sources estimated. The late Max Allen, grandson of Terrell

decoy guerrilla Lieutenant Horace Allen, insisted his grandfather was the man history forgot. He told author Thomas Shelby Watson that Horace should get credit for taking Quantrill's life and that the Larue County native had a pocket watch with Quantrill's name engraved inside. He did not know what happened to the watch. Langford's late grandson, also named John Langford, told Watson that his grandfather clipped off a lock of Quantrill's reddish-blonde hair after learning it was Quantrill he had shot. Grandson Langford's widow gave Thomas Shelby Watson a small curl of the hair.

13. Interview, Max Allen, while visiting home of Thomas Shelby Watson, 1979.

14. Interview, Elmer Stephens, quoting his uncle Ben Stevens.

15. Ibid. Stephens said his uncle told him the worthless parole was placed under a mantle clock by Terrell.

16. Connelley, p. 480.

17. Letter to the Editor, *Louisville Courier-Journal*, June 13, 1937. Edith Ross said the women of Missouri idolized Quantrill and that "aunt Harriet nursed him until he died in a Louisville hospital." Harriet Ross was the mother of the Quantrill guerrilla John Ross and later married a Lobb.

18. The Kansas State Historical Society determined that a teenager's bones became mixed with Quantrill's when they fell into his Louisville grave from an adjacent grave.

19. A photo of Quantrill once owned by the late Lowell Ashe of Louisville, belonged to Ashe's great-uncle, Quantrill guerrilla Donnie Pence, then to Pence's nephew Fred Miles of Samuels, Ky. The Pence-Miles photo has been confirmed to be a legitimate image of Quantrill by the Kentucky Historical Society. An identical image of Quantrill was found in an album in the Peck family of Louisville, also relatives of the Pences, and references to some of the photos in this book are to the Fred Miles-Pauline Peck Collection. The late Lowell Ashe, who willed the Quantrill picture to the Kentucky Historical Society, was Donnie

Pence's great-nephew and wore Pence's heavy gold wedding band.

Chapter 36

1. Statements of Private Jno. O. Smith, Co. G, 54th Rgt. Ky. Mtd. Infantry Provost who was picketing the west end of Taylorsville at Brashears Creek near the Wootton house; citizen George Mason and others. Provost Marshal files, National Archives.
2. Ibid.
3. Palmer, *Personal Recollections*. Palmer said the real name of "Texas" was "probably Jonathan Billingsboy." John Newman Edwards, in *Noted Guerrillas or the Warfare of the Border*, said, "His true name was probably Jonathan Billingboy (the 's' excluded)." Edwards was prone to embellishment that sometimes bordered on exaggeration. "Hoskins" was also spelled "Haskins" in other accounts and "Texas" was identified as Thomas Vickers in the *Louisville Journal* after the war. Mary Clarke gave a description of Brothers as the man "in the house" and one of "Texas" as the man "in the yard."
4. Letter. Dept of Kentucky, Record Group 393, Part 1, Register of Letters Received, Entry 2172, Vol. 3, page 408, C-143. Mary A. Clark confirmed that the attack on her occurred April 25, 1865.
5. Edwards, p. 444.
6. *U.S. vs. Samuel O. Berry*. Witness Joseph F. Watson testified that he delivered messages from Berry to Kirk and that Kirk was the liaison who carried messages to the federal authorities. Watson said Berry, Mitchell and Tom Henry met at the home of his father, Thomas Watson, a mile east of Taylorsville on Salt River to formulate their communications. Thomas Watson was the great-great-grandfather of Thomas Shelby Watson, author of this book.
7. Ibid. *U.S. vs. Samuel O. Berry*, witness Thomas E. Green.
8. *U.S. vs. Samuel O. Berry*, testimony of Cyrus J. Wilson.

Epilogue

1. Letter to J. Winston Coleman, Jr., Lexington, April 9, 1953, from Wand B. Duncan, Bowling Green, Ky.
2. Letter to author. Oct. 4, 1971, from Carrie Masden, Lebanon Junction, and Magruder family tradition.
3. Letter, Daniel Sanders of Mercer County, complaint to military authorities April 5, 1865, Kentucky Military History Museum.
4. Clipping, Casey County Library, Liberty, Ky. Saunders told authorities Bridgewater had shot him in the shoulder and stole his ring during an earlier encounter. Saunders said he had a doctor save the bullet so he could have it remolded and use it to kill Bridgewater.
5. *Weekly Courier*, Louisville, July 31, 1867, p. 2, c. 8.
6. Clipping, Casey County Library, Liberty, Ky.
7. David Gambrel, article, *Danville Advocate-Messenger*, Aug. 1996.
8. *Louisville Daily Journal*, April 30, 1865, p. 3, c. 6.
9. Ed Shinnick, *Some Old Time History of Shelbyville and Shelby County* (Frankfort: Blue Grass Press, 1974).
10. Interview. Ottis Goodwin, 1972. Goodwin married Catherine Gray, a daughter of Abe Gray and Alice Terrell, Ed Terrell's sister.
11. Shinnick.
12. *Owensboro Messenger and Examiner*, Feb. 9, 1888, p. 1, c. 6.
13. *U.S. vs. Francis Payne Stone*.
14. *U.S. vs. J.H. Vincell*.
15. *U.S. vs. Henry Spaulding*.
16. *McLean County News*, "Jake Bennett becomes a good citizen," June 12, 1980.
17. *U.S. vs. Joseph Jonigan*.
18. *U.S. vs. Elias Garrett*.
19. *U.S. vs. Dave Martin*.
20. *U.S. vs. Tom Henry*.
21. Letter, Wand B. Duncan to J. Winston Coleman, April 9, 1953.

Bibliography

Allardice, Bruce S. *More Generals in Gray.* Baton Rouge: Louisiana State University Press, 1995.

Allison, Young E. *Select Works of Young E. Allison.* Louisville: John P. Morton & Co., 1935.

Balance, James L. Journal. Shakertown (Shaker Village) Collection, Pleasant Hill, Ky.

Barton, O.S. *Three Years with Quantrill: A True Story Told by His Scout John McCorkle.* 1914. Norman: University of Oklahoma Press, 1998.

Boling, John. *Guerilla Times in Meade County.* Utica, Ky: McDowell Publications, n.d.

Bowmar III, Dan M. *Giants of the Turf.* Lexington: The Blood-Horse, 1960.

Brownlee, Richard S. *Gray Ghosts of the Confederacy.* Baton Rouge: Louisiana State University Press, 1958.

Clark, Champ. *My Quarter Century of American Politics.* New York: Harper & Brothers Publishers, 1920.

Clark, Thomas D. *Pleasant Hill in the Civil War.* Harrodsburg, Ky.: Pleasant Hill Press, 1972.

Coleman, J. Winston. *Lexington During the Civil War.* Lexington: Henry Clay Press, 1968.

Collins, Lewis. *History of Kentucky.* Louisville: John P. Morton & Co., 1924.

Connelley, William Elsey. *Quantrill and the Border Wars.* Cedar Rapids, Iowa: Torch Press, 1909.

Daughters of the Confederacy. *Minutes of the Eighth Annual Convention of the Kentucky Division.* Louisville: Press of George G. Fetter Co., 1905.

Davis, William C. *The Orphan Brigade: The Kentucky Confederates Who Couldn't Go Home.* New York: Doubleday & Co., 1980.

Drane, Maude Johnston. *History of Henry County, Ky.* Louisville: Franklin Printing Co., 1948.

Duke, Basil Wilson. *Morgan's Cavalry.* Cincinnati: Miami Printing and Publishing Co., 1867.

_____. *Reminiscences of General Basil W. Duke, C.S.A.* New York: Doubleday, 1911.

Bibliography

Dunlavy, Benjamin. *East Family Journal.* Shakertown (Shaker Village) Collection, Pleasant Hill, Ky.

Edwards, John N. *Noted Guerrillas or the Warfare of the Border.* St. Louis: Brand & Co., 1877.

Hardin, Bayless. *Brigadier General John Hunt Morgan of Kentucky.* Kentucky Historical Society, undated.

Harmon, Geraldine Crain. *Chaplin Hills: History of Perryville, Kentucky.* Danville, Ky.: Bluegrass Printing Co., 1971.

Harrison, Dr. Lowell H. *The Civil War in Kentucky.* Lexington: University Press of Kentucky; reprint edition, January 1987.

_____. "Governor Magoffin and the Secession Crisis." Kentucky Historical Society Register 72.

Heady, Peyton. *Union County, Kentucky in the Civil War, 1861–65.* Morganfield, Ky.: Self-published, 1985.

Hervey, John. *Racing in America 1665 — 1865.* New York: Privately printed by the Jockey Club, 1944.

Horan, James. *Confederate Agent.* New York: Crown Publishers, 1954.

_____. *Desperate Men.* Bonanza Books. Crown Publishers, 1949.

Johnson, Adam Rankin. *The Partisan Rangers of the Confederate States Army.* Edited by William J. Davis. Austin: State House Press, 1995.

Journal of the Congress of the Confederate States of America, 1861–65. 58th Congress, 2d Session, Senate Document 234; Serials 4610–4616. National Archives, Washington DC.

Journals of the Kentucky General Assembly. Kentucky Historical Society, May 16, 1861.

Kerr, Charles. *History of Kentucky.* Chicago: American Historical Society, 1922.

Louisville & Nashville Railroad records. University of Louisville Archives.

Magee, M. Juliette. *Ballard's Brave Boys.* Wickliffe, Ky.: The Advance-Yeoman, 1974.

Magruder, Henry C. *Three Years in the Saddle: The Life and Confession of Henry C. Magruder, the Original "Sue Munday," the Scourge of Kentucky.* Louisville: Published by his Captor, Maj. Cyrus J. Wilson, 1865.

McDowell, Robert E. *City of Conflict: Louisville in the Civil War, 1861–1865.* Louisville: Louisville Civil War Round Table, 1962.

Merrifield, Dr. Alexander Hamilton. "Wartime in the Bloomfield Country." *Kentucky Standard,* July 9, 1903.

Messmer, Charles. "Louisville During the Civil War." *Filson Club History Quarterly* 52, No. 2 (April 1978).

Millard, Joseph. "The Spy Who Saved the Union." In *True Civil War Stories.* Greenwich, Conn.: Fawcett Publications, 1961.

Mosgrove, George Dallas. *Kentucky Cavaliers in Dixie: Reminiscences of a Confederate Cavalryman.* Louisville Courier-Journal Job Printing Co., 1895; reprint, Jackson, Tenn.: McCowat-Mercer Press, 1957.

Myers, Raymond E. *The Zollie Tree.* Louisville: Filson Club Press, 1964.

Palmer, John M. *Personal Recollections of John M. Palmer: The Story of an Earnest Life.* Cincinnati: Roberts Clarke Co., 1901.

Prichard, James M. "General Orders No. 59: Kentucky's Reign of Terror." *Civil War Quarterly* 10, n.d.

_____. *Tree Shaker*. Civil War pamphlet. Louisville, undated.

Rizk, Estelle S. *No More Muffled Hoof Beats*. Philadelphia: Dorrance & Company, 1960.

Sensing, Thurman. *Champ Ferguson, Confederate Guerrilla*. Nashville, Tenn.: Vanderbilt University Press,1942.

Shinnick, Ed. *Some Old Time History of Shelbyville and Shelby County*. Frankfort: Blue Grass Press, 1974.

Smith, Sarah B. *Historic Nelson County*. Louisville: Gateway Press, 1971.

Southern Bivouac 2 (Sept. 1883–Aug. 1884). Wilmington, N.C.: Broadfoot Publishing Co.

Tapp, Hambleton, and James C. Klotter. *Kentucky's Decades of Discord, 1865–1900*. Kentucky Historical Society, 1977.

Thomas, Edison H. *John Hunt Morgan and his Raiders*. Lexington: University Press of Kentucky, 1975.

Tinsley, Harry D. *History of No Creek*. Frankfort: Roberts Printing, 1953.

United States versus Samuel O. Berry. Courts-Martial. National Archives, Old Military Records.

United States versus Jerome Clarke, alias Sue Mundy. Courts-Martial. National Archives, Old Military Records.

United States versus James W. Davis. Courts-Martial. National Archives, Old Military Records.

United States versus Elias Garrett. Courts-Martial. National Archives, Old Military Records.

United States versus Tom Henry. Courts-Martial. National Archives, Old Military Records.

United States versus Joseph Jonigan. Courts-Martial, National Archives, Old Military Records.

United States versus Henry Magruder. Courts-Martial. National Archives, Old Military Records.

United States versus Dave Martin. Courts-Martial. National Archives, Old Military Records.

United States versus Henry Metcalf. Courts-Martial. National Archives, Old Military Records.

United States versus Henry Spaulding. Courts-Martial. National Archives, Old Military Records.

United States versus Francis Payne Stone. Courts-Martial. National Archives, Old Military Records.

United States versus Solomon Thompson. Courts-Martial. National Archives, Old Military Records.

United States versus Henry Turner. Courts-Martial. National Archives, Old Military Records.

United States versus J.H. Vincell. Courts-Martial. National Archives, Old Military Records.

Bibliography

War of the Rebellion: A Compilation of the Official Records of the Union and Confederate Armies. National Archives.

Willis, George L. *Kentucky Democracy.* 3 vols. Louisville: Democratic Historical Society, 1935.

Index

Index

233

Index

Index

Index